CIVIL DISOBEDIENCE
in focus

How can civil disobedience be defined and distinguished from revolution or lawful protest? What, if anything, justifies civil disobedience? Can nonviolent civil disobedience ever be effective?

The issues surrounding civil disobedience have been discussed since at least 399 BC and, in the wake of such recent events as the protest at Tiananmen Square, are still of great relevance. By presenting classic and current philosophical reflections on the issues, this book presents all the basic materials needed for a philosophical assessment of the nature and justification of civil disobedience. The pieces included range from classic statements by Plato, Thoreau, and Martin Luther King, to essays by leading contemporary thinkers such as Rawls, Raz, and Singer. Hugo Adam Bedau's introduction sets out the issues and shows how the various authors shed light on each aspect of them.

Hugo Adam Bedau is Austin Fletcher Professor of Philosophy at Tufts University.

ROUTLEDGE PHILOSOPHERS IN FOCUS SERIES

General Editor: Stanley Tweyman
York University, Toronto

CIVIL DISOBEDIENCE
in focus

Edited by Hugo Adam Bedau

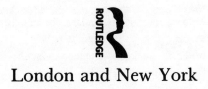

London and New York

First published 1991
by Routledge
11 New Fetter Lane, London EC4P 4EE

Simultaneously published in the USA and Canada
by Routledge
29 West 35th Street, New York, NY 10001

Reprinted 1994, 1995

Typeset in Baskerville by Witwell Ltd, Southport
Printed and bound in Great Britain by
TJ Press (Padstow) Ltd, Padstow, Cornwall

British Library Cataloguing in Publication Data
A catalogue record for this book is available from the British Library

Library of Congress Cataloguing in Publication Data
A catalogue record for this book is available from the Library of Congress

ISBN 0-415-05055-3

CONTENTS

ACKNOWLEDGEMENTS

I am grateful to the following publishers for their permission to reprint material as follows:

Plato, *Crito*, from G. M. A. Grube, trans., *Plato: Five Dialogues*, 1981, by permission of Hackett Publishing Co., Indianapolis, IN.

H. A. Bedau, 'Civil Disobedience and Personal Responsibility for Injustice,' *The Monist*, 54 (1970), pp. 517–35, by permission of the editor.

Martin Luther King, Jr., 'Letter from Birmingham City Jail,' © 1963 Martin Luther King, Jr. Copyright renewed 1991 by Corretta Scott King. Reprinted by arrangement with The Heirs to the Estate of Martin Luther King, Jr. c/o Joan Daves Agency as agent for the proprietor.

Herbert J. Storing, 'The Case Against Civil Disobedience,' in Robert A. Goldwin (ed.), *On Civil Disobedience: Essays Old and New*, Rand McNally, 1969, pp. 95–106, 114–20, reprinted by permission of Kenyon College, Gambier, OH.

John Rawls, 'Civil Disobedience,' reprinted by permission of the publishers from sections 55, 57, and 59 of *A Theory of Justice*, by John Rawls, Cambridge, Mass.: The Belknap Press of Harvard University Press, Copyright © 1971 by the President and Fellows of Harvard College. All rights reserved.

Peter Singer, 'Disobedience as a Plea for Reconsideration,' © Oxford University Press 1973. Reprinted from *Democracy and Disobedience*, pp. 84–92, by Peter Singer (1973) by permission of Oxford University Press.

John Morreall, 'The Justifiability of Violent Civil Disobedience,' *Canadian Journal of Philosophy*, 6 (1976), pp. 35–47, reprinted by permission of the editor.

Vinit Haksar, 'Civil Disobedience and Non-Cooperation,' from Vinit Haksar, *Civil Disobedience, Threats and Offers*, New Delhi, Oxford University Press, 1986, pp. 29–41, by permission of the publisher.

Joseph Raz, 'Civil Disobedience,' © Oxford University Press 1979. Reprinted from *The Authority of Law* by Joseph Raz (1979), pp. 266–75, by permission of Oxford University Press.

Kent Greenawalt, 'Justifying Nonviolent Disobedience,' from *Conflicts of Law and Morality*, pp. 226–43, by Kent Greenawalt. Copyright © 1987 by Oxford University Press, Inc.

Brian Smart, 'Defining Civil Disobedience,' *Inquiry*, 21 (1978), pp. 249–69, reprinted by permission of the editor.

INTRODUCTION

I

Civil disobedience - disobeying the law in a good cause - is as old as Prometheus' disobedience of Zeus in order to give fire to mankind and Antigone's defiance of Creon's edict denying proper burial to her brother Polynices. It is as current as these recent headline events:

1 In the United States, Operation Rescue organizes trespass actions at abortion clinics.
2 In China, university students in Beijing's Tiananmen Square stage a sit-in to protest on behalf of freedom and democracy.
3 In South Africa, opponents of apartheid and the brutal policy tactics used to enforce it march in downtown Cape Town.

The problem of the individual's relation to the state and its government - its authority and its laws - and the appropriate response to offensive or unjust laws - meek compliance, protest, disobedience, rebellion - has been debated at least since 399 BC, when Crito argued that Socrates should flee from prison to avoid an undeserved death penalty. Jews and Christians, at the risk of their lives, disobeyed the demands of Roman law and its claims of supreme authority by refusing to place a pinch of incense on the altar of Caesar. Religious consciousness, with its doctrine of 'passive obedience,' has a long history of conscientious refusal when faced with arrogant secular demands.[1]

The theory of civil disobedience, freed from its religious setting, does not emerge as a distinctive subject for secular thought until the middle of the last century. It is introduced

1 See David Daube, *Civil Disobedience in Antiquity* (Edinburgh: Edinburgh University Press, 1972).

1

(along with the term, 'civil disobedience,' itself) in the nonpareil essay by the American naturalist Henry David Thoreau. Thoreau's refusal in the 1840s to pay his poll tax was intended to be symbolic of his objections to the federal government's aggressive war against Mexico, support for chattel slavery in the southern states, and continued violation of the rights of the native Indian population. Thoreau's disobedience had no discernible effect on these injustices, but his ideas were none the less a good example of how actual practice can yield a reflective theoretical product.[2]

Half a century later Thoreau's ideas were brought to international attention first through the writings of Leo Tolstoy and subsequently by Mohandas Gandhi. Tolstoy defended the right to refuse to bear arms, and his counsels were addressed to conscientious objectors and their critics on both sides of the Atlantic. Gandhi's concern was quite different. He realized that carefully planned mass nonviolent resistance, in conjunction with other political and moral pressures, could advance the cause of Indian nationalism and bring the British Raj to its knees. After a struggle that lasted four decades, foreign rule in India came to an end in 1947 - and Gandhi was assassinated in the following year.[3]

Despite its historic American origin in Thoreau's practice and writings, civil disobedience did not become a household term or a topic of interest to political and legal philosophy until the early 1950s. In the United States, the Montgomery Bus Boycott (1955) became the opening salvo in a decade-long struggle by black Americans to achieve civil rights under law equal to those of white Americans. In England, the Committee for Nonviolent Action advocated 'nuclear pacifism' and under the leadership of the ageing Bertrand Russell used civil disobedience mainly in order to secure publicity for its cause.[4] In the United States, the leading figure in the Civil Rights Movement was Martin Luther

2 See Walter Harding and Michael Meyer, *The New Thoreau Handbook* (New York: NYU Press, 1980), pp. 41-2, 80-1, 135-9; Walter Harding, *The Variorum Civil Disobedience* (New York: Twayne, 1967).

3 See Mohandas K. Gandhi, *Non-Violent Resistance* (New York: Schocken, 1961).

4 See Bertrand Russell, 'Civil Disobedience and the Threat of Nuclear Warfare,' in Clara Urquhart (ed.), *A Matter of Life* (London: Jonathan Cape, 1963), pp. 189-96, and reprinted in H. A. Bedau (ed.), *Civil Disobedience: Theory and Practice* (New York: Pegasus, 1969), pp. 153-9. See also his essays, 'Civil Disobedience,' *New Statesman* (Feb. 17, 1961), 245-6, and 'On Civil Disobedience,' in Arthur and Lila Weinberg (eds.), *Instead of Violence* (Boston: Beacon, 1965), pp. 51-7.

King, Jr. He and his associates taught the nation the power of nonviolent disobedience to change the law. King, like Gandhi, became a martyr to the cause when he was assassinated in 1968. By tradition and temperament, Americans were even less attuned to nonviolence than were the masses of India, and any prophet of radical reform, however nonviolent his tactics, evidently put his own life at risk.[5]

Even before King's death, civil disobedience in the United States was aimed at new targets and enlisted new practitioners as a consequence of the government's deepening military involvement in Southeast Asia. Draft refusal and war protest soon engaged the attention of the nation, and the tumult spilled over into violence against property and persons. Violent disruptions in the late 1960s marked the end of the Civil Rights Movement and the escalation of conflict in and over Vietnam.[6]

The slow response by philosophers to the practice of civil disobedience is but one more illustration of the truth of Hegel's observation that the owl of Minerva flies only at dusk. In 1961, the American Philosophical Association organized a symposium on 'Political Obligation and Civil Disobedience,' perhaps the first occasion on which the whole subject received official attention from the academic community.[7] During the rest of that decade, however, political theorists, legal philosophers, and moralists of various persuasions subjected civil disobedience to intensive scrutiny. By the mid-1980s, a dozen books and another dozen anthologies, along with scores of articles, provided a wide range of discussion on every important aspect of the subject.[8]

5 On civil disobedience in the Civil Rights Movement and Martin Luther King, Jr., see Juan Williams, *Eyes on the Prize: America's Civil Rights Years 1954-65* (New York: Viking, 1987); Arthur Wascow, *From Race-Riot to Sit-In* (New York: Anchor, 1966); Howard Zinn, *SNCC: The New Abolitionists* (Boston: Beacon, 1965).

6 On the circumstances of civil disobedience and related protests during the Vietnam War, see 'Trials of the Resistance' (New York NY: *New York Review of Books*, 1970); Alice Lynd (ed.), *We Won't Go* (Boston: Beacon, 1968).

7 See Richard A. Wasserstrom, Hugo A. Bedau, and Stuart M. Brown, Jr., 'Symposium: Political Obligation and Civil Disobedience,' *Journal of Philosophy*, 58 (1961), 641-65, 669-81.

8 No comprehensive bibliography on civil disobedience has been published; see, however, the bibliographies in Paul Harris (ed.), *Civil Disobedience* (Lanham MD: University Press of America, 1989), pp. 287-92; Elliot M. Zashin, *Civil Disobedience and Democracy* (New York: Free Press, 1972), pp. 351-5; Jeffrie G. Murphy (ed.), *Civil Disobedience and Violence* (Belmont CA: Wadsworth, 1971), pp. 146-51.

II

The selections included in this book are divided into two groups. The first includes what are arguably the three most influential sources for discussion of the whole topic – Socrates's argument with Crito and the Laws of Athens; Thoreau's essay originally published under the title 'Resistance to Government' but better known as 'Civil Disobedience'; and King's 'Letter from Birmingham City Jail,' drafted while he was behind bars for violating an injunction against participating in a Civil Rights demonstration. Whereas Socrates's argument is a classic explanation of why it would be wrong to disobey even an unjust law, both Thoreau and King endeavor to explain why it would be wrong to obey such laws. To these classic essays I have added two others. One is my own attempt to examine what I call Thoreau's principle, that it is morally necessary not to be an instrument of injustice to others. The other is a critique of King and of civil disobedience on behalf of civil rights by Herbert J. Storing.

The second group of essays focuses on the most influential contemporary philosophical discussion of civil disobedience, that by John Rawls in his *A Theory of Justice* (1971). For the past two decades, Rawls's definition and defense of civil disobedience in liberal democracy has served to frame the major issues and provoke valuable criticism. I have chosen essays or excerpts from books by Kent Greenawalt, Vinit Haksar, John Morreall, Joseph Raz, Peter Singer, and Brian Smart because they shed critical and constructive light on Rawls and thereby on the whole subject itself.

Between the classic views of Socrates, Thoreau, and King, their modern interpreters, and the discussions by academic philosophers that focuses on Rawls's views, the present volume contains enough of what is needed to examine if not to answer the major questions that arise whenever civil disobedience is advocated, discussed, or carried out.

III

What are those major questions? Consider any law – edict, rule, command, order, statute, regulation, etc. – to which you are subject and that you thus are supposed to obey. If you are indifferent to its requirements or approve of them, then you will probably comply. But if you don't agree with the law, then you must decide what to do. You can choose among several possibilities.

One is to comply after all, keeping your disapproval quiet, perhaps out of prudent fear of punishment for noncompliance or out of distaste for public attention and criticism as a dissenter. Another option is to comply but only after voicing disapproval, insofar as such dissent is itself not unlawful. Compliance, even if done under open protest, and after efforts to avert or nullify the law, is not civil disobedience – for nothing illegal has been done, no law has been *disobeyed*.

(As an aside, we should notice that it is sometimes difficult to state what the law in a particular case *is*. During the Civil Rights Movement, protesters often argued that segregation laws and injunctions in restraint of demonstrations were themselves unlawful because unconstitutional. Lawyers friendly to the cause of equal rights, like Archibald Cox, tended to agree.[9] Opponents of the Vietnam War, notably Ronald Dworkin, argued in a somewhat parallel fashion that it was inappropriate to prosecute protesters for illegal conduct when the constitutional status of the draft and of the war itself was so uncertain.[10])

What holds for lawful protest generally thus holds for strikes, boycotts, poster parades, and refusal to accept government employment: Where these acts are methods of lawful protest they do not count as civil disobedience, as that term has standardly come to be used.

Another obvious alternative when confronted with a law with which one does not agree is to refuse to comply, but to keep one's noncompliance hidden, again in a prudent desire to avoid the unpleasant consequences – arrest and trial, conviction and punishment, perhaps public opprobrium – that typically ensue when one's unlawful conduct is done openly. Can conduct of this sort ever be regarded as civil disobedience?

It certainly meets the test of disobedience, but is it *civil*? As the

9 See Archibald Cox, 'Direct Action, Civil Disobedience, and the Constitution,' in his *Civil Rights, the Constitution and the Courts* (Cambridge MA: Harvard, 1967); also Charles L. Black, Jr., 'The Problem of the Compatibility of Civil Disobedience with American Institutions of Government,' *Texas Law Review*, 43 (1965), 492–506.
10 Ronald Dworkin, 'On Not Prosecuting Civil Disobedience' (1968), reprinted in his *Taking Rights Seriously* (Cambridge MA: Harvard, 1977), pp. 206–22.

readings in this volume show, neither King nor Rawls think so, and their shared view is the dominant one. But the position of Socrates and Thoreau is less clear. In Socrates' case, the sole issue he examines is whether he should bribe his jailer to escape the death sentence, unfairly but lawfully imposed by the people of Athens for his (alleged) crimes. As Gregory Vlastos has noted, 'The disobedient action contemplated in the *Crito* would not have been open defiance of the law, but fraudulent evasion of it, involving lying and the corruption of public servants.'[11] And one must wonder whether Socrates or any of his contemporaries even had the concept of civil disobedience as we have come to understand it. 'The Greeks did not go on protest marches; Socrates never engaged in a sit-in.'[12] Yet we know from Plato's *Apology* that Socrates did have the concept of justified disobedience of the law and, as *Crito* amply proves, he certainly had the concept of unjustified disobedience. As for Thoreau, it appears that he made no effort whatever for several years to make public his noncompliance with the poll tax law. Since his own conduct was never far from his mind when he later lectured and wrote in defense of 'civil disobedience,' it seems unlikely that he meant to exclude his own illegal conduct – consisting of silent evasion of taxes – from the reach of his argument.

The matter is not so easily disposed of, however. Crucial to the question under discussion is what one believes to be the point, or purpose, or aim of one's lawbreaking. What is it, in other words, that turns some but not all disobedience into *civil* disobedience? If one's disobedience is nothing more than the attempt to avoid having to comply with a given law, then covert disobedience can often accomplish that end quite well. This is true whether or not one believes the law disobeyed to be unjust (think, for example, of those who gave aid to Jews in Nazi-occupied Europe) and whether or not one is right. But in the conduct of Gandhi as well as King, and in Rawls's and virtually all other modern discussions of the subject (even if not in Thoreau's), there is a distinctive purpose to civil disobedience: Its purpose is to frustrate and then change the law itself, by making an *appeal to conscience*, the conscience of the authorities and especially the

11 Gregory Vlastos, 'Socrates on Political Obedience and Disobedience,' *Yale Review* (Summer 1974), 517–34, at 531.
12 Richard Kraut, *Socrates and the State* (Princeton NJ: Princeton University Press, 1984), p. 75.

conscience of the majority of the public – the conscience, in short, of whoever it is that issues, enforces, and supports the law being broken. Civil disobedience thus conceived must be viewed as an exercise in *public* moral education, as a tactic to achieve law reform. Hence the disobedience is properly called 'civil' because it is part of the civic life of the society. But no such appeal to the public conscience can be made unless the illegal conduct is done openly, in the public forum, as a political act.

We should pause to notice a chronic problem that arises whenever civil disobedience is discussed today. The relative respectability of Gandhian civil disobedience in our time encourages many who break the law and wish to secure public approval for it to describe their conduct – whether correctly or not – as 'civil disobedience.' (I myself began this introduction by offering Prometheus' theft of fire as an example, provisionally, of civil disobedience!) As there is no way to avoid the misappropriation and abuse of this or any other political term, one constantly needs to be on the alert to keep distinct in one's own thinking the nature of the act under discussion, not merely what its advocates or critics call it, the criteria for the justification of illegal conduct, and the judgment whether the act under discussion, or any other like it, is justified.

For these reasons, then, it is unlikely that illegal conduct done covertly is to be regarded as civil disobedience. Or at least it is clear why, if one regards the purpose of civil disobedience to be in part the moral education of society at large, it is impossible to achieve that aim while keeping hidden the fact that one has broken the law.

Once we settle on the purpose of civil disobedience, we can face some ancillary questions about its nature and justification. First, we can contrast civil disobedience with *conscientious objection*, by arguing that the two differ in their primary purpose. The primary purpose of conscientious objection is not public education but private exemption, not political change but (to put it bluntly) personal hand-washing. When the conscientious objector violates the law, he or she does so primarily in order to avoid conduct condemned by personal conscience even though required by public law. Setting an example for others or forcing them to re-evaluate their support for the law is a secondary consideration. Thoreau's essay on civil disobedience, taken in the context of his own tax evasion, is perennially confusing; it more nearly constitutes an argument for conscientious refusal than an argument for civil disobedience understood as action designed to change the law through public moral education.[13]

Second, we can see that the place of *nonviolence* in civil disobedience is problematic. Understandably, pacifists like Gandhi and King reject on principled grounds the use of violence to resist even unjust laws. But for others, and that includes most of the philosophers who have written on the subject, the decision whether to act violently (and whether to confine violence to destroying property, as in the Boston Tea Party of 1773, or ruining draft board files, as the Catonsville Nine did in 1968[14]) emerges as a tactical, not a principled, matter. Ideal political discourse is, of course, nonviolent – rational, tolerant of disagreement, and patient. To the extent that civil disobedience should imitate, as well as it can, the kind of discourse its advocates presumably acknowledge for ideal politics, to that extent it must be nonviolent – nonviolent in intention as well as in actual effect. Anything else shifts public attention to the violent act itself and away from the laws or policies under protest. Those who support the legal status quo – as the city and state governments in the South did in the face of the Civil Rights Movement of the 1960s, and as the Communist Party chiefs in Beijing did when confronting the students in Tiananmen Square – have no hesitation in putting down nonviolent illegal protest with virtually uncontrolled violent countermeasures. As the protesters typically see it, however, they accept the lawful consequences of their illegal conduct, including nonresistance to arrest, trial, and punishment in order to testify to their own sincerity and to show that they respect the rule of law generally.[15]

Does this suffice to mark off civil disobedience not only from rebellion and revolution but also from ordinary criminal con-

---

13 On conscientious objection and the appeal to conscience, see John Rawls, *A Theory of Justice* (Cambridge MA: Harvard), pp. 368–71, 377–81; Lillian Schlissel (ed.), *Conscience in America: A Documentary History of Conscientious Objection in America, 1757–1967* (New York: Dutton, 1968).

14 See Francine du Plessix Gray, *Divine Disobedience: Profiles in Catholic Radicalism* (New York: Knopf, 1970); William VanEtten Casey and Philip Nobile (eds.), *The Berrigans* (New York: Avon, 1971).

15 On nonviolent protest, see Arthur and Lila Weinberg (eds.), *Instead of Violence* (Boston: Beacon, 1965); Staughton Lynd (ed.), *Nonviolence in America: A Documentary History* (Indianapolis: Bobbs-Merrill, 1966).

duct? Two decades ago, critics of the civil rights and anti-war movements were often quite insistent in objecting that it was self-serving of the protesters to cloak their illegal conduct in the language of civility, when in fact their behavior was no different from that of common criminals. The charge looks more tempting when, as was true in many cases, the protesters (blacks in the South, draft-age men in the North) had something personal to gain, some benefit for themselves, in the successful outcome of their protest. The reply usually made on behalf of the protesters is that their illegal conduct was *conscientious*. It was motivated by respect for some moral principle which, in the judgment of the protesters, was violated by the law and which deserved greater respect than the law itself. Ordinary criminal conduct is not so governed, it is argued, and quite apart from the nonviolence of civil disobedience, it is its conscientiousness that sets it apart from ordinary criminality. (Whether the conscientiousness of civil disobedience makes it not only akin to but a species of conscientious objection we may ignore here.)

It is beyond dispute that Thoreau, Gandhi, and King rested the legitimacy of their civil disobedience on an appeal to moral principle. (Whether they also stood to gain personally from the success of their endeavors is a quite separate issue and irrelevant to the justification of their conduct.) However, saying more than this by specifying the nature or the content of the moral principles that may or must be appealed to if the illegal conduct is to be regarded as civil disobedience may well be impossible. All that can be required is that the protester be sincerely committed to *some* moral principle whose importance in his eyes overrides the claim on him made by the law. (Rawls, following both Gandhi and King, stresses the importance of *shared* moral principles that tie together the protesters and the authorities as well as the general public. But this point bears on the justification of civil disobedience, not its nature.)

IV

When we turn to the issue of the *justification* of civil disobedience, the nature of the moral principles relied on by the protester is obviously crucial. Presumably not just *any* moral principle will suffice to justify illegal conduct, even if it does suffice to make the conduct into civil disobedience. (And not even the right principles in the wrong circumstances will suffice for justification, either.) For surely some acts of civil disobedience are unjustified, and the reason is that sound moral principles do not permit, much less require, illegal conduct of certain kinds in certain kinds of circumstances. Exactly what these justifying principles are is a matter of some disagreement.

In Socrates' case, it appears that justifiable illegal conduct – at least for him, in his circumstances – is virtually impossible. This is the burden of the argument he puts into the mouth of the Laws of Athens. Its adequacy turns largely on how appropriate and convincing an account the Laws give of the origin and strength of Socrates' obligation to obey the law, which turns on the adequacy of the particular version of the social contract theory that the Laws advance (a large topic and one not pursued in any detail in this book).[16]

In Thoreau's case, what justifies his refusal to pay the poll tax, he believes, is that he avoids becoming a party to (if not an actual instrument of) injustices to others. The extent to which Thoreau's reasoning is convincing depends in part on what we are to make of his principle that 'What I have to do is to see . . . that I do not lend myself to the wrong I condemn.'

In King's case, several different principles are mentioned, all of which King claims establish the injustice of legally enforced racial segregation. As Storing's criticisms indicate, he is not convinced that the principles King invokes really vindicate his conduct.[17]

It must be conceded, I believe, that a truly adequate approach to the justification of civil disobedience cannot be found in the classic writings of Socrates, Thoreau, and King, nor can a clear impression be formed of what such a justification would look like. For progress on this important matter we are principally indebted to John Rawls, who was perhaps the first philosopher

---

16 See A. John Simmons, *Moral Principles and Political Obligations* (Princeton NJ: Princeton University Press, 1979).

17 For other criticisms of King, see Louis Waldman, 'Civil Rights – Yes; Civil Disobedience – No (A Reply to Dr. Martin Luther King)' (1965), reprinted in H. A. Bedau (ed.), *Civil Disobedience: Theory and Practice* (New York: Pegasus, 1969), pp. 106–15; Herbert Brownell, 'Civil Disobedience – A Lawyer's Challenge,' *American Criminal Law Quarterly*, 3 (Fall 1964), 27–32; Morris Liebman, 'Civil Disobedience – A Threat to our Law Society,' *American Bar Association Journal* (July 1965), 645–47; Charles Rice, 'Civil Disobedience: Formula for Chaos,' *Alabama Lawyer*, 27 (1966), pp. 249–79.

really to devote careful thought to the nature and justification of civil disobedience from within the framework of a general theory of social justice and liberal democracy.[18] The issues raised by Rawls's approach concern not only all those already noticed but several others as well.

Paramount among these issues is the question whether civil disobedience is ever justifiable in a constitutional democracy, such as Great Britain or the United States. This is tantamount to asking whether my breaking the law can ever be consistent with my respect for majority rule under a constitution that protects minority rights. Rawls argues that it can be, and none of his commentators reprinted here disagrees. But Rawls also agrees with Sidney Hook and many other critics of civil disobedience in the 1960s, that principled law-breaking and respect for majority rule is consistent only if the law-breaker willingly accepts his punishment.[19] Peter Singer, in chapter 7, argues against this constraint.

Rawls also distinguishes having the *right* to commit civil disobedience from being *justified* in acting on this right. Joseph Raz, in chapter 10, accepts this distinction (as most philosophers would) but understands it quite differently from Rawls (whose views he does not expressly mention). The result is a rather different picture of justified civil disobedience.

Rawls thinks of civil disobedience as noncoercive because it is nonviolent. Vinit Haksar, with his eye on Gandhian civil disobedience (and he could have made the same point with reference to King's mass demonstrations), argues in chapter 9 that there is a continuum from the coercive to the noncoercive, and that acts of civil disobedience can in theory occur at any point on this continuum. John Morreall, in chapter 8, openly defends violent (and to that extent coercive) civil disobedience against Rawls's arguments limiting it to nonviolent action.

Rawls (as was noted in passing above) thinks the justification of civil disobedience requires that the protesters appeal to moral or constitutional principles shared with the general public. Peter Singer finds this far too restrictive.

18 For other views of civil disobedience in a constitutional democracy, see Burton Zweibach, *Civility and Disobedience* (New York, Cambridge University Press, 1975); Zashin, op. cit., note 8; Carl Cohen, *Civil Disobedience: Conscience, Tactics, and the Law* (New York, Columbia, 1971).
19 Sidney Hook, *The Paradoxes of Freedom* (Berkeley CA: University of California Press, 1964), pp. 106–39.

Rawls writes as if a line between nonviolent and violent disobedience can be drawn, and claims that within a constitutional democracy only nonviolent disobedience is justifiable. Morreall, along with some other writers who are reluctant to condemn political violence out of hand, finds this unconvincing.[20]

Rawls endeavours to lay down what amounts to a set of necessary and sufficient conditions for the justification of civil disobedience. Kent Greenawalt, in chapter 11, examines sympathetically but critically these (and other) criteria for justification. His essay, along with those by Morreall and Raz in particular, provides an account of the justification of civil disobedience subtly different from Rawls's.

Finally, any account of the justification of civil disobedience of course turns on the prior issue of how the term has been defined. Rawls recognizes that the term is used to refer to different kinds of political activity, and that any definition (including his) is somewhat arbitrary. But he does not explore other possible definitions or the interaction between his definition and his justification of civil disobedience. Brian Smart, in chapter 12, does do this in a novel way by borrowing from the semantic theories of Paul Grice.

One might well complain that the evaluation of civil disobedience has a dimension not represented by the writings selected for this volume, namely the assessment of the actual effects (for good or ill) on the political community in which acts of civil disobedience have been committed. I would agree. Neither advocates and activists, such as Thoreau and King, nor academic philosophers, such as Rawls, provide such an account, and one cannot fully understand civil disobedience without some attention to its political results. My response, apart from this willing concession, is to point out that another whole book at least would be needed to fulfil this task. And that book – say, a more comprehensive and up-to-date version of Jerome Skolnick's useful volume, *The Politics of Protest* (1969) – must be left for others to edit and write.

---

20 For a useful discussion of violence and its justifications, see Jerome A. Shaffer (ed.), *Violence* (New York: McKay, 1971).

1

CRITO

Plato

SOCRATES: Here already, Crito? Surely it is still early?

CRITO: Indeed it is.

SOCRATES: About what time?

CRITO: Just before dawn.

SOCRATES: I wonder that the warder paid any attention to you.

CRITO: He is used to me now, Socrates, because I come here so often. Besides, he is under some small obligation to me.

SOCRATES: Have you only just come, or have you been here for long?

CRITO: Fairly long.

SOCRATES: Then why didn't you wake me at once, instead of sitting by my bed so quietly?

CRITO: I wouldn't dream of such a thing, Socrates. I only wish I were not so sleepless and depressed myself. I have been wondering at you, because I saw how comfortably you were sleeping, and I deliberately didn't wake you because I wanted you to go on being as comfortable as you could. I have often felt before in the course of my life how fortunate you are in your disposition, but I feel it more than ever now in your present misfortune when I see how easily and placidly you put up with it.

SOCRATES: Well, really, Crito, it would be hardly suitable for a man of my age to resent having to die.

CRITO: Other people just as old as you are get involved in these misfortunes, Socrates, but their age doesn't keep them from resenting it when they find themselves in your position.

SOCRATES: Quite true. But tell me, why have you come so early?

CRITO: Because I bring bad news, Socrates - not so bad from your point of view, I suppose, but it will be very hard to bear for

From: *Plato: The Last Days of Socrates*, translated by Hugh Tredennick (Harmondsworth: Penguin Books, 1959) pp. 79-96.

me and your other friends, and I think that I shall find it hardest of all.

SOCRATES: Why, what is this news? Has the boat come in from Delos – the boat which ends my reprieve when it arrives?

CRITO: It hasn't actually come in yet, but I expect it will be here today, judging from the report of some people who have just arrived from Sunium and left it there. It's quite clear from their account that it will be here today, and so by tomorrow, Socrates, you will have to . . . to end your life.

SOCRATES: Well, Crito, I hope that it may be for the best. If the gods will it so, so be it. All the same, I don't think it will arrive today.

CRITO: What makes you think that?

SOCRATES: I will try to explain. I think I am right in saying that I have to die on the day after the boat arrives?

CRITO: That's what the authorities say, at any rate.

SOCRATES: Then I don't think it will arrive on this day that is just beginning, but on the day after. I am going by a dream that I had in the night, only a little while ago. It looks as though you were right not to wake me up.

CRITO: Why, what was the dream about?

SOCRATES: I thought I saw a gloriously beautiful woman dressed in white robes, who came up to me and addressed me in these words: 'Socrates, To the pleasant land of Phthia on the third day thou shalt come.'

CRITO: Your dream makes no sense, Socrates.

SOCRATES: To my mind, Crito, it is perfectly clear.

CRITO: Too clear, apparently. But look here, Socrates, it is still not too late to take my advice and escape. Your death means a double calamity for me. I shall not only lose a friend whom I can never possibly replace, but besides a great many people who don't know you and me very well will be sure to think that I let you down, because I could have saved you if I had been willing to spend the money. And what could be more contemptible than to get a name for thinking more of money than of your friends? Most people will never believe that it was you who refused to leave this place although we tried our hardest to persuade you.

SOCRATES: But my dear Crito, why should we pay so much attention to what 'most people' think? The really reasonable people, who have more claim to be considered, will believe that the facts are exactly as they are.

CRITO: You can see for yourself, Socrates, that one has to think of popular opinion as well. Your present position is quite enough to show that the capacity of ordinary people for causing trouble is not confined to petty annoyances, but has hardly any limits if you once get a bad name with them.

SOCRATES: I only wish that ordinary people *had* an unlimited capacity for doing harm; then they might have an unlimited power for doing good, which would be a splendid thing, if it were so. Actually they have neither. They cannot make a man wise or stupid; they simply act at random.

CRITO: Have it that way if you like, but tell me this, Socrates. I hope that you aren't worrying about the possible effects on me and the rest of your friends, and thinking that if you escape we shall have trouble with informers for having helped you to get away, and have to forfeit all our property or pay an enormous fine, or even incur some further punishment? If any idea like that is troubling you, you can dismiss it altogether. We are quite entitled to run that risk in saving you, and even worse, if necessary. Take my advice, and be reasonable.

SOCRATES: All that you say is very much in my mind, Crito, and a great deal more besides.

CRITO: Very well, then, don't let it distress you. I know some people who are willing to rescue you from here and get you out of the country for quite a moderate sum. And then surely you realize how cheap these informers are to buy off; we shan't need much money to settle them, and I think you've got enough of my money for yourself already. And then even supposing that in your anxiety for my safety you feel that you oughtn't to spend my money, there are these foreign gentlemen staying in Athens who are quite willing to spend theirs. One of them, Simmias of Thebes, has actually brought the money with him for this very purpose, and Cebes and a number of others are quite ready to do the same. So, as I say, you mustn't let any fears on these grounds make you slacken your efforts to escape, and you mustn't feel any misgivings about what you said at your trial – that you wouldn't know what to do with yourself if you left this country. Wherever you go, there are plenty of places where you will find a welcome, and if you choose to go to Thessaly, I have friends there who will make much of you and give you complete protection, so that no one in Thessaly can interfere with you.

Besides, Socrates, I don't even feel that it is right for you to try to do what you are doing, throwing away your life when you might save it. You are doing your best to treat yourself in exactly the same way as your enemies would, or rather did, when they wanted to ruin you. What is more, it seems to me that you are letting your sons down too. You have it in your power to finish their bringing-up and education, and instead of that you are proposing to go off and desert them, and so far as you are concerned they will have to take their chance. And what sort of chance are they likely to get? The sort of thing that usually happens to orphans when they lose their parents. Either one ought not to have children at all, or one ought to see their upbringing and education through to the end. It strikes me that you are taking the line of least resistance, whereas you ought to make the choice of a good man and a brave one, considering that you profess to have made goodness your object all through life. Really, I am ashamed, both on your account and on ours, your friends'. It will look as though we had played something like a coward's part all through this affair of yours. First there was the way you came into court when it was quite unnecessary – that was the first act. Then there was the conduct of the defense – that was the second. And finally, to complete the farce, we get this situation, which makes it appear that we have let you slip out of our hands through some lack of courage and enterprise on our part, because we didn't save you, and you didn't save yourself, when it would have been quite possible and practicable, if we had been any use at all.

There, Socrates, if you aren't careful, besides the suffering there will be all this disgrace for you and us to bear. Come, make up your mind. Really it's too late for that now; you ought to have it made up already. There is no alternative; the whole thing must be carried through during this coming night. If we lose any more time, it can't be done; it will be too late. I appeal to you, Socrates, on every ground; take my advice and please don't be unreasonable!

SOCRATES: My dear Crito, I appreciate your warm feelings very much – that is, assuming that they have some justification. If not, the stronger they are, the harder they will be to deal with. Very well, then, we must consider whether we ought to follow your advice or not. You know that this is not a new idea of mine; it has always been my nature never to accept advice from any of my friends unless reflection shows that it is the best course that reason offers. I cannot abandon the principles which I used to hold in the past simply because this accident has happened to me; they seem to me to be much as they were, and I respect and regard the same principles now as before. So unless we can find better principles on this occasion, you can be quite sure that I shall not agree with you – not even if the power of the people conjures up fresh hordes of bogies to terrify our childish minds, by subjecting us to chains and executions and confiscations of our property.

Well, then, how can we consider the question most reasonably? Suppose that we begin by reverting to this view which you hold about people's opinions. Was it always right to argue that some opinions should be taken seriously but not others? Or was it always wrong? Perhaps it was right before the question of my death arose, but now we can see clearly that it was a mistaken persistence in a point of view which was really irresponsible nonsense. I should like very much to inquire into this problem, Crito, with your help, and to see whether the argument will appear in any different light to me now that I am in this position, or whether it will remain the same, and whether we shall dismiss it or accept it.

Serious thinkers, I believe, have always held some such view as the one which I mentioned just now, that some of the opinions which people entertain should be respected, and others should not. Now I ask you, Crito, don't you think that this is a sound principle? You are safe from the prospect of dying tomorrow, in all human probability, and you are not likely to have your judgment upset by this impending calamity. Consider, then, don't you think that this is a sound enough principle, that one should not regard all the opinions that people hold, but only some and not others? What do you say? Isn't that a fair statement?

CRITO: Yes, it is.

SOCRATES: In other words, one should regard the good ones and not the bad?

CRITO: Yes.

SOCRATES: The opinions of the wise being good, and the opinions of the foolish bad?

CRITO: Naturally.

SOCRATES: To pass on, then, what do you think of the sort of illustration that I used to employ? When a man is in training, and taking it seriously, does he pay attention to all praise and criticism and opinion indiscriminately, or only when it comes from the one qualified person, the actual doctor or trainer?

CRITO: Only when it comes from the one qualified person.

SOCRATES: Then he should be afraid of the criticism and welcome the praise of the one qualified person, but not those of the general public.

CRITO: Obviously.

SOCRATES: So he ought to regulate his actions and exercises and eating and drinking by the judgment of his instructor, who has expert knowledge, rather than by the opinions of the rest of the public.

CRITO: Yes, that is so.

SOCRATES: Very well. Now if he disobeys the one man and disregards his opinion and commendations, and pays attention to the advice of the many who have no expert knowledge, surely he will suffer some bad effect?

CRITO: Certainly.

SOCRATES: And what is this bad effect? Where is it produced? I mean, in what part of the disobedient person?

CRITO: His body, obviously; that is what suffers.

SOCRATES: Very good. Well now, tell me, Crito - we don't want to go through all the examples one by one - does this apply as a general rule, and above all to the sort of actions which we are trying to decide about, just and unjust, honorable and dishonorable, good and bad? Ought we to be guided and intimidated by the opinion of the many or by that of the one - assuming that there is someone with expert knowledge? Is it true that we ought to respect and fear this person more than all the rest put together, and that if we do not follow his guidance we shall spoil and mutilate that part of us which, as we used to say, is improved by right conduct and destroyed by wrong? Or is this all nonsense?

CRITO: No, I think it is true, Socrates.

SOCRATES: Then consider the next step. There is a part of us which is improved by healthy actions and ruined by unhealthy ones. If we spoil it by taking the advice of nonexperts, will life be worth living when this part is once ruined? The part I mean is the body. Do you accept this?

CRITO: Yes.

SOCRATES: Well, is life worth living with a body which is worn out and ruined in health?

CRITO: Certainly not.

SOCRATES: What about the part of us which is mutilated by wrong actions and benefited by right ones? Is life worth living with this part ruined? Or do we believe that this part of us, whatever it may be, in which right and wrong operate, is of less importance than the body?

CRITO: Certainly not.

SOCRATES: It is really more precious?

CRITO: Much more.

SOCRATES: In that case, my dear fellow, what we ought to consider is not so much what people in general will say about us but how we stand with the expert in right and wrong, the one authority, who represents the actual truth. So in the first place your proposition is not correct when you say that we should consider popular opinion in questions of what is right and honorable and good, or the opposite. Of course one might object. All the same, the people have the power to put us to death.

CRITO: No doubt about that! Quite true, Socrates. It is a possible objection.

SOCRATES: But so far as I can see, my dear fellow, the argument which we have just been through is quite unaffected by it. At the same time I should like you to consider whether we are still satisfied on this point, that the really important thing is not to live, but to live well.

CRITO: Why, yes.

SOCRATES: And that to live well means the same thing as to live honorably or rightly?

CRITO: Yes.

SOCRATES: Then in the light of this agreement we must consider whether or not it is right for me to try to get away without an official discharge. If it turns out to be right, we must make the attempt; if not, we must let it drop. As for the considerations you raise about expense and reputation and bringing up children, I am afraid, Crito, that they represent the reflections of the ordinary public, who put people to death, and would bring them back to life if they could, with equal indifference to reason. Our real duty, I fancy, since the argument leads that way, is to consider one question only, the one which we raised just now. Shall we be acting rightly in paying money and showing gratitude to these people who are going to rescue me, and in escaping or arranging the escape ourselves, or shall we really be acting wrongly in doing all this? If it becomes clear that such conduct is wrong, I cannot help thinking that the question whether we are sure to die, or to suffer other ill effect for that matter, if we stand our ground and take no action, ought not to weigh with us at all in comparison with the risk of doing what is wrong.

CRITO: I agree with what you say, Socrates, but I wish you would consider what we ought to *do*.

SOCRATES: Let us look at it together, my dear fellow; and if you can challenge any of my arguments, do so and I will listen to you; but if you can't, be a good fellow and stop telling me over and over again that I ought to leave this place without official permission. I am very anxious to obtain your approval before I adopt the course which I have in mind. I don't want to act against your convictions. Now give your attention to the starting point of this inquiry – I hope that you will be satisfied with my way of stating it – and try to answer my questions to the best of your judgment.

CRITO: Well, I will try.

SOCRATES: Do we say that one must never willingly do wrong, or does it depend upon circumstances? Is it true, as we have often agreed before, that there is no sense in which wrongdoing is good or honorable? Or have we jettisoned all our former convictions in these last few days? Can you and I at our age, Crito, have spent all these years in serious discussions without realizing that we were no better than a pair of children? Surely the truth is just what we have always said. Whatever the popular view is, and whether the alternative is pleasanter than the present one or even harder to bear, the fact remains that to do wrong is in every sense bad and dishonorable for the person who does it. Is that our view, or not?

CRITO: Yes, it is.

SOCRATES: Then in no circumstances must one do wrong.

CRITO: No.

SOCRATES: In that case one must not even do wrong when one is wronged, which most people regard as the natural course.

CRITO: Apparently not.

SOCRATES: Tell me another thing, Crito. Ought one to do injuries or not?

CRITO: Surely not, Socrates.

SOCRATES: And tell me, is it right to do an injury in retaliation, as most people believe, or not?

CRITO: No, never.

SOCRATES: Because, I suppose, there is no difference between injuring people and wronging them.

CRITO: Exactly.

SOCRATES: So one ought not to return a wrong or an injury to any person, whatever the provocation is. Now be careful, Crito, that in making these single admissions you do not end by admitting something contrary to your real beliefs. I know that there are and always will be few people who think like this, and consequently between those who do think so and those who do not there can be no agreement on principle; they must always feel contempt when they observe one another's decisions. I want even you to consider very carefully whether you share my views and agree with me, and whether we can proceed with our discussion from the established hypothesis that it is never right to do a wrong or return a wrong or defend oneself against injury by retaliation, or whether you dissociate yourself from any share in this view as a basis for discussion. I have held it for a long time, and still hold it, but if you have formed any other opinion, say so and tell me what it is. If, one the other hand, you stand by what we have said, listen to my next point.

CRITO: Yes, I stand by it and agree with you. Go on.

SOCRATES: Well, here is my next point, or rather question. Ought one to fulfil all one's agreements, provided that they are right, or break them?

CRITO: One ought to fulfil them.

SOCRATES: Then consider the logical consequence. If we leave this place without first persuading the state to let us go, are we or are we not doing an injury, and doing it in a quarter where it is least justifiable? Are we or are we not abiding by our just agreements?

CRITO: I can't answer your question, Socrates. I am not clear in my mind.

SOCRATES: Look at it in this way. Suppose that while we were preparing to run away from here - or however one should describe it - the laws and constitution of Athens were to come and confront us and ask this question. Now, Socrates, what are you proposing to do? Can you deny that by this act which you are contemplating you intend, so far as you have the power, to destroy us, the laws, and the whole state as well? Do you imagine that a city can continue to exist and not be turned upside down, if the legal judgments which are pronounced in it have no force but are nullified and destroyed by private persons?

How shall we answer this question, Crito, and others of the same kind? There is much that could be said, especially by a professional advocate, to protest against the invalidation of this law which enacts that judgments once pronounced shall be binding. Shall we say, Yes, I do intend to destroy the laws, because the state wronged me by passing a faulty judgment at my trial? Is this to be our answer, or what?

CRITO: What you have just said, by all means, Socrates.

SOCRATES: Then what supposing the laws say, Was there provision for this in the agreement between you and us, Socrates? Or did you undertake to abide by whatever judgments the state pronounced?

If we expressed surprise at such language, they would probably say, Never mind our language, Socrates, but answer our questions; after all, you are accustomed to the method of question and answer. Come now, what charge do you bring against us and the state, that you are trying to destroy us? Did we not give you life in the first place? Was it not through us that your father married your mother and begot you? Tell us, have you any complaint against those of us laws that deal with marriage?

No, none, I should say.

Well, have you any against the laws which deal with children's urbringing and education, such as you had yourself? Are you not grateful to those of us laws which were instituted for this end, for requiring your father to give you a cultural and physical education?

Yes, I should say.

Very good. Then since you have been born and brought up and educated, can you deny, in the first place, that you were our child and servant, both you and your ancestors? And if this is so, do you imagine that what is right for us is equally right for you, and that whatever we try to do to you, you are justified in retaliating? You did not have equality of rights with your father, or your employer - supposing that you had had one - to enable you to retaliate. You were not allowed to answer back when you were scolded or to hit back when you were beaten, or to do a great many other things of the same kind. Do you expect to have such license against your country and its laws that if we try to put you to death in the belief that it is right to do so, you on your part will try your hardest to destroy your country and us its laws in return?

And will you, the true devotee of goodness, claim that you are justified in doing so? Are you so wise as to have forgotten that compared with your mother and father and all the rest of your ancestors your country is something far more precious, more venerable, more sacred, and held in greater honor both among gods and among all reasonable men? Do you not realize that you are even more bound to respect and placate the anger of your country than your father's anger? That if you cannot persuade your country you must do whatever it orders, and patiently submit to any punishment that it imposes, whether it be flogging or imprisonment? And if it leads you out to war, to be wounded or killed, you must comply, and it is right that you should do so. You must not give way or retreat or abandon your position. Both in war and in the law courts and everywhere else you must do whatever your city and your country command, or else persuade them in accordance with universal justice, but violence is a sin even against your parents, and it is a far greater sin against your country,

What shall we say to this, Crito – that what the laws say is true, or not?

CRITO: Yes, I think so.

SOCRATES: Consider, then, Socrates, the laws would probably continue, whether it is also true for us to say that what you are now trying to do to us is not right. Although we have brought you into the world and reared you and educated you, and given you and all your fellow citizens a share in all the good things at our disposal, nevertheless by the very fact of granting our permission we openly proclaim this principle, that any Athenian, on attaining to manhood and seeing for himself the political organization of the state and us its laws, is permitted, if he is not satisfied with us, to take his property and go away wherever he likes. If any of you chooses to go to one of our colonies, supposing that he should not be satisfied with us and the state, or to emigrate to any other country, not one of us laws hinders or prevents him from going away wherever he likes, without any loss of property. On the other hand, if any one of you stands his ground when he can see how we administer justice and the rest of our public organization, we hold that by so doing he has in fact undertaken to do anything that we tell him. And we maintain that anyone who disobeys is guilty of doing wrong on three separate counts: first because we are his parents, and secondly because we are his guardians, and thirdly because, after promising obedience, he is neither obeying us nor persuading us to change our decision if we are at fault in any way. And although all our orders are in the form of proposals, not of savage commands, and we give him the choice of either persuading us or doing what we say, he is actually doing neither. These are the charges, Socrates, to which we say that you will be liable if you do what you are contemplating, and you will not be the least culpable of your fellow countrymen, but one of the most guilty.

If I asked why, they would no doubt pounce upon me with perfect justice and point out that there are very few people in Athens who have entered into this agreement with them as explicitly as I have. They would say, Socrates, we have substantial evidence that you are satisfied with us and with the state. You would not have been so exceptionally reluctant to cross the borders of your country if you had not been exceptionally attached to it. You have never left the city to attend a festival or for any other purpose, except on some military expedition. You have never traveled abroad as other people do, and you have never felt the impulse to acquaint yourself with another country or constitution. You have been content with us and with our city. You have definitely chosen us, and undertaken to observe us in all your activities as a citizen, and as the crowning proof that you are satisfied with our city, you have begotten children in it. Furthermore, even at the time of your trial you could have proposed the penalty of banishment, if you had chosen to do so – that is, you could have done then with the sanction of the state what you are now trying to do without it. But whereas at that time you made a noble show of indifference if you had to die, and in fact preferred death, as you said, to banishment, now you show no respect for your earlier professions, and no regard for us, the laws, whom you are trying to destroy. You are behaving like the lowest type of menial, trying to run away in spite of the contracts and undertakings by which you agreed to live as a member of our state. Now first answer this question. Are we or are we not speaking the truth when we say that you have undertaken, in deed if not in word, to live your life as a citizen in obedience to us?

What are we to say to that, Crito? Are we not bound to admit it?

CRITO: We cannot help it, Socrates.

SOCRATES: It is a fact, then, they would say, that you are

breaking covenants and undertakings made with us, although you made them under no compulsion or misunderstanding, and were not compelled to decide in a limited time. You had seventy years in which you could have left the country, if you were not satisfied with us or felt that the agreements were unfair. You did not choose Sparta or Crete – your favourite models of good governments – or any other Greek or foreign state. You could not have absented yourself from the city less if you had been lame or blind or decrepit in some other way. It is quite obvious that you stand by yourself above all other Athenians in your affection for this city and for us its laws. Who would care for a city without laws? And now, after all this, are you not going to stand by your agreement? Yes, you are, Socrates, if you will take our advice, and then you will at least escape being laughed at for leaving the city.

We invite you to consider what good you will do to yourself or your friends if you commit this breach of faith and stain your conscience. It is fairly obvious that the risk of being banished and either losing their citizenship or having their property confiscated will extend to your friends as well. As for yourself, if you go to one of the neighboring states, such as Thebes or Megara, which are both well governed, you will enter them as an enemy to their constitution, and all good patriots will eye you with suspicion as a destroyer of law and order. Incidentally you will confirm the opinion of the jurors who tried you that they gave a correct verdict; a destroyer of laws might very well be supposed to have a destructive influence upon young and foolish human beings. Do you intend, then, to avoid well-governed states and the higher forms of human society? And if you do, will life be worth living? Or will you approach these people and have the impudence to converse with them? What arguments will you use, Socrates? The same which you used here, that goodness and integrity, institutions and laws, are the most precious possessions of mankind? Do you not think that Socrates and everything about him will appear in a disreputable light? You certainly ought to think so.

But perhaps you will retire from this part of the world and go to Crito's friends in Thessaly? That is the home of indiscipline and laxity, and no doubt they would enjoy hearing the amusing story of how you managed to run away from prison by arraying yourself in some costume or putting on a shepherd's smock or some other conventional runaway's disguise, and altering your personal appearance. And will no one comment on the fact that an old man of your age, probably with only a short time left to live, should dare to cling so greedily to life, at the price of violating the most stringent laws? Perhaps not, if you avoid irritating anyone. Otherwise, Socrates, you will hear a good many humiliating comments. So you will live as the toady and slave of all the populace, literally 'roistering in Thessaly,' as though you had left this country for Thessaly to attend a banquet there. And where will your discussions about goodness and uprightness be then, we should like to know? But of course you want to live for your children's sake, so that you may be able to bring them up and educate them. Indeed! By first taking them off to Thessaly and making foreigners of them, so that they may have that additional enjoyment? Or if that if not your intention, supposing that they are brought up here with you still alive, will they be better cared for and educated without you, because of course your friends will look after them? Will they look after your children if you go away to Thessaly, and not if you go away to the next world? Surely if those who profess to be your friends are worth anything, you must believe that they would care for them.

No, Socrates, be advised by us your guardians, and do not think more of your children or of your life or of anything else than you think of what is right, so that when you enter the next world you may have all this to plead in your defense before the authorities there. It seems clear that if you do this thing, neither you nor any of your friends will be the better for it or be more upright or have a cleaner conscience here in this world, nor will it be better for you when you reach the next. As it is, you will leave this place, when you do, as the victim of a wrong done not by us, the laws, but by your fellow men. But if you leave in that dishonorable way, returning wrong for wrong and evil for evil, breaking your agreements and covenants with us, and injuring those whom you least ought to injure - yourself, your friends, your country, and us - then you will have to face our anger in your lifetime, and in that place beyond when the laws of the other world know that you have tried, so far as you could, to destroy even us their brothers, they will not receive you with a kindly welcome. Do not take Crito's advice, but follow ours.

That, my dear friend Crito, I do assure you, is what I seem to hear them saying, just as a mystic seems to hear the strains of music, and the sound of their arguments rings so loudly in my head that I cannot hear the other side. I warn you that, as my opinion stands at present, it will be useless to urge a different view. However, if you think that you will do any good by it, say what you like.

CRITO: No, Socrates, I have nothing to say.

SOCRATES: Then give it up, Crito, and let us follow this course, since God points out the way.

2

CIVIL DISOBEDIENCE

Henry David Thoreau

I heartily accept the motto – 'That government is best which governs least'; and I should like to see it acted up to more rapidly and systematically. Carried out, it finally amounts to this, which also I believe – 'That government is best which governs not at all'; and when men are prepared for it, that will be the kind of government which they will have. Government is at best but an expedient; but most governments are usually, and all governments are sometimes, inexpedient. The objections which have been brought against a standing army, and they are many and weighty, and deserve to prevail, may also at last be brought against a standing government. The standing army is only an arm of the standing government. The government itself, which is only the mode which the people have chosen to execute their will, is equally liable to be abused and perverted before the people can act through it. Witness the present Mexican war, the work of comparatively a few individuals using the standing government as their tool; for, in the outset, the people would not have consented to this measure.

This American government – what is it but a tradition, though a recent one, endeavouring to transmit itself unimpaired to posterity, but each instant losing some of its integrity? It has not the vitality and force of a single man; for a single man can bend it to his will. It is a sort of wooden gun to the people themselves.

From: H. D. Thoreau, *A Yankee in Canada with Anti-Slavery and Reform Papers* (Boston: Ticknor & Fields, pp.123-51. Originally delivered in January 1848 as a lecture under the title 'On the Relation of the Individual to the State,' and first published in Elizabeth Peabody (ed.), *Aesthetic Papers* (Boston: privately printed, 1849), under the title, 'Resistance to Civil Government.'

But it is not the less necessary for this; for the people must have some complicated machinery or other, and hear its din, to satisfy that idea of government which they have. Governments show thus how succesfully men can be imposed on, even impose on themselves, for their own advantage. It is excellent, we must all allow. Yet this government never of itself furthered any enterprise, but by the alacrity with which it got out of its way. *It* does not keep the country free. *It* does not settle the West. *It* does not educate. The character inherent in the American people has done all that has been accomplished; and it would have done somewhat more, if the government had not sometimes got in its way. For government is an expedient by which men would fain succeed in letting one another alone; and, as has been said, when it is most expedient, the governed are most let alone by it. Trade and commerce, if they were not made of India-rubber, would never manage to bounce over the obstacles which legislators are continually putting in their way; and, if one were to judge these men wholly by the effects of their actions and not partly by their intentions, they would deserve to be classed and punished with those mischievous persons who put obstructions on the railroads.

But, to speak practically and as a citizen, unlike those who call themselves no-government men, I ask for, not at once no government, but *at once* a better government. Let every man make known what kind of government would command his respect, and that will be one step toward obtaining it.

After all, the practical reason why, when the power is once in the hands of the people, a majority are permitted, and for a long period continue, to rule, is not because they are most likely to be in the right, nor because this seems fairest to the minority, but because they are physically the strongest. But a government in which the majority rule in all cases cannot be based on justice, even as far as men understand it. Can there not be a government in which majorities do not virtually decide right and wrong, but conscience? – in which majorities decide only those questions to which the rule of expediency is applicable? Must the citizen ever for a moment, or in the least degree, resign his conscience to the legislator? Why has every man a conscience, then? I think that we should be men first, and subjects afterward. It is not desirable to cultivate a respect for the law, so much as for the right. The only obligation which I have a right to assume, is to do at any time what I think right. It is truly enough said, that a corporation has no conscience; but a corporation of conscientious men is a corporation *with* a conscience. Law never made men a whit more just; and, by means of their respect for it, even the well-disposed are daily made the agents of injustice. A common and natural result of an undue respect for law is, that you may see a file of soldiers, colonel, captain, corporal, privates, powder-monkeys, and all, marching in admirable order over hill and dale to the wars, against their wills, ay, against their common sense and consciences, which makes it very steep marching indeed, and produces a palpitation of the heart. They have no doubt that it is a damnable business in which they are concerned; they are all peaceably inclined. Now, what are they? Men at all? or small movable forts and magazines, at the service of some unscrupulous man in power? Visit the Navy-Yard, and behold a marine, such a man as an American government can make, or such as it can make a man with its black arts - a mere shadow and reminiscence of humanity, a man laid out alive and standing, and already, as one may say, buried under arms with funeral accompaniments, though it may be -

> Not a drum was heard, not a funeral note,
> As his corpse to the rampart we hurried;
> Not a soldier discharged his farewell shot
> O'er the grave where our hero we buried.

The mass of men serve the state thus, not as men mainly, but as machines, with their bodies. They are the standing army, and the militia, jailers, constables, posse comitatus, &c. In most cases there is no free exercise whatever of the judgment or of the moral sense; but they put themselves on a level with wood and earth and stones; and wooden men can perhaps be manufactured that will serve the purpose as well. Such command no more respect than men of straw or a lump of dirt. They have the same sort of worth only as horses and dogs. Yet such as these even are commonly esteemed good citizens. Others - as most legislators, politicians, lawyers, ministers, and officeholders - serve the state chiefly with their heads; and, as they rarely make any moral distinctions, they are as likely to serve the Devil, without *intending* it, as God. A very few, as heroes, patriots, martyrs, reformers in the great sense, and *men*, serve the state with their consciences also, and so necessarily resist it for the most part; and they are commonly treated as enemies by it. A wise man will only be useful as a man, and will not submit to be 'clay,' and 'stop a hole to keep the wind away,' but leave that office to his dust at least:

> I am too high-born to be propertied,
> To be a secondary at control,
> Or useful serving-man and instrument
> To any sovereign state throughout the world.

He who gives himself entirely to his fellow-men appears to them useless and selfish; but he who gives himself partially to them is pronounced a benefactor and philanthropist.

How does it become a man to behave toward this American government to-day? I answer, that he cannot without disgrace be associated with it. I cannot for an instant recognize the political organization as *my* government which is the *slave's* government also.

All men recognize the right of revolution; that is, the right to refuse allegiance to, and to resist, the government, when its tyranny or its inefficiency are great and endurable. But almost all say that such is not the case now. But such was the case, they think, in the Revolution of '75. If one were to tell me that this was a bad government because it taxed certain foreign commodities brought to its ports, it is most probable that I should not make an ado about it, for I can do without them. All machines have their friction; and possibly this does enough good to counterbalance the evil. At any rate, it is a great evil to make a stir about it. But when the friction comes to have its machine, and oppression and robbery are organized, I say, let us not have such a machine any longer. In other words, when a sixth of the population of a nation which has undertaken to be the refuge of liberty are slaves, and a whole country is unjustly overrun and conquered by a foreign army, and subjected to military law, I think that it is not too soon for honest men to rebel and revolutionize. What makes this duty the more urgent is the fact, that the country so overrun is not our own, but ours is the invading army.

Paley, a common authority with many on moral questions, in his chapter on the 'Duty of Submission to Civil Government,' resolves all civil obligations into expediency; and he proceeds to say, 'that so long as the interest of the whole society requires it, that is, so long as the established government cannot be resisted or changed without public inconveniency, it is the will of God that the established government be obeyed, and no longer. . . . This principle being admitted, the justice of every particular case of resistance is reduced to a computation of the quantity of the danger and grievance on the one side, and of the probability and expense of redressing it on the other.' Of this, he says, every man shall judge for himself. But Paley appears never to have contemplated those cases to which the rule of expediency does not apply, in which a people, as well as an individual, must do justice, cost what it may. If I have unjustly wrested a plank from a drowning man, I must restore it to him though I drown myself. This, according to Paley, would be inconvenient. But he that would save his life, in such a case, shall lose it. This people must cease to hold slaves, and to make war on Mexico, though it cost them their existence as a people.

In their practice, nations agree with Paley; but does any one think that Massachusetts does exactly what is right at the present crisis?

A drab of state, a cloth-o'-silver slut,
To have her train borne up, and her soul trail in the dirt.

Practically speaking, the opponents to a reform in Massachusetts are not a hundred thousand politicians at the South, but a hundred thousand merchants and farmers here, who are more interested in commerce and agriculture than they are in humanity, and are not prepared to do justice to the slave and to Mexico, *cost what it may*. I quarrel not with far-off foes, but with those who, near at home, co-operate with, and do the bidding of, those far away, and without whom the latter would be harmless. We are accustomed to say, that the mass of men are unprepared; but improvement is slow, because the few are not materially wiser or better than the many. It is not so important that many should be as good as you, as that there be some absolute goodness somewhere; for that will leaven the whole lump. There are thousands who are *in opinion* opposed to slavery and to the war, who yet in effect do nothing to put an end to them; who, esteeming themselves children of Washington and Franklin, sit down with their hands in their pockets, and say that they know not what to do, and do nothing; who even postpone the question of freedom to the question of free-trade, and quietly read the prices-current along with the latest advices from Mexico, after dinner, and, it may be, fall asleep over them both. What is the price-current of an honest man and patriot to-day? They hesitate, and they regret, and sometimes they petition; but they do nothing in earnest and with effect. They will wait, well disposed, for others to remedy the evil, that they may no longer have it to regret. At most, they give only a cheap vote, and a feeble countenance and God-speed, to the right, as it goes by them. There are nine hundred and ninety-nine patrons of virtue to one virtuous man. But it is easier to deal with the real possessor of a thing than with the temporary guardian of it.

All voting is a sort of gaming, like checkers or backgammon, with a slight moral tinge to it, a playing with right and wrong, with moral questions; and betting naturally accompanies it. The character of the voters is not staked. I cast my vote, perchance, as I think right; but I am not vitally concerned that that right should prevail. I am willing to leave it to the majority. Its obligation, therefore, never exceeds that of expediency. Even voting *for the right* is *doing* nothing for it. It is only expressing to men feebly your desire that it should prevail. A wise man will not leave the right to the mercy of chance, nor wish it to prevail through the power of the majority. There is but little virtue in the action of masses of men. When the majority shall at length vote for the abolition of slavery, it will be because they are indifferent to slavery, or because there is but little slavery left to be abolished by their vote. *They* will then be the only slaves. Only *his* vote can hasten the abolition of slavery who asserts his own freedom by his vote.

I hear of a convention to be held at Baltimore, or elsewhere, for the selection of a candidate for the Presidency, made up chiefly of editors, and men who are politicians by profession; but I think, what is it to any independent, intelligent; and respectable man what decision they may come to? Shall we not have the advantage of his wisdom and honesty, nevertheless? Can we not count upon some independent votes? Are there not many individuals in the country who do not attend conventions? But no: I find that the respectable man, so called, has immediately drifted from his position, and despairs of his country, when his country has more reason to despair of him. He forthwith adopts one of the candidates thus selected as the only *available* one, thus proving that he is himself *available* for any purposes of the demagogue.

His vote is of no more worth than that of any unprincipled foreigner or hireling native, who may have been bought. O for a man who is a *man*, and, as my neighbour says, has a bone in his back which you cannot pass your hand through! Our statistics are at fault: the population has been returned too large. How many *men* are there to a square thousand miles in this country? Hardly one. Does not America offer any inducement for men to settle here? The American has dwindled into an Odd Fellow – one who may be known by the development of his organ of gregariousness, and a manifest lack of intellect and cheerful self-reliance; whose first and chief concern, on coming into the world, is to see that the Almshouses are in good repair; and, before yet he has lawfully donned the virile garb, to collect a fund for the support of the widows and orphans that may be; who, in short, ventures to live only by the aid of the Mutual Insurance Company, which has promised to bury him decently.

It is not a man's duty, as a matter of course, to devote himself to the eradication of any, even the most enormous wrong; he may still properly have other concerns to engage him; but it is his duty, at least, to wash his hands of it, and, if he gives it no thought longer, not to give it practically his support. If I devote myself to other pursuits and contemplations, I must first see, at least, that I do not pursue them sitting upon another man's shoulders. I must get off him first, that he may pursue his contemplations too. See what gross inconsistency is tolerated. I have heard some of my townsmen say, 'I should like to have them order me out to help put down an insurrection of the slaves, or to march to Mexico – see if I would go'; and yet these very men have each, directly by their allegiance, and so indirectly, at least, by their money, furnished a substitute. The soldier is applauded who refuses to serve in an unjust war by those who do not refuse to sustain the unjust government which makes the war; is applauded by those whose own act and authority he disregards and sets at naught; as if the State were penitent to that degree that it hired one to scourge it while it sinned, but not to that degree that it left off sinning for a moment. Thus, under the name of Order and Civil Government, we are all made at last to pay homage to and support our own meanness. After the first blush of sin comes its indifference; and from immoral it becomes, as it were, *un*moral, and not quite unnecessary to that life which we have made.

The broadest and most prevalent error requires the most disinterested virtue to sustain it. The slight reproach to which the virtue of patriotism is commonly liable, the noble are most likely to incur. Those who, while they disapprove of the character and measures of a government, yield to it their allegiance and support, are undoubtedly its most conscientious supporters, and so frequently the most serious obstacles to reform. Some are petitioning the State to dissolve the Union, to disregard the requisitions of the President. Why do they not dissolve it themselves – the union between themselves and the State – and refuse to pay their quota into its treasury? Do not they stand in the same relation to the State, that the State does to the Union? And have not the same reasons prevented the State from resisting the Union, which have prevented them from resisting the State?

How can a man be satisfied to entertain an opinion merely, and enjoy *it*? Is there any enjoyment in it, if his opinion is that he is aggrieved? If you are cheated out of a single dollar by your neighbor, you do not rest satisfied with knowing that you are cheated, or with saying that you are cheated, or even with petitioning him to pay you your due; but you take effectual steps at once to obtain the full amount, and see that you are never cheated again. Action from principle, the perception and the performance of right, changes things and relations; it is essentially revolutionary, and does not consist wholly with anything which was. It not only divides states and churches, it divides families; ay, it divides the *individual*, separating the diabolical in him from the divine.

Unjust laws exist: shall we be content to obey them, or shall we endeavor to amend them, and obey them until we have succeeded, or shall we transgress them at once? Men generally, under such a government as this, think that they ought to wait until they have persuaded the majority to alter them. They think that, if they should resist, the remedy would be worse than the evil. But it is the fault of the government itself that the remedy *is* worse than the evil. *It* makes it worse. Why is it not more apt to anticipate and provide for reform? Why does it not cherish its wise minority? Why does it cry and resist before it is hurt? Why does it not encourage its citizens to be on the alert to point out its faults, and *do* better than it would have them? Why does it always crucify Christ, and excommunicate Copernicus and Luther, and pronounce Washington and Franklin rebels?

One would think, that a deliberate and practical denial of its authority was the only offence never contemplated by government; else, why has it not assigned its definite, its suitable and proportionate penalty? If a man who has no property refuses but once to earn nine shillings for the State, he is put in prison for a period unlimited by any law that I know, and determined only by the discretion of those who placed him there; but if he should steal ninety times nine shillings from the State, he is soon permitted to go at large again.

If the injustice is part of the necessary friction of the machine of governments, let it go, let it go: perchance it will wear smooth – certainly the machine will wear out. If the injustice has a spring, or a pulley, or a rope, or a crank, exclusively for itself, then perhaps you may consider whether the remedy will not be worse than the evil; but if it is of such a nature that it requires you to be the agent of injustice to another, then, I say, break the law. Let your life be a counter friction to stop the machine. What I have to do is to see, at any rate, that I do not lend myself to the wrong which I condemn.

As for adopting the ways which the State has provided for remedying the evil, I know not of such ways. They take too much time, and a man's life will be gone. I have other affairs to attend to. I came into this world, not chiefly to make this a good place to live in, but to live in it, be it good or bad. A man has not everything to do, but something; and because he cannot do *everything*, it is not necessary that he should do *something* wrong. It is not my business to be petitioning the Governor or the Legislature any more than it is theirs to petition me; and, if they should not hear my petition, what should I do then? But in this case the state has provided no way: its very Constitution is the evil. This may seem to be harsh and stubborn and unconciliatory; but it is to treat with the utmost kindness and consideration the only spirit that can appreciate or deserves it. So is all change for the better, like birth and death, which convulse the body.

I do not hesitate to say, that those who call themselves Abolitionists should at once effectually withdraw their support, both in person and property, from the government of Massachusetts, and not wait till they constitute a majority of one, before they suffer the right to prevail through them. I think that it is enough if they have God on their side, without waiting for that other one. Moreover, any man more right than his neighbors constitutes a majority of one already.

I meet this American government, or its representative, the State government, directly, and face to face, once a year – no more – in the person of its tax-gatherer; this is the only mode in which a man situated as I am necessarily meets it; and it then says distinctly, Recognize me; and the simplest, the most effectual, and, in the present posture of affairs, the indispensablest mode of treating with it on this head, of expressing your little satisfaction with and love for it, is to deny it then. My civil neighbor, the tax-gatherer, is the very man I have to deal with – for it is, after all, with men and not with parchment that I quarrel – and he has voluntarily chosen to be an agent of the government. How shall he ever know well what he is and does as an officer of the government, or as a man, until he is obliged to consider whether he shall treat me, his neighbor, for whom he has respect, as a neighbor and well-disposed man, or as a maniac and disturber of the peace, and see if he can get over this obstruction to his neighborliness without a ruder and more impetuous thought or speech corresponding with his action. I know this well, that if one thousand, if one hundred, if ten men whom I could name – if ten *honest* men only – ay, if *one* HONEST man, in this State of Massachusetts, *ceasing to hold slaves*, were actually to withdraw from this copartnership, and be locked up in the county jail therefor, it would be the abolition of slavery in America. For it matters not how small the beginning may seem to be: what is once well done is done forever. But we love better to talk about it: that we say in our mission. Reform keeps many scores of newspapers in its service, but not one man. If my esteemed neighbor, the State's ambassador, who will devote his days to the settlement of the question of human rights in the Council Chamber, instead of being threatened with the prisons of Carolina, were to sit down the prisoner of Massachusetts, that State which is so anxious to foist the sin of slavery upon her sister – though at present she can discover only an act of inhospitality to be the ground of a quarrel with her – the Legislature would not wholly waive the subject the following winter.

Under a government which imprisons any unjustly, the true place for a just man is also a prison. The proper place to-day, the only place which Massachusetts has provided for her freer and less desponding spirits, is in her prisons, to be put out and locked out of the State by her own act, as they have already put themselves out by their principles. It is there that the fugitive slave, and the Mexican prisoner on parole, and the Indian come to plead the wrongs of his race, should find them; on that separate, but more free and honorable ground, where the State places those who are not *with* her, but *against* her – the only house in a slave State in which a free man can abide with honor. If any think that their influence would be lost there, and their voices no longer afflict the ear of the State, that they would not be as an enemy within its walls, they do not know by how much truth is stronger than error, nor how much more eloquently and effectively he can combat injustice who has experienced a little in his own person. Cast your whole vote, not a strip of paper merely, but your whole influence. A minority is powerless while it conforms to the majority; it is not even a minority then; but it is irresistible when it clogs by its whole weight. If the alternative is to keep all just men in prison, or give up war and slavery, the State will not hesitate which to choose. If a thousand men were not to pay their tax-bills this year, that would not be a violent and bloody measure, as it would be to pay them, and enable the State to commit violence and shed innocent blood. This is, in fact, the definition of a peaceable revolution, if any such is possible. If the tax-gatherer, or any other public officer, asks me, as one has done, 'But what shall I do?' my answer is, 'If you really wish to do anything, resign your office.' When the subject has refused allegiance, and the officer has resigned his office, then the revolution is accomplished. But even suppose blood should flow. Is there not a sort of blood shed when the conscience is wounded? Through this wound a man's real manhood and immortality flow out, and he bleeds to an everlasting death. I see this blood flowing now.

I have contemplated the imprisonment of the offender, rather than the seizure of his goods – though both will serve the same purpose – because they who assert the purest right, and consequently are most dangerous to a corrupt State, commonly have not spent much time in accumulating property. To such the State renders comparatively small service, and a slight tax is wont appear exorbitant, particularly if they are obliged to earn it by special labor with their hands. If there were one who lived wholly without the use of money, the State itself would hesitate to demand it of him. But the rich man – not to make any invidious comparison – is always sold to the institution which makes him rich. Absolutely speaking, the more money, the less virtue; for money comes between a man and his objects, and obtains them for him; and it was certainly no great virtue to obtain it. It puts to rest many questions which he would otherwise be taxed to answer; while the only new question which it puts is the hard but superfluous one, how to spend it. Thus his moral ground is taken from under his feet. The opportunities of living are diminished in proportion as what are called the 'means' are increased. The best thing a man can do for his culture when he is rich is to endeavour to carry out those schemes which he entertained when he was poor. Christ answered the Herodians according to their condition. 'Show me the tribute-money,' said he – and one took a penny out of his pocket; if you use money which has the image of Caesar on it, and which he has made current and valuable, that is, *if you are men of the State,* and gladly enjoy the advantages of Caesar's government, then pay him back some of his own when he demands it; 'Render therefore to Caesar that which is Caesar's, and to God those things which are God's' – leaving them no wiser than before as to which was which; for they did not wish to know.

When I converse with the freest of my neighbors, I perceive that, whatever they may say about the magnitude and seriousness of the question, and their regard for the public tranquility, the long and the short of the matter is, that they cannot spare the protection of the existing government, and they dread the consequences to their property and families of disobedience to it. For my own part, I should not like to think that I ever rely on the protection of the State. But, if I deny the authority of the State when it presents its tax-bill, it will soon take and waste all my property, and so harass me and my children without end. This is hard. This makes it impossible for a man to live honestly, and at the same time comfortably, in outward respects. It will not be worth the while to accumulate property; that would be sure to go again. You must hire or squat somewhere, and raise but a small crop, and eat that soon. You must live within yourself, and depend upon yourself always tucked up and ready for a start, and not have many affairs. A man may grow rich in Turkey even, if he will be in all respects a good subject of the Turkish govern-ment. Confucius said: 'If a state is governed by the principles of reason, poverty and misery are subjects of shame; if a state is not governed by the principles of reason, riches and honors are the subjects of shame.' No: until I want the protection of Massachusetts to be extended to me in some distant Southern port, where my liberty is endangered, or until I am bent solely on building up an estate at home by peaceful enterprise, I can afford to refuse allegiance to Massachusetts, and her right to my property and life. It costs me less in every sense to incur the penalty of disobedience to the State, than it would to obey. I should feel as if I were worth less in that case.

Some years ago, the State met me in behalf of the Church, and commanded me to pay a certain sum toward the support of a clergyman whose preaching my father attended, but never I myself. 'Pay,' it said, 'or be locked up in the jail.' I declined to pay. But, unfortunately, another man saw fit to pay it. I did not see why the schoolmaster should be taxed to support the priest, and not the priest the schoolmaster; for I was not the State's schoolmaster, but I supported myself by voluntary subscription. I did not see why the lyceum should not present its tax-bill, and have the State to back its demand, as well as the Church. However, at the request of the selectmen, I condescended to make some such statement as this in writing: 'Know all men by these presents, that I, Henry Thoreau, do not wish to be regarded as a member of any incorporated society which I have not joined.' This I gave to the town clerk; and he has it. The State, having thus learned that I did not wish to be regarded as a member of that church, has never made a like demand on me since; though it said that it must adhere to its original presumption that time. If I had known how to name them, I should then have signed off in detail from all the societies which I never signed on to; but I did not know where to find a complete list.

I have paid no poll-tax for six years. I was put into a jail once on this account, for one night; and, as I stood considering the walls of solid stone, two or three feet thick, the door of wood and iron, a foot thick, and the iron grating which strained the light, I could not help being struck with the foolishness of that institution which treated me as if I were mere flesh and blood and bones, to be locked up. I wondered that it should have concluded at length that this was the best use it could put me to, and had never thought to avail itself of my services in some way. I saw that, if there was a wall of stone between me and my townsmen, there was a still more difficult one to climb or break through, before they could get to be as free as I was. I did not for a moment feel confined, and the walls seemed a great waste of stone and mortar. I felt as if I alone of all my townsmen had paid my tax. They plainly did not know how to treat me, but behaved like persons who are underbred. In every threat and in every compliment there was a blunder; for they thought that my chief desire was to stand the other side of that stone wall. I could not but smile to see how industriously they locked the door on my meditations, which followed them out again without let or hindrance, and *they* were really all that was dangerous. As they could not reach me, they had resolved to punish my body; just as boys, if they cannot come at some person against whom they have a spite, will abuse his dog. I saw that the State was half-witted, that it was timid as a lone woman with her silver spoons, and that it did not know its friends from its foes, and I lost all my remaining respect for it, and pitied it.

Thus the State never intentionally confronts a man's sense, intellectual or moral, but only his body, his senses. It is not armed with superior wit or honesty, but with superior physical strength. I was not born to be forced. I will breathe after my own fashion. Let us see who is the strongest. What force has a multitude? They can only force me who obey a higher law than I. They force me to become like themselves. I do not hear of *men* being *forced* to live this way or that by masses of men. What sort of life were that to live? When I meet a government which says to me, 'Your money or your life,' why should I be in haste to give it my money? It may be in a great strait, and not know what to do: I cannot help that. It must help itself; do as I do. It is not worth the while to snivel about it. I am not responsible for the successful working of the machinery of society. I am not the son of the engineer. I perceive that, when an acorn and a chestnut fall side by side, the one does not remain inert to make way for the other, but both obey their own laws, and spring and grow and flourish as best they can, till one, perchance, overshadows and destroys the other. If a plant cannot live according to its nature, it dies; and so a man.

The night in prison was novel and interesting enough. The prisoners in their shirtsleeves were enjoying a chat and the evening air in the doorway, when I entered. But the jailer said, 'Come, boys, it is time to lock up'; and so they dispersed, and I heard the sound of their steps returning into the hollow apartments. My roommate was introduced to me by the jailer, as 'a first-rate fellow and a clever man.' When the door was locked, he showed me where to hang my hat, and how he managed matters there. The rooms were whitewashed once a month; and this one, at least, was the whitest, most simply furnished, and probably the neatest apartment in the town. He naturally wanted to know where I came from, and what brought me there; and, when I had told him, I asked him in my turn how he came there, presuming him to be an honest man, of course; and, as the world goes, I believe he was. 'Why', said he, 'they accuse me of burning a barn; but I never did it.' As near as I could discover, he had probably gone to bed in a barn when drunk, and smoked his pipe there; and so a barn was burnt. He had the reputation of being a clever man, had been there some three months waiting for his trial to come on, and would have to wait as much longer; but he was quite domesticated and contented, since he got his board for nothing, and thought that he was well treated.

He occupied one window, and I the other; and I saw, that, if one stayed there long, his principal business would be to look out the window. I had soon read all the tracts that were left there, and examined where former prisoners had broken out, and where a grate had been sawed off, and heard the history of the various occupants of that room; for I found that even here there was a history and a gossip which never circulated beyond the walls of the jail. Probably this is the only house in the town where verses are composed, which are afterward printed in a circular form, but not published. I was shown quite a long list of verses which were composed by some young men who had been detected in an attempt to escape, who avenged themselves by singing them.

I pumped my fellow-prisoner as dry as I could, for fear I should never see him again; but at length he showed me which was my bed, and left me to blow out the lamp.

It was like traveling into a far country, such as I had never expected to behold, to lie there for one night. It seemed to me that I never had heard the town-clock strike before, nor the evening sounds of the village; for we slept with the windows open, which were inside the grating. It was to see my native village in the light of the Middle Ages, and our Concord was turned into a Rhine stream, and visions of knights and castles passed before me. They were the voices of old burghers that I heard in the streets. I was an involuntary spectator and auditor of whatever was done and said

42

in the kitchen of the adjacent village-inn – a wholly new and rare experience to me. It was a closer view of my native town. I was fairly inside of it. I never had seen its institutions before. This is one of its peculiar institutions; for it is a shire town. I began to comprehend what its inhabitants were about.

In the morning, our breakfasts were put through the hole in the door, in small oblong-square tin pans, made to fit, and holding a pint of chocolate, with brown bread, and an iron spoon. When they called for the vessels again, I was green enough to return what bread I had left; but my comrade seized it, and said that I should lay that up for lunch or dinner. Soon after he was let out to work at haying in a neighboring field, whither he went every day, and would not be back till noon; so he bade me good-day, saying that he doubted if he should see me again.

When I came out of prison – for some one interfered, and paid that tax – I did not perceive that great changes had taken place on the common, such as he observed who went in a youth, and emerged a tottering and gray-headed man; and yet a change had to my eyes come over the scene – the town, and State, and country – greater than any that mere time could effect. I saw yet more distinctly the State in which I lived. I saw to what extent the people among whom I lived could be trusted as good neighbors and friends; that their friendship was for summer weather only; that they did not greatly propose to do right; that they were a distinct race from me by their prejudices and superstitions, as the Chinamen and Malays are; that, in their sacrifices to humanity, they ran no risks, not even to their property; that, after all, they were not so noble but they treated the thief as he had treated them, and hoped, by a certain outward observance and a few prayers, and by walking in a particular straight though useless path from time to time, to save their souls. This may be to judge my neighbors harshly; for I believe that many of them are not aware that they have such an institution as the jail in their village.

It was formerly the custom in our village, when a poor debtor came out of jail, for his acquaintances to salute him, looking through their fingers, which were crossed to represent the grating of a jail window, 'How do ye do? ' My neighbors did not thus salute me, but first looked at me, and then at one another, as if I had returned from a long journey. I was put into jail as I was going to the shoemaker's to get a shoe which was mended. When

I was let out the next morning, I proceeded to finish my errand, and having put on my mended shoe, joined a huckleberry party, who were impatient to put themselves under my conduct; and in half an hour – for the horse was soon tackled – was in the midst of a huckleberry field, on one of our highest hills, two miles off, and then the State was nowhere to be seen.

This is the whole history of 'My Prisons.'

I have never declined paying the highway tax, because I am as desirous of being a good neighbor as I am of being a bad subject; and, as for supporting schools, I am doing my part to educate my fellow-countrymen now. It is for no particular item in the tax-bill that I refuse to pay it. I simply wish to refuse allegiance to the State, to withdraw and stand aloof from it effectually. I do not care to trace the course of my dollar, if I could, till it buys a man or a musket to shoot one with – the dollar is innocent – but I am concerned to trace the effects of my allegiance. In fact, I quietly declare war with the State, after my fashion, though I will still make what use and get what advantage of her I can, as is usual in such cases.

If others pay the tax which is demanded of me, from a sympathy with the State, they do but what they have already done in their own case, or rather they abet injustice to a greater extent than the State requires. If they pay the tax from a mistaken interest in the individual taxed, to save his property, or prevent his going to jail, it is because they have not considered wisely how far they let their private feelings interfere with the public good.

This, then, is my position at present. But one cannot be too much on his guard in such a case, lest his action be biased by obstinacy, or an undue regard for the opinions of men. Let him see that he does only what belongs to himself and to the hour.

I think sometimes, Why, this people mean well; they are only ignorant; they would do better if they knew how: why give your neighbors this pain to treat you as they are not inclined to? But I think again, this is no reason why I should do as they do, or permit others to suffer much greater pain of a different kind. Again, I sometimes say to myself, When many millions of men, without heat, without ill will, without personal feeling of any kind, demand of you a few shillings only, without the possibility, such is their constitution, of retracting or altering their present demand, and without the possibility, on your side, of appeal to any other millions, why expose yourself to this overwhelming brute force? You do not resist cold and hunger, the winds and the waves, thus obstinately; you quietly submit to a thousand similar necessities. You do not put your head into the fire. But just in proportion as I regard this as not wholly a brute force, but partly a human force, and consider that I have relations to those millions as to so many millions of men, and not of mere brute or inanimate things, I see that appeal is possible, first and instantaneously, from them to the Maker of them, and secondly, from them to themselves. But, if I put my head deliberately into the fire, there is no appeal to fire or to the Maker of fire, and I have only myself to blame. If I could convince myself that I have any right to be satisfied with men as they are, and to treat them accordingly, and not according, in some respects, to my requisitions and expectations of what they and I ought to be, then, like a good Mussulman and fatalist, I should endeavor to be satisfied with things as they are, and say it is the will of God. And, above all, there is this difference between resisting this and a purely brute or natural force, that I can resist this with some effect; but I cannot expect, like Orpheus, to change the nature of the rocks and trees and beasts.

I do not wish to quarrel with any man or nation. I do not wish to split hairs, to make fine distinctions, or set myself up as better than my neighbors. I seek rather, I may say, even an excuse for conforming to the laws of the land. I am but too ready to conform to them. Indeed, I have reason to suspect myself on this head; and each year, as the tax-gatherer comes round, I find myself disposed to review the acts and position of the general and State governments, and the spirit of the people, to discover a pretext for conformity.

> We must affect our country as our parents;
> And if at any time we alienate
> Our love or industry from doing it honor,
> We must respect effects and teach the soul
> Matter of conscience and religion,
> And not desire of rule or benefit.

I believe that the State will soon be able to take all my work of this sort out of my hands, and then I shall be no better a patriot than my fellow-countrymen. Seen from a lower point of view, the Constitution, with all its faults, is very good; the law and the courts are very respectable; even this State and this American government are, in many respects, very admirable and rare things, to be thankful for, such as a great many have described them; but seen from a point of view a little higher, they are what I have described them; seen from a higher still, and the highest, who shall say what they are, or that they are worth looking at or thinking of at all?

However, the government does not concern me much, and I shall bestow the fewest possible thoughts on it. It is not many moments that I live under a government, even in this world. If a man is thought-free, fancy-free, imagination-free, that which is *not* never for a long time appearing *to be* to him, unwise rulers or reformers cannot fatally interrupt him.

I know that most men think differently from myself; but those whose lives are by profession devoted to the study of these or kindred subjects, content me as little as any. Statesmen and legislators, standing so completely within the institution, never distinctly and nakedly behold it. They speak of moving society, but have no resting-place without it. They may be men of a certain experience and discrimination, and have no doubt invented ingenious and even useful systems, for which we sincerely thank them; but all their wit and usefulness lie within certain not very wide limits. They are wont to forget that the world is not governed by policy and expediency. Webster never goes behind government, and so cannot speak with authority about it. His words are wisdom to those legislators who contemplate no essential reform in the existing government; but for thinkers, and those who legislate for all time, he never once glances at the subject. I know of those whose serene and wise speculations on this theme would soon reveal the limits of his mind's range and hospitality. Yet, compared with the cheap professions of most reformers, and the still cheaper wisdom and eloquence of politicians in general, his are almost the only sensible and valuable words, and we thank Heaven for him. Comparatively, he is always strong, original, and, above all, practical. Still his quality is not wisdom, but prudence. The lawyer's truth is not Truth, but consistency, or a consistent expediency. Truth is always in harmony with herself, and is not concerned chiefly to reveal the justice that may consist with wrong-doing. He well deserves to be called, as he has been called, the Defender of the Constitution. There are really no blows to be given by him but defensive ones. He is not a leader, but a follower. His leaders are the men of '87. 'I have never made an effort,' he says, 'and never propose to make an effort; I have never countenanced an effort, and never mean to countenance an effort, to disturb the arrangement as originally made, by which the various States came into the Union.' Still thinking of the sanction which the Constitution gives to slavery, he says, 'Because it was a part of the original compact – let it stand.' Notwithstanding his special acuteness and ability, he is unable to take a fact out of its merely political relations, and behold it as it lies absolutely to be disposed of by the intellect – what, for instance, it behooves a man to do here in America today with regard to slavery, but ventures, or is driven, to make some such desperate answer as the following, while professing to speak absolutely, and as a private man – from which what new and singular code of social duties might be inferred? 'The manner,' says he, 'in which the governments of those States where slavery exists are to regulate it, is for their own consideration, under their responsibility to their constituents, to the general laws of propriety, humanity, and justice, and to God. Associations formed elsewhere, springing from a feeling of humanity, or any other cause, have nothing whatever to do with it. They have never received any encouragement from me, and they never will.'

They who know of no purer sources of truth, who have traced up its stream no higher, stand, and wisely stand, by the Bible and the Constitution, and drink at it there with reverence and humility; but they who behold where it comes trickling into this lake or that pool, gird up their loins once more, and continue their pilgrimage towards its fountain-head.

No man with a genius for legislation has appeared in America. They are rare in the history of the world. There are orators, politicians, and eloquent men, by the thousand; but the speaker has not yet opened his mouth to speak, who is capable of settling the much-vexed questions of the day. We love eloquence for its own sake, and not for any truth which it may utter, or any heroism it may inspire. Our legislators have not yet learned the comparative value of free-trade and of freedom, of union, and of rectitude, to a nation. They have no genius or talent for comparatively humble questions of taxation and finance, commerce and manufactures and agriculture. If we were left solely to the wordy wit of legislators in Congress for our guidance, uncorrected by the seasonable experience and the effectual complaints of the people, America would not long retain her rank among the nations. For eighteen hundred years, though perchance I have no right to say it, the New Testament has been written, yet where is the legislator who has wisdom and practical talent enough to avail himself of the light which it sheds on the science of legislation?

The authority of government, even such as I am willing to submit to - for I will cheerfully obey those who know and can do better than I, and in many things even those who neither know nor can do so well - is still an impure one: to be strictly just, it must have the sanction and consent of the governed. It can have no pure right over my person and property but what I concede to it. The progress from an absolute to a limited monarchy, from a limited monarchy to a democracy, is a progress toward a true respect for the individual. Even the Chinese philosopher was wise enough to regard the individual as the basis of the empire. Is a democracy, such as we know it, the last improvement possible in government? Is it not possible to take a step further toward recognizing and organizing the rights of man? There will never be a really free and enlightened State, until the State comes to recognize the individual as a higher and independent power, from which all its own power and authority are derived, and treats him accordingly.

I please myself with imagining a State at last which can afford to be just to all men, and to treat the individual with respect as a neighbor; which even would not think it inconsistent with its own repose, if a few were to live aloof from it, not meddling with it, nor embraced by it, who fulfilled all the duties of neighbors and fellow-men. A State which bore this kind of fruit, and suffered it to drop off as fast as it ripened, would prepare the way for a still more perfect and glorious State, which also I have imagined, but not yet anywhere seen.

3

CIVIL DISOBEDIENCE AND PERSONAL RESPONSIBILITY FOR INJUSTICE

H. A. Bedau

I. Recent discussions of civil disobedience show the world of scholarship and public affairs in disarray. Not only is there considerable disagreement over how civil disobedience is to be justified (one would expect that), there is hardly less disagreement over what civil disobedience is. Can it be violent, or must it be nonviolent, in intention and in outcome? Can civil disorder be a special case of mass civil disobedience? Must civil disobedience proceed within the framework of the existing politico-legal system or may it be revolutionary in intention? Could it be anarchistic? Should the authorities endeavor to prosecute and punish the civil disobedient as though he were a common criminal? Is disobedience which results in no punishment of the disobedient not civil disobedience after all? Because of disagreements over the answers to these questions, the description of an act as an act of civil disobedience is likely to be ambiguous and controversial not only for the general public and the government but even in some cases for the protesters themselves. Confusion rooted in honest misunderstanding is compounded by bad faith, by basic disagreements over the ideal and the actual relations between the individual and the state, and by obscurity in the facts surrounding the intentions of the protesters and the consequences of their acts.

It is not possible here to review in detail all these disagreements, nor to undertake the socio-historical analysis of particular controversies in order to illuminate the issues involving civil disobedience and our understanding of them. I do wish, however,

From: H. A. Bedau, 'Civil Disobedience and Personal Responsibility for Injustice,' *The Monist*, 54 (1970), pp. 517–35.

to single out for investigation yet another of these basic disagreements. The one I have in mind arises because of a duality in the conception of the purpose of civil disobedience. It is now clear, even if a few years ago it was not, that civil disobedience may be undertaken to *prevent* the operation of some law or policy thought unjust; but it may also be undertaken in order to *protest* the operation of some unjust law or policy. The former purpose typically has as its mode of action what can be called *direct* resistance, e.g., a draftee refuses to report for induction, a black insists on being seated at a segregated lunch counter. The latter purpose is likely to have as its mode *indirect* resistance, disobedience at one (or even several) remove(s), e.g., blacks violate a trespass ordinance to protest racial injustices, students interrupt a commencement ceremony in order to protest the military-industrial-university complex. (Lest my choice of examples be misleading, let me add that of course individual as distinct from mass civil disobedience may be undertaken for either purpose, and that the prevention/protest distinction should not be thought of as either exhaustive or exclusive.)

What gives urgency to the study of these distinctions and their correlation is that the use of indirect civil disobedience for the purpose of protest has come under explicit and sharp attack by various writers, including two prominently placed legal spokesmen, viz., the current Solicitor General and a (then) Associate Justice of the Supreme Court. Writing within a few weeks of each other, Mr. Erwin Griswold concluded that '. . . it is illicit to violate otherwise valid laws either as a symbol of protest or in the course of protest . . .';[1] and Mr. Justice Fortas agreed, saying that '. . . civil disobedience . . . is never justified in our nation where the law being violated is not itself the focus or target of the protest.' [2] 'The law violation is excused only if the law which is violated . . . *itself* is unconstitutional or invalid' (F, 16). The common thesis of Fortas and Griswold is that indirect civil

---

1 Erwin N. Griswold, 'Dissent – 1968,' *Tulane Law Review*, 42 (1968), 726–39, at 735. Hereinafter cited in the text as G.
2 Abe Fortas, *Concerning Dissent and Civil Disobedience* (New York: Signet Broadside, 1968), p. 62. Hereinafter cited in the text as F. (NB: This booklet has appeared in two different paginations with unaltered text; my references are to the first printing in sixty-four pages.) For further criticism of indirect civil disobedience, see, e.g., Francis A. Allen, 'Civil Disobedience and the Legal Order,' *University of Cincinnati Law Review*, 36 (1967), 12–13, and Charles Frankel, *Education and the Barricades* (New York: W. W. Norton and Co., 1968), p. 65.

disobedience – at least, in a constitutional democracy and by a person who understands and accepts its principles (a set of qualifications which neither Griswold nor Fortas mentions but which each assumes and which we may grant) – is never justified.[3] But even the casual observer during the past decade must know that much, if not most, civil disobedience (as well as much illegal conduct not to be understood as civil disobedience) in this country was indirect and presumably thought to be justified by those who undertook it. Plainly, there is on this point a major disagreement between these critics and a large number of activists. I think it is worth attempting to clarify the basic issues on both sides.

At the outset, let me declare that the central or paradigm cases of civil disobedience I take to be acts which are illegal (or presumed to be so by those committing them, or by those coping with them, at the time), committed openly (not evasively or covertly), nonviolently (not intentionally or negligently destructive of property or harmful of persons), and conscientiously (not impulsively, unwillingly, thoughtlessly, etc.) within the framework of the rule of law (and thus with a willingness on the part of the disobedient to accept the legal consequences of his act, save in the special case where his act is intended to overthrow the government) and with the intention of frustrating or protesting some law, policy, or decision (or the absence thereof) of the government (or of some of its officers).[4] It is sufficient for present purposes to report that all of the parties to the argument about to be examined seem to accept essentially such a conception of civil disobedience (especially that it is illegal, not violent, conscientious, not covert), and do so without thinking they have prejudged any issue as to the justifiability of particular acts of civil disobedience (or, for that matter, of other sorts of acts, e.g., of violent protest, including rebellion).

3 Fortas, it will be noticed, refers first to 'justified' civil disobedience and then to 'excusable' civil disobedience; this should, but does not, mark a change in his objection. For a concise statement that indicates the importance of this distinction, see H. L. A. Hart, *Punishment and Responsibility* (Oxford: Oxford University Press, 1968), pp. 13–14.

4 This is a somewhat broader definition than the one offered some years ago in my article, 'On Civil Disobedience,' *Journal of Philosophy*, 58 (1961), 661. For a sample of recent definitions and their divergence from one another, see H. A. Bedau (ed.), *Civil Disobedience* (New York: Pegasus, 1969), pp. 217–19.

II. Why does anyone consider committing indirect civil disobedience? Possible reasons are legion, e.g., the wish to disrupt otherwise legal and justifiable practices in order to foment confusion and disorder, fear of the consequences of committing direct civil disobedience, frustration and impatience. But surely the main and obvious reason is the undeniable fact that some injustices are *inaccessible* to direct resistance by some who would protest them. In this regard as in others, it is convenient to reconsider Thoreau's case. It will be recalled that Thoreau refused to pay his state poll tax, not as a protest or obstruction to this particular (admittedly unpopular) tax law or to the principle of personal taxation. On the contrary, he pointedly conceded that in general taxation is fully justified.[5] Rather, it was his inaccessibility to the precincts of injustice which led Thoreau to his tax refusal: no one was trying to return him to a slave plantation, no one was forcing him to join in the expeditionary forces invading Mexico, no one was mistreating him in Indian territory. Yet it was precisely these injustices which his tax resistance was aimed at.[6] If the Fortas–Griswold theory (as I shall call it) were correct, the only persons who could commit civil disobedience justifiably would be those who are directly involved in injustice. This would limit the class of prospective disobedients to two sorts: those who are the direct *victims* of injustice (e.g., fugitive slaves, Indians) or those who are the direct *agents* of injustice (e.g., bounty hunters, soldiers). But the typical citizen, not being in either of these positions with regard to many social injustices, may neither attempt to frustrate nor even protest these injustices by means of civil disobedience. The individual's right of conscientious dissent, which both Fortas and Griswold profess to recognize (G, 728; F, 48 ff.), and its peremptory authority justifies the disobedient only for resisting the precise act he is ordered by law to accept or to enforce; this and this only he may conscientiously resist through civil disobedience.

A theory with such consequences is a bit daunting. At first impression it seems as though *any* government ought to be able to be subjected to justified conscientious resistance, in one way or

5 Henry David Thoreau, 'Civil Disobedience,' in his *A Yankee in Canada with Anti-Slavery and Reform Papers* (Boston: Ticknor and Fields, 1866), p. 145.
6 Thoreau, op. cit., p. 136. What constitutes an injustice I cannot attempt to discuss here. Suffice to say that Thoreau himself shows that he thinks his civil disobedience is justified because his protest is against the systematic violation of others' human rights. See Thoreau, op. cit., pp. 127-8, 151.

another, within or without the law, on account of *any* of its laws or policies (including its failure to pass or to enforce certain laws or certain policies) by *anyone* in the society, whether or not he is directly affected by those laws or policies. The Fortas–Griswold theory implicitly denies this and would severely restrict the number of persons in a position to make such a protest through illegal but justifiable acts. I submit it is strange and needs argument which, as we shall see, neither Fortas nor Griswold provide, to show that the proper relation between an individual and his government, especially when he is a committed democrat and his government a professing constitutional democracy, is such that the vast majority of the injustices perpetrated and perpetuated by his government are forever beyond his protest through justifiable civil disobedience. He may, thanks to his civil rights, protest at the polls and, thanks to his civil liberties, protest from a soap-box. He may even protest through civil disobedience with justification provided it is his ox that is gored or forced to do the goring. But beyond this he may not go.

I suspect that one of the unavowed reasons why Fortas and Griswold come to this conclusion is that they think a person remote from a social injustice can have little or no responsibility for it. Such a person does not in any way authorize or sanction it, he or she does not in any way cause or contribute to it; therefore, he or she has no reason to take matters into his or her own hands so as to act illegally to protest it. If this is their view, it is in sharp contrast with Thoreau's. As he put it, 'What I have to do is to see . . . that I do not lend myself to the wrong which I condemn.' [7] Such a concern invites inquiry into causal and other connections more subtle than those manifested in being the direct agent of injustice or its direct victim. A few years ago, the same concern Thoreau expressed was put in this way: each of us must accept 'personal responsibility for injustice.' [8] If the Fortas–Griswold theory is correct, the principle involved here – which I shall call henceforth, partly for brevity's sake, Thoreau's Principle – must be mistaken. On their theory, it must be true that each individual bears so little responsibility for the acts of his government that he need not mitigate or acquit himself of blame and fault for injustices authorized by his government, because no blame or

7 Thoreau, op. cit., p. 134.
8 Harris Wofford, Jr., 'Non-Violence and the Law,' *Journal of Religious Thought*, 15 (1957–58), 29.

fault accrues to him at all. Griswold, it is true, quotes favorably an author who asserts, 'In a democracy . . . every citizen bears a measure of personal responsibility for misgovernment, bad laws, or wrong policies . . .' But the quotation immediately continues '. . . unless he has played his full part in trying to get a better government into power, better laws on the statute book, and better policies adopted' [9] (G, 729). Presumably, all such efforts are to be conducted entirely within the law as it stands and without recourse to Thoreauvian disobedience. Such is the position of the Fortas–Griswold theory.

III. By what arguments, by appeal to what principles, does the Fortas–Griswold theory arrive at its universal and unqualified condemnation of all (though not only) acts of indirect civil disobedience? Nowhere does either author offer any direct argument to show precisely how his conclusion is reached. But if one scrutinizes their remarks, it is possible to conjecture several arguments, some or all of which they may have thought to be sufficient to establish their position. And, in addition, one can think of other arguments, in light of the discussion so far, which might even be superior to those detectable in their texts. Altogether, I find seven arguments for consideration.

(1) The only way in which indirect civil disobedience could be justified is under the 'symbolic speech' doctrine of the First Amendment, whereby since the 'Red Flag' case[10] various objects and acts other than the mere written or spoken word are to be accorded the status of protected 'speech'. But all acts of indirect civil disobedience involve destruction of property, interference with the safety and liberty of others, assault on public decorum, and thus cannot receive such constitutional protection. Since the Constitution cannot protect such acts, nothing can: they are not justified (F, 16–19; G, 730–31).

9 The source Griswold quotes is J. N. D. Anderson, *Into the World–the Need and Limits of Christian Involvement* (London: 1968), p. 41.
10 Stromberg v. California, 283 U.S. 359 (1931), cited in Griswold, op. cit., p. 730. The Court held that a California statute banning display of any flag as a symbol of opposition to organized government was inconsistent with the right of free speech as guaranteed under the First and Fourteenth Amendments. For a perceptive discussion of constitutional protections afforded and denied non-speech acts, see Louis Henkin in *Harvard Law Review*, 82 (1968), 76–82; also Fred P. Graham, 'Is It Action or "Symbolic Speech"? ,' *The New York Times*, June 2, 1968, p. E5; and Note, 'Symbolic Conduct,' *Columbia Law Review*, 68 (1968), 1091–126.

(2) The sole excuse for civil disobedience in a constitutional democracy is as an ingredient in securing judicial review of the constitutionality or validity of a given law thought to be unjust or otherwise objectionable. But where the law broken is not the law protested, even the invalidity or unconstitutionality of the latter will not excuse the conduct in violation of the former, because there is no logical or legal relation between the two laws (F, 16).

(3) Indirect civil disobedience is always an 'act of rebellion, not merely of dissent' (F, 63). But rebellion cannot be justified in a constitutional democracy 'so long as our government obeys the mandate of the constitution' and provides full 'facility and protection' for dissent within the law. Therefore, indirect civil disobedience 'is never justified in our nation' (F, 63).

(4) Any justification of indirect civil disobedience will also justify social chaos, but this is a *reductio ad absurdum*; therefore indirect civil disobedience cannot be justified. Put somewhat less abruptly, there is no logical limit to the laws someone might choose to break in the name of protesting a given injustice inaccessible to his direct protest. Some such acts would clearly be absurd, e.g., refusing to obey an eviction notice in New York in May 1969 in order to protest the execution of Sacco and Vanzetti in Massachusetts in August 1927 (a hypothetical case), or obstructing traffic at the rush hour on a major metropolitan thoroughfare in order to protest discriminatory hiring practices by a city-sponsored consessionaire some miles away (an actual case, the Triborough Bridge 'stall-in' of 1964). Since there is no logical way to distinguish the plainly absurd cases from the other cases, civil disobedience of this sort must be categorically unjustified. It is impossible to 'distinguish in principle the legal quality of the determination to halt a troop train to protest the Vietnam war or to block workmen from entering a segregated job site to protest employment discrimination, from the determination to fire shots into a civil rights leader's home to protest integration' (G, 733-34).

(5) If the purpose of civil disobedience is primarily an 'educative' one,[11] and if mass civil disobedience especially is typically an

---

11 Richard Wasserstrom, in *Civil Disobedience* (Santa Barbara: Center for the Study of Democratic Institutions, 1966), p. 18.

'important effort at communication,' [12] then indirect civil disobedience fails to accomplish this purpose, or fails to accomplish it sufficiently well, given its failure to affect directly the injustice being protested and the confusion and other harm it causes. Such acts convey a mixed message, which is precisely what good propaganda should not do.

(6) Personal responsibility for injustice, such as there is anything of this sort at all, is sufficiently met by playing one's full part within the existing political and legal system, with its constitutional provisions for minority rights, and without breaking any laws not themselves the object of protest as unjust, in order to obtain a government which will undo by exercise of its constitutional powers whatever injustices its predecessor may have perpetrated or perpetuated (G, 729).

(7) The only acts of civil disobedience which could be justified are those which interrupt the enabling or authorizing relationship between the protester and those inflicting or suffering injustice. No act of indirect civil disobedience does this. Therefore, no such act can be justified.

These arguments are of distinctly uneven merit, save that all are alike in being unsound; their errors, however, are of varied interest and significance. In (1), the factual premise as to interference with the liberties or safety of others is simply false, even if it is true in some cases. Nor is it persuasive that what the Constitution cannot justify (or what the Justices will not read as the meaning of the Constitution) settles the question of justification, barring prior proof that the Constitution itself is truly just. The argument in (2) simply relies on an arbitrary assumption, and moreover one which the Supreme Court has elsewhere already eroded, notably in many of the Civil Rights cases of the early 1960s. The claim of rebellion in argument (3) is simply gratuitous, false, and question-begging. The argument in (4) is the product of willful and culpable blindness to distinctions (between violence and nonviolence, between risk of harm to others and risk of harm to oneself) which not only a philosopher should be able to see. Along these lines, and no doubt others, a thorough refutation of the first four of the above arguments can be advanced, and I forbear any further development of these

12 Harris Wofford, Jr., as quoted in *The New York Times*, August 11, 1968, p. E 11.

counter-arguments out of the desire not to belabor the obvious and from residual qualms that I may have misunderstood Fortas and Griswold. Argument (5) is not one of their arguments, but it is much in the air today; it has its point, but it cannot suffice to provide sweeping and universal condemnation of indirect civil disobedience. This leaves arguments (6) and (7) for closer study, and I intend to devote the rest of the paper to examining them. Instead, however, of any further quarrel directly with these two arguments and with the Fortas–Griswold theory,[13] I shall turn to an explication and interpretation of their opponents' position, so far as I understand it, and insofar as it rests upon the principle I have called Thoreau's Principle, a principle of doubtful clarity and plausibility.

IV. At the beginning, we should notice an ambiguity in the notion of accepting personal responsibility for injustice. One might construe this not as an accusatory phrase declaring that the addressees *are* responsible for certain injustices, but as an admonitory phrase urging them to *take* responsibility for certain injustices, to take it upon themselves to protest and alleviate, if possible, certain injustices for which they bear no responsibility and deserve no blame whatsoever. It is possible to understand Thoreau's Principle in this way. But on this interpretation, acceptance of responsibility does not imply any fault; nor, presumably, would rejection of responsibility deserve rebuke or condemnation. Since I think imputation of fault is a crucial feature of Thoreau's Principle, I shall put this possible interpretation aside.

Thoreau, then, I take it, sees himself as responsible for certain injustices which (a) he knows he has not intentionally, know-

13 The entire argument of Fortas, op. cit., has been subjected to point-for-point criticism by Howard Zinn, *Disobedience and Democracy* (New York: Vintage Books, 1968). The insufficiencies of Zinn's own critique have been concisely canvassed in a review by Carl Cohen, *The Nation* (December 2, 1968), 597–600. Zinn's objection to Fortas' position on indirect civil disobedience (a topic ignored by Cohen in his review) is that it 'guarantees that the most fundamental ills of American society will remain unassailable by civil disobedience' (pp. 36–37), that 'poverty, racism, war (the most persistent and basic evils of our time) are held sacrosanct against civil disobedience by Fortas' rule' (p. 38). To conclude this is to assume that no one at all is in the position of directly imposing or directly suffering these 'basic evils,' and that none of these evils is built into the system of laws and governmental policies so as to be accessible to direct resistance, and that if not everyone can make direct protest no one can. All these assumptions are, of course, false.

ingly, or in his own person directly inflicted, and (b) are not inflicted by someone acting as the executor of his intention. I assume also that Thoreau does not implicitly single out himself as especially responsible for the injustices he protests: he is responsible only if Emerson, Alcott, Hawthorne and the rest are responsible, too. They are all responsible, perhaps equally, in the same way and for the same reasons, viz., both (a) and (b) are true of them, no exculpating or exonerating conditions protect them, and certain inculpating conditions make them subject to Thoreau's Principle. What line of reasoning establishes the application of such a principle with its imputation of individual vicarious responsibility with fault and its culmination in indirect civil disobedience? Consider the following argument, which Thoreau might have addressed to himself:

(1) Certain particular persons (federal marshals, local sheriffs, Indian agents, soldiers) continue to commit acts, knowingly and deliberately, which violate the human rights of others, e.g., they cheat Indian tribes, hunt fugitive Negro slaves, serve voluntarily in the armed assault on Mexicans in Mexican territory. (Never mind that these persons do not think of themselves as having inflicted injustices in such acts.)

(2) These persons do not act gratuitously on their own, but as the paid agents of their government with full authorization for their acts. (Never mind that they would be liable for punishment or loss of employment if they failed to perform their duties, which included such acts.)

(3) Therefore, the government is itself responsible for those injustices. (Never mind that the government does not view these acts or the policies they implement as unjust.)

Let us say that the principle that allows the inference of (3) from (2) is a Principle of Governmental Responsibility, simply a special case of a principal's responsibility for the authorized acts of his agent. Now, one way to proceed from this point is by means of two further principles.

(4) If a political community continues to accept a government knowing the acts it commits to implement its policies, then the community itself becomes responsible for those acts whether or not it knew and approved of them before the fact. Let us say that (4) expresses a Principle of Collective Responsibility. I shall ignore the obvious need to supply criteria

for 'continues to accept' and to delimit the 'political community' in question. The next step in the argument is this:

(5) If an individual continues to accept membership in a political community in the knowledge of what that community authorizes, then the individual himself becomes responsible for those acts whether or not he knew and approved of them before the fact.

Let us call (5) a Principle of Distributive Responsibility, which yields individual vicarious responsibility for the acts of one's government. Presumably, (5) needs to be qualified in its antecedent so as to provide only *partial*, not complete, vicarious responsibility. This leads to questions of how degrees of partial vicarious responsibility are to be measured (on the assumption that not all persons partially responsible are equally responsible), but I forego pursuit of further specification on this point here. (Similarly, I ignore the need here, as in (4), for a criterion of 'continues to accept;' as for 'membership,' however, *vide infra*.) Notice that (3)–(5) are not principles of *strict* responsibility: (3) relies on the notion, expressed in (2), that the principal knows and intends, and so orders or directs, his agents to act in the manner in question; whereas (4) and (5) simply require, respectively, collective and individual knowledge of these acts after the fact. Likewise, whereas the application of (2) will be negatived by a showing of no intention in the principal, that will not suffice to negative the application of (4) or (5). Also, it is clear that if (1)–(5) are true and that if they show that a Thoreau is responsible for the injustices cited in (1), they also suffice to show that his neighbors and kinsmen are responsible, too. Finally, I take it that the thrust of the argument establishes responsibility *with fault* in (3)–(5). In (5), fault accrues because subsequent to the unjust acts and to one's knowledge of them, one has done nothing to alter one's position with regard to the circumstances which bring these injustices into being and which continue them.

Anyone who accepts (5) has imposed on himself a much more demanding burden than any established by the conventional principle of democratic political responsibility endorsed by Griswold (above, Section II). In fact (5) may be false and it may have unwelcome consequences. No doubt it is high-minded and lays the basis for acts which can only be regarded as supererogatory, acts of 'ultra obligation.' [14] Point (5) is not a popular principle of morality. But it is not unknown today. A recent statement issued by student protesters on behalf of their disruptive activities nicely expresses this point of view. Their statement read in part:

> As white Americans, we bear a special responsibility with regard to the Selective Service System and the war machine it feeds; and we can no longer allow that system to function smoothly in our name, for we cannot tolerate the atrocities it perpetrates upon our brothers in America, in Vietnam, and in other parts of the world.[15]

Only persons who accept (5) or some similar principle could sincerely issue such a statement.

Yet (5) as it stands is insufficient to express Thoreau's Principle, for two reasons. It fails to bring out explicitly the nature of the linkage between the individual and the government in virtue of which vicarious responsibility is established. And it fails to contain the injunction to act out of concern for one's responsibilities. Both these deficiencies can be remedied if we consider how one might (and how Thoreau did) view his own act of tax withholding.

One might argue that it is only by paying taxes that a person satisfies the membership condition in the antecedent of (5). Or, it might be argued that payment of taxes, though not necessary, is a sufficient condition of membership. It is also possible to argue that membership is established in other ways (e.g., by acceptance of conferred benefits, by voting, by continued residency), and therefore that tax payment is an aggravation of the responsibility already established under (5). A rather different line of argument, which allows us to bypass (4)-(5), and one which comes closer to Thoreau's own remarks as well as to the nature of tax paying, might be framed in terms of the following principle:

(6) If an individual pays taxes, knowing how they have been spent and will be spent, he becomes responsible for whatever are the deliberate acts on behalf of which those taxes are levied, collected, and spent. (Never mind that he is under a

14 The phrase is from Russell Grice, *The Grounds of Moral Judgment* (Cambridge University Press, 1967), pp. 36, 155ff.
15 *The New York Times*, May 26, 1969, p. 8.

legal obligation to pay the taxes, i.e., they are not his voluntary contribution to defray his share of the costs of government.)

Thoreau makes much of the way payment of taxes signifies 'allegiance' to government; he makes nothing of the way in which tax payment consanguinifies the commonwealth (to use Hobbes's phrase) and thus enables government to carry out its business. Today, the latter is far more significant than the former, and far more significant than in Thoreau's day. The state poll tax which he refused to pay probably had little economic relation, even indirectly, with any of the injustices of the federal government he wished to protest. Nevertheless, I think it is fair to emphasize the twofold *authorizing* and *enabling* functions which an individual's tax payments can be taken to serve. It is this twofold result of tax payment as a measure of allegiance which Thoreau in effect acknowledged when he wrote, 'I do not care to trace the course of my [tax] dollar . . . but I am concerned to trace the effects of my allegiance.' [16] Thoreau's Principle, I suggest, should be so framed as to bring out explicitly just these features as the ones which link the individual to his government and its agents. So I propose:

(7) A person becomes responsible for the acts of another (person, government) if and only if (and to the degree that) he (a) has authorized that other to act, or (b) has enabled that other to act, (c) knows how that other has used his position and authority to act, and (d) he continues to do (a) and (b), i.e., he does not act to revoke the authority granted or to prevent its abuse.

Now (7) is not only a more elaborate version of (5); it expresses Thoreau's Principle insofar as it is a principle of nonstrict partial individual vicarious responsibility with fault. It is not to be supposed, of course, that this principle is a principle of *legal* fault, that is, that someone of whom (7) is true is to be held legally accountable and liable for criminal punishment or civil damages. This is no objection to (7), however, as a sound principle of moral responsibility or as one actually held by

16 Thoreau, op. cit., p. 145.

Thoreau and others.[17] Furthermore, although tax paying is a specially vivid sort of act in virtue of which a person could become responsible under (7), (7) is sufficiently broad so that other acts, too, could have this consequence; e.g., voting to re-elect a government, or accepting appointment in the government, could be construed as fulfilling these conditions.

One advantage from (6) and (7) is that they help us to see, in a way which (4)-(5) obscure, that the responsibility imposed by Thoreau's Principle is not as vicarious as it originally seemed. For (6)-(7) make out the injustices in question as standing in a not wholly obscure or imaginary causal and authorized relation to the person to be held responsible under them. This result also helps make plausible the claim that the moral responsibility imposed under (7) imputes fault, since as ordinarily conceived, vicarious responsibility is thought of as faultless responsibility.[18]

The rest of Thoreau's Principle, which is admonitory or injunctive in character, can be conjoined to (7) and expressed in this way:

(8) Anyone at all responsible for unjust acts, whether of his own or of another's, must act so as to acquit himself of the fault incurred by that responsibility.

Thoreau remarks, 'If the injustice is part of the necessary friction of the machine of government, let it go, let it go . . . but if it is of such a nature that it requires you to be the agent of injustice to another, then I say, break the law.'[19] This passage, better than any other, shows us that Thoreau's justification of tax

---

17 The degree to which principles such as (4)-(7) depart from those whereby partial responsibility and criminal liability are established may be gauged from consulting Glanville Williams, *Criminal Law: The General Part*, 2nd edn (London: Stevens & Sons, 1961). For a recent discussion of both collective and distributive legal and moral responsibility, but with no defense of Thoreauvian principles, see Joel Feinberg, 'Collective Responsibility,' *Journal of Philosophy*, 45 (1968), 674-88. Although it is not addressed to the justification of civil disobedience, nor usefully applicable to that subject, the line of argument used by Karl Jaspers in his *The Question of German Guilt* (New York: Capricorn Books, 1961), has some interesting contrasts with Thoreauvian reasoning as I reconstruct it. This is especially true of Jaspers' 'Scheme of Distinctions' (pp. 31-46), in which ordinary 'criminal' guilt is contrasted progressively with 'political', 'moral', and 'metaphysical' guilt. None of these notions of 'guilt' quite coincides with the fault which results from (4)-(7).

18 See Hart, op. cit., p. 223.

19 Thoreau, op. cit., p. 134.

withholding turns out to depend on showing that tax paying is a form of agency responsibility after all, albeit a remote and indirect one.

Now it is clear that anyone who accepts (8) is bound to contemplate illegal activity, so long as purely legal activities prove insufficient to affect the injustices for which he is responsible under (7). That such activities are insufficient, for whatever reason, is an important factual assumption needed before (7)-(8) can be thought to require civil disobedience. It is also fairly clear that any acts taken in response to (8) are not going to be acts only of protest or obstruction; they are going to be in part exculpatory and even expiatory. It is this feature in particular about acts of civil disobedience that the Fortas–Griswold theory fails to take into account. If one of the fundamental reasons why persons are driven to undertake indirect civil disobedience is not only the inaccessibility of injustice to their direct action but also their desire to exculpate themselves from further complicity in injustice, as a result of the unjust acts of others and of their own implication therein – an implication established by the facts and by their acceptance of moral principles such as (4) and (5) or (7) and (8) – then the critic will have to recognize this and will have to show what (if anything) is faulty in the convictions or reasoning of his opponents. As it is, the Fortas–Griswold theory is simply unaware of what I suggest is one of the crucial features of the position it would criticize.

Given (7) as a specification of *all* the conditions under which vicarious individual responsibility with fault is incurred, then if one accepts (8) it is sufficient and necessary to act so as to defeat at least one of the conditions (a)-(d) in (7). But given (6), refusing to pay one's taxes is necessary to achieve this result. (Thoreau clearly thinks it is also sufficient, in his case, and perhaps it was. He said that 'the only mode in which a man situated as I am necessarily meets [his] government . . . directly, and face to face, . . . [is] in the person of its tax-gatherer. . . .'[20] Few could say this today.) Tax refusal will signify withdrawal of allegiance. It will also disable government, though admittedly only to the pro rata share of the total tax burden assigned to the disobedient. As for condition (c), this does not come into play in discharging fault; although one may not incur responsibility if he is (not culpably)

20 Thoreau, op. cit., p. 135.

ignorant of his government's policies and acts, he obviously cannot hope to remove fault already incurred by becoming ignorant of what he knows.

V. The argument of the preceding section shows, I hope, that since responsibility for injustice can be incurred not only by committing injustice directly and not only by someone else acting as one's direct agent under explicit orders, but also more remotely, it is superficial to regard all indirect civil disobedience as essentially alike in those respects bearing on its justification. For we have seen that an argument can be made out to show that an otherwise perfectly valid law or institution can serve both to authorize and to enable acts whereby ordinary persons who neither commit, direct, nor approve of those acts are nevertheless to be faulted if they do not withdraw their implicit support for such acts. It must be conceded, however, that if such reasoning shows that it is foolish to condemn all indirect civil disobedience, it also fails to vindicate all indirect civil disobedience. Not every purely 'symbolic' act of illegal nonviolent protest will succeed in negating one or more of the conditions set forth in (7), and therefore cannot be thought justified by anyone who understands his act along Thoreauvian lines. Since so much civil disobedience has been indirect and cannot be rationally understood as undertaken so as to negate the conditions of (7), one can only conclude either that these acts are not justified (and that to this extent Fortas and Griswold are correct in condemning them) or that Thoreau's Principle has been incorrectly explicated, because it should show that these acts are justified; or, as I myself believe, that much indirect civil disobedience must be understood by its practitioners as falling outside the protection of Thoreau's Principle and therefore still awaits some other interpretation and defense than that provided in the previous section. It seems likely to me that many of those who commit 'symbolic', indirect civil disobedience do not see themselves as having any responsibility for the injustices they wish to protest. If they did, they would be more concerned to establish, in their own minds at least, that their acts of protest sever one or more links in the chain which connects them, via their participation in government, with government's injustices. Obviously, so long as one does not see himself as implicated in the injustices he wishes to protest, he need not worry whether his civil disobedience cancels that implication; and this will free him to undertake a much wider variety of acts of protest than if he were under the constraint of Thoreau's Principle. Yet if Thoreau's Principle is sound, then it is quite clear that almost everyone, either under (6) or under (7), in fact does bear some vicarious responsibility for the injustices of his government. It remains morally dubious, at the least, how that implication in injustice can be left intact by resisters who would at the same time be ready to undertake purely 'symbolic' civil disobedience. I should think that Thoreau would join Fortas and Griswold in shaking his head at the spectacle.

Quite apart from the insufficiency of Thoreau's Principle as a general justification for indirect civil disobedience, there are certain difficulties in (7)–(8) themselves even under the most favorable circumstances. One is that a protester must be honestly bewildered by the difficulty of knowing how to escape the onus placed upon him once he accepts (7). Given Thoreau's own view of his situation, it is understandable why he might think this onus is removed by simply not paying taxes; but it is almost impossible for anyone today to think that a comparable act of indirect civil disobedience would accomplish the same result for himself. The difficulty is created by the absence of any measure for the degree of partial responsibility one incurs for the injustice in question, and of the extent of one's indirect responsibility for acts of government. There seems to be no obvious way for the would-be protester to be free from doubt whether the quantum of his protest falls short or exceeds the quantum of his responsibility for the injustice he is protesting. The absence of any tribunal to assess such matters, i.e., the fact that no question of legal responsibility is involved, makes the whole matter such as to encourage one to deny any responsibility of this sort at all, i.e., to repudiate (6) and (7), or else to look foolish in attempting to apportion one's resistance to his self-assessed responsibility.

There is a further problem in all cases of tax resistance, as the mode of response under (8). If it is argued that a partial responsibility for the unjust acts of government is incurred by paying taxes, then it seems arbitrary not to grant under the same principles a partial responsibility for the just acts of government. But if this is granted, then the tax withholder must also grant that the very act by which he exculpates his responsibility for injustice is also an act by which he removes support for his share of the just practices of government. Tax withholding is a very blunt social instrument; to shift the cliché, its effects fall, as does the rain, on the just and unjust alike. What this suggests is that principles such as (5)–(7), given the way taxes support all acts of government, force a would-be resister either to blind himself to the injustice which results from his resistance under (8), or to recognize an inescapably tragic dilemma in which he finds himself: he is damned if he does resist by withholding taxes, and he is damned if he doesn't.

Finally, Thoreau's Principle as it stands provides no reason why one should try to fight injustice through *nonviolent* acts. But unless this can be done, Thoreau's Principle seems to have little or no relevance to civil disobedience in contrast to other forms of illegal resistance to government. To this objection, one might reply that anyone likely to accept principles such as (5)–(8) is likely also to believe that (a) it cannot be right to discharge responsibility for injustice by becoming the direct agent of a new wrong or injustice, and that (b) this is precisely what results from any act of violence, even when it is aimed at those who (by their own acts or inaction) have implicated others in their injustices; (a) is a familiar principle of morality commended to us from more than one quarter; but we have already seen that violating (a) may be required if we are to act under (8). Whether (b) is true is not so clear. At best it may be only a useful rule of thumb for political tactics. Whatever its status, if Thoreau's Principle is to be usable in the task of justifying civil disobedience, (b) must be assumed as well. In any case, what this objection brings out, and I think correctly, is that Thoreau's Principle as it stands is not categorically nonviolent in its implementation; it is not a principle to which a pacifist is necessarily committed nor one the commitment to which makes one a pacifist.

Two things I have not tried to do in this essay. One is to show that Thoreau's Principle by itself justifies indirect civil disobedience, the other is to show that all indirect civil disobedience is justified. I have in fact all but explicitly denied both these generalizations. What I have tried to show is that important as the distinctions are between direct and indirect civil disobedience, and between protesting and obstructing injustice through civil disobedience, there are principles of moral responsibility which some (conspicuously, but not only and not originally, Thoreau) accept and which, in conjunction with the actual complexities of our relationship with our government, cut across these distinctions and which can go some distance toward justifying certain kinds of indirect civil disobedience for persons who accept such principles.

4

LETTER FROM BIRMINGHAM CITY JAIL

Martin Luther King, Jr

My dear Fellow Clergymen,
While confined here in the Birmingham City Jail, I came across your recent statement calling our present activities 'unwise and untimely.' Seldom, if ever, do I pause to answer criticism of my work and ideas. If I sought to answer all of the criticisms that cross my desk, my secretaries would be engaged in little else in the course of the day, and I would have no time for constructive work. But since I feel that you are men of genuine goodwill and your criticisms are sincerely set forth, I would like to answer your statement in what I hope will be patient and reasonable terms.

I think I should give the reason for my being in Birmingham, since you have been influenced by the argument of 'outsiders coming in.' I have the honor of serving as president of the Southern Christian Leadership Conference, an organization operating in every Southern state, with headquarters in Atlanta, Georgia. We have some eighty-five affiliate organizations all across the South – one being the Alabama Christian Movement for Human Rights. Whenever necessary and possible we share staff, educational and financial resources with our affiliates. Several months ago our local affiliate here in Birmingham invited us to be on call to engage in a nonviolent direct action program if such were deemed necessary. We readily consented and when the hour came we lived up to our promises. So I am here, along with several members of my staff, because we were invited here. I am here because I have basic organizational ties here.

From: M. L. King, Jr., *Why We Can't Wait* (New York: Harper & Row, 1963), pp. 77–100. Originally published in a slightly different version in *Liberation* (June 1963), pp. 10–16.

Beyond this, I am in Birmingham because injustice is here. Just as the eighth-century prophets left their little villages and carried their 'thus saith the Lord' far beyond the boundaries of their home towns; and just as the Apostle Paul left his little village of Tarsus and carried the gospel of Jesus Christ to practically every hamlet and city of the Graeco-Roman world, I too am compelled to carry the gospel of freedom beyond my particular home town. Like Paul, I must constantly respond to the Macedonian call for aid.

Moreover, I am cognizant of the interrelatedness of all communities and states. I cannot sit idly by in Atlanta and not be concerned about what happens in Birmingham. Injustice anywhere is a threat to justice everywhere. We are caught in an inescapable network of mutuality, tied in a single garment of destiny. Whatever affects one directly affects all indirectly. Never again can we afford to live with the narrow, provincial 'outside agitator' idea. Anyone who lives inside the United States can never be considered an outsider anywhere in this country.

You deplore the demonstrations that are presently taking place in Birmingham. But I am sorry that your statement did not express a similar concern for the conditions that brought the demonstrations into being. I am sure that each of you would want to go beyond the superficial social analyst who looks merely at effects, and does not grapple with underlying causes. I would not hesitate to say that it is unfortunate that so-called demonstrations are taking place in Birmingham at this time, but I would say in more emphatic terms that it is even more unfortunate that the white power structure of this city left the Negro community with no other alternative.

In any nonviolent campaign there are four basic steps: (1) Collection of the facts to determine whether injustices are alive. (2) Negotiation. (3) Self-purification and (4) Direct Action. We have gone through all of these steps in Birmingham. There can be no gainsaying of the fact that racial injustice engulfs this community.

Birmingham is probably the most thoroughly segregated city in the United States. Its ugly record of police brutality is known in every section of this country. Its unjust treatment of Negroes in the courts is a notorious reality. There have been more unsolved bombings of Negro homes and churches in Birmingham than in any city in this nation. These are the hard, brutal and unbelievable facts. On the basis of these conditions Negro leaders sought to negotiate with the city fathers. But the political leaders consistently refused to engage in good faith negotiation.

Then came the opportunity last September to talk with some of the leaders of the economic community. In these negotiating sessions certain promises were made by the merchants – such as the promise to remove the humiliating racial signs from the stores. On the basis of these promises Rev. Shuttlesworth and the leaders of the Alabama Christian Movement for Human Rights agreed to call a moratorium on any type of demonstrations. As the weeks and months unfolded we realized that we were the victims of a broken promise. The signs remained. Like so many experiences of the past we were confronted with blasted hopes, and the dark shadow of a deep disappointment settled upon us. So we had no alternative except that of preparing for direct action, whereby we would present our very bodies as a means of laying our case before the conscience of the local and national community. We were not unmindful of the difficulties involved. So we decided to go through a process of self-purification. We started having workshops on nonviolence and repeatedly asked ourselves the questions, 'Are you able to accept blows without retaliating?' 'Are you able to endure the ordeals of jail?' We decided to set our direct action program around the Easter season, realizing that with the exception of Christmas, this was the largest shopping period of the year. Knowing that a strong economic withdrawal program would be the by-product of direct action, we felt that this was the best time to bring pressure on the merchants for the needed changes. Then it occurred to us that the March election was ahead and so we speedily decided to postpone action until after election day. When we discovered that Mr. Connor was in the run-off, we decided again to postpone action so that the demonstrations could not be used to cloud the issues. At this time we agreed to begin our nonviolent witness the day after the run-off.

This reveals that we did not move irresponsibly into direct action. We too wanted to see Mr. Connor defeated; so we went through postponement after postponement to aid in this community need. After this we felt that direct action could be delayed no longer.

You may well ask, 'Why direct action? Why sit-ins, marches, etc.? Isn't negotiation a better path?' You are exactly right in your call for negotiation. Indeed, this is the purpose of direct action. Nonviolent direct action seeks to create such a crisis and establish such creative tension that a community that has constantly refused to negotiate is forced to confront the issue. It seeks so to dramatize the issue that it can no longer be ignored. I just referred to the creation of tension as a part of the work of the nonviolent resister. This may sound rather shocking. But I must confess that I am not afraid of the word tension. I have earnestly worked and preached against violent tension, but there is a type of constructive nonviolent tension that is necessary for growth. Just as Socrates felt that it was necessary to create a tension in the mind so that individuals could rise from the bondage of myths and half-truths to the unfettered realm of creative analysis and objective appraisal, we must see the need of having nonviolent gadflies to create the kind of tension in society that will help men to rise from the dark depths of prejudice and racism to the majestic heights of understanding and brotherhood. So the purpose of the direct action is to create a situation so crisis-packed that it will inevitably open the door to negotiation. We, therefore, concur with you in your call for negotiation. Too long has our beloved Southland been bogged down in the tragic attempt to live in monologue rather than dialogue.

One of the basic points in your statement is that our acts are untimely. Some have asked, 'Why didn't you give the new administration time to act?' The only answer that I can give to this inquiry is that the new administration must be prodded about as much as the outgoing one before it acts. We will be sadly mistaken if we feel that the election of Mr. Boutwell will bring the millennium to Birmingham. While Mr. Boutwell is much more articulate and gentle than Mr. Connor, they are both segregationists, dedicated to the task of maintaining the status quo. The hope I see in Mr. Boutwell is that he will be reasonable enough to see the futility of massive resistance to desegregation. But he will not see this without pressure from the devotees of civil rights. My friends, I must say to you that we have not made a single gain in civil rights without determined legal and nonviolent pressure. History is the long and tragic story of the fact that privileged groups seldom give up their privileges voluntarily. Individuals may see the moral light and voluntarily give up their unjust posture; but as Reinhold Niebuhr has reminded us, groups are more immoral than individuals.

71

We know through painful experience that freedom is never voluntarily given by the oppressor; it must be demanded by the oppressed. Frankly, I have never yet engaged in a direct action movement that was 'well timed,' according to the timetable of those who have not suffered unduly from the disease of segregation. For years now I have heard the words 'Wait!' It rings in the ear of every Negro with a piercing familiarity. This 'Wait' has almost always meant 'Never'. It has been a tranquilizing thalidomide, relieving the emotional stress for a moment, only to give birth to an ill-formed infant of frustration. We must come to see with the distinguished jurist of yesterday that 'justice too long delayed is justice denied.' We have waited for more than three hundred and forty years for our constitutional and God-given rights. The nations of Asia and Africa are moving with jet-like speed toward the goal of political independence, and we still creep at horse-and-buggy pace toward the gaining of a cup of coffee at a lunch counter. I guess it is easy for those who have never felt the stinging darts of segregation to say, 'Wait'. But when you have seen vicious mobs lynch your mothers and fathers at will and drown your sisters and brothers at whim; when you have seen hate-filled policemen curse, kick, brutalize and even kill your black brothers and sisters with impunity; when you see the vast majority of your twenty million Negro brothers smothering in an air-tight cage of poverty in the midst of an affluent society; when you suddenly find your tongue twisted and your speech stammering as you seek to explain to your six-year-old daughter why she can't go to the public amusement park that has just been advertised on television, and see tears welling up in her little eyes when she is told that Funtown is closed to colored children, and see the depressing clouds of inferiority begin to form in her little mental sky, and see her begin to distort her little personality by unconsciously developing a bitterness toward white people; when you have to concoct an answer for a five-year-old son asking in agonizing pathos: 'Daddy, why do white people treat colored people so mean?'; when you take a cross-country drive and find it necessary to sleep night after night in the uncomfortable corners of your automobile because no motel will accept you; when you are humiliated day in and day out by nagging signs reading 'white' and 'colored'; when your first name becomes 'nigger' and your middle name becomes 'boy' (however old you are) and your last name becomes 'John', and when your wife and mother are never given the respected title 'Mrs.'; when you are harried by day and haunted at night by the fact that you are a Negro, living constantly at tip-toe stance never quite knowing what to expect next, and plagued with inner fears and outer resentments; when you are forever fighting a degenerating sense of 'nobodiness'; then you will understand why we find it difficult to wait. There comes a time when the cup of endurance runs over, and men are no longer willing to be plunged into an abyss of injustice where they experience the blackness of corroding despair. I hope, sirs, you can understand our legitimate and unavoidable impatience.

You express a great deal of anxiety over our willingness to break laws. This is certainly a legitimate concern. Since we so diligently urge people to obey the Supreme Court's decision of 1954 outlawing segregation in the public schools, it is rather strange and paradoxical to find us consciously breaking laws. One may well ask, 'How can you advocate breaking some laws and obeying others?' The answer is found in the fact that there are two types of laws: There are *just* and there are *unjust* laws. I would agree with Saint Augustine that 'An unjust law is no law at all.'

Now what is the difference between the two? How does one determine when a law is just or unjust? A just law is a man-made code that squares with the moral law or the law of God. An unjust law is a code that is out of harmony with the moral law. To put it in the terms of Saint Thomas Aquinas, an unjust law is a human law that is not rooted in eternal and natural law. Any law that uplifts human personality is just. Any law that degrades human personality is unjust. All segregation statutes are unjust because segregation distorts the soul and damages the personality. It gives the segregator a false sense of superiority, and the segregated a false sense of inferiority. To use the words of Martin Buber, the great Jewish philosopher, segregation substitutes an 'I-it' relationship for the 'I-thou' relationship, and ends up relegating persons to the status of things. So segregation is not only politically, economically and sociologically unsound, but it is morally wrong and sinful. Paul Tillich has said that sin is separation. Isn't segregation an existential expression of man's tragic separation, an expression of his awful estrangement, his terrible sinfulness? So I can urge men to disobey segregation ordinances because they are morally wrong.

73

Let us turn to a more concrete example of just and unjust laws. An unjust law is a code that a majority inflicts on a minority that is not binding on itself. This is difference made legal. On the other hand a just law is a code that a majority compels a minority to follow that it is willing to follow itself. This is sameness made legal.

Let me give another explanation. An unjust law is a code inflicted upon a minority which that minority had no part in enacting or creating because they did not have the unhampered right to vote. Who can say that the legislature of Alabama which set up the segregation laws was democratically elected? Throughout the state of Alabama all types of conniving methods are used to prevent Negroes from becoming registered voters and there are some counties without a single Negro registered to vote despite the fact that the Negro constitutes a majority of the population. Can any law set up in such a state be considered democratically structured?

These are just a few examples of unjust and just laws. There are some instances when a law is just on its face and unjust in its application. For instance, I was arrested Friday on a charge of parading without a permit. Now there is nothing wrong with an ordinance which requires a permit for a parade, but when the ordinance is used to preserve segregation and to deny citizens the First Amendment privilege of peaceful assembly and peaceful protest, then it becomes unjust.

I hope you can see the distinction I am trying to point out. In no sense do I advocate evading or defying the law as the rabid segregationist would do. This would lead to anarchy. One who breaks an unjust law must do it *openly, lovingly* (not hatefully as the white mothers did in New Orleans when they were seen on television screaming 'nigger, nigger, nigger'), and with a willingness to accept the penalty. I submit that an individual who breaks a law that conscience tells him is unjust, and willingly accepts the penalty by staying in jail to arouse the conscience of the community over its injustice, is in reality expressing the very highest respect for law.

Of course, there is nothing new about this kind of civil disobedience. It was seen sublimely in the refusal of Shadrach, Meshach and Abednego to obey the laws of Nebuchadnezzar because a higher moral law was involved. It was practiced superbly by the early Christians who were willing to face hungry lions and the excruciating pain of chopping blocks, before submitting to certain unjust laws of the Roman empire. To a degree academic freedom is a reality today because Socrates practiced civil disobedience.

We can never forget that everything Hitler did in Germany was 'legal' and everything the Hungarian freedom fighters did in Hungary was 'illegal'. It was 'illegal' to aid and comfort a Jew in Hitler's Germany. But I am sure that if I had lived in Germany during that time I would have aided and comforted my Jewish brothers even though it was illegal. If I lived in a Communist country today where certain principles dear to the Christian faith are suppressed, I believe I would openly advocate disobeying these anti-religious laws. I must make two honest confessions to you, my Christian and Jewish brothers. First, I must confess that over the last few years I have been gravely disappointed with the white moderate. I have almost reached the regrettable conclusion that the Negro's great stumbling-block in the stride toward freedom is not the White Citizen's Council-er or the Ku Klux Klanner, but the white moderate who is more devoted to 'order' than to justice; who prefers a negative peace which is the absence of tension to a positive peace which is the presence of justice; who constantly says, 'I agree with you in the goal you seek, but I can't agree with your methods of direct action'; who paternalistically feels that he can set the timetable for another man's freedom; who lives by the myth of time and who constantly advises the Negro to wait until a 'more convenient season.' Shallow understanding from people of goodwill is more frustrating than absolute misunderstanding from people of ill will. Lukewarm acceptance is much more bewildering than outright rejection.

I had hoped that the white moderate would understand that law and order exist for the purpose of establishing justice, and that when they fail to do this they become dangerously structured dams that block the flow of social progress. I had hoped that the white moderate would understand that the present tension of the South is merely a necessary phase of the transition from an obnoxious negative peace, where the Negro passively accepted his unjust plight, to a substance-filled positive peace, where all men will respect the dignity and worth of human personality. Actually, we who engage in nonviolent direct action are not the creators of tension. We merely bring to the surface the hidden tension that is already alive. We bring it out in the open where it can be seen and dealt with. Like a boil that can never be cured as long as it is covered up but must be opened with all its pus-flowing ugliness to the natural medicines of air and light, injustice must likewise be exposed, with all of the tension its exposing creates, to the light of human conscience and the air of national opinion before it can be cured.

In your statement you asserted that our actions, even though peaceful, must be condemned because they precipitate violence. But can this assertion be logically made? Isn't this like condemning the robbed man because his possession of money precipitated the evil act of robbery? Isn't this like condemning Socrates because his unswerving commitment to truth and his philosophical delvings precipitated the misguided popular mind to make him drink the hemlock? Isn't this like condemning Jesus because His unique God-Consciousness and never-ceasing devotion to His will precipitated the evil act of crucifixion? We must come to see, as federal courts have consistently affirmed, that it is immoral to urge an individual to withdraw his efforts to gain his basic constitutional rights because the quest precipitates violence. Society must protect the robbed and punish the robber.

I had also hoped that the white moderate would reject the myth of time. I received a letter this morning from a white brother in Texas which said: 'All Christians know that the colored people will receive equal rights eventually, but it is possible that you are in too great of a religious hurry. It has taken Christianity almost 2000 years to accomplish what it has. The teachings of Christ take time to come to earth'. All that is said here grows out of a tragic misconception of time. It is the strangely irrational notion that there is something in the very flow of time that will inevitably cure all ills. Actually time is neutral. It can be used either destructively or constructively. I am coming to feel that the people of ill will have used time much more effectively than the people of goodwill. We will have to repent in this generation not merely for the vitriolic words and actions of the bad people, but for the appalling silence of the good people. We must come to see that human progress never rolls in on wheels of inevitability. It comes through the tireless efforts and persistent work of men willing to be co-workers with God, and without this hard work time itself becomes an ally of the forces of social stagnation. We must use time creatively, and forever realize that the time is always ripe to do right. Now is the time to make real the promise of democracy, and transform our pending national elegy into a creative psalm of brotherhood. Now is the time to lift our national policy from the quicksand of racial injustice to the solid rock of human dignity.

You spoke of our activity in Birmingham as extreme. At first I was rather disappointed that fellow clergymen would see my nonviolent efforts as those of the extremist. I started thinking about the fact that I stand in the middle of two opposing forces in the Negro community. One is a force of complacency made up of Negroes who, as a result of long years of oppression, have been so completely drained of self-respect and a sense of 'somebodiness' that they have adjusted to segregation, and, of a few Negroes in the middle class who, because of a degree of academic and economic security, and because at points they profit by segregation, have unconsciously become insensitive to the problems of the masses. The other force is one of bitterness and hatred, and comes perilously close to advocating violence. It is expressed in the various black nationalist groups that are springing up over the nation, the largest and best known being Elijah Muhammad's Muslim movement. This movement is nourished by the contemporary frustration over the continued existence of racial discrimination. It is made up of people who have lost faith in America, who have absolutely repudiated Christianity, and who have concluded that the white man is an incurable 'devil'. I have tried to stand between these two forces, saying that we need not follow the 'do-nothingism' of the complacent or the hatred and despair of the black nationalist. There is the more excellent way of love and nonviolent protest. I'm grateful to God that, through the Negro church, the dimension of nonviolence entered our struggle. If this philosophy had not emerged, I am convinced that by now many streets of the South would be flowing with floods of blood. And I am further convinced that if our white brothers dismiss as 'rabble rousers' and 'outside agitators' those of us who are working through the channels of nonviolent direct action and refuse to support our nonviolent efforts, millions of Negroes, out of frustration and despair, will seek solace and security in black nationalist ideologies, a development that will lead inevitably to a frightening racial nightmare.

Oppressed people cannot remain oppressed forever. The urge for freedom will eventually come. This is what happened to the

American Negro. Something within has reminded him of his birthright of freedom; something without has reminded him that he can gain it. Consciously and unconsciously, he has been swept in by what the Germans call the *Zeitgeist*, and with his black brothers of Africa, and his brown and yellow brothers of Asia, South America and the Caribbean, he is moving with a sense of cosmic urgency toward the promised land of racial justice. Recognizing this vital urge that has engulfed the Negro community, one should readily understand public demonstrations. The Negro has many pent-up resentments and latent frustrations. He has to get them out. So let him march sometime; let him have his prayer pilgrimages to the city hall; understand why he must have sit-ins and freedom rides. If his repressed emotions do not come out in these nonviolent ways, they will come out in ominous expressions of violence. This is not a threat; it is a fact of history. So I have not said to my people 'get rid of your discontent.' But I have tried to say that this normal and healthy discontent can be channelized through the creative outlet of nonviolent direct action. Now this approach is being dismissed as extremist. I must admit that I was initially disappointed in being so categorized.

But as I continued to think about the matter I gradually gained a bit of satisfaction from being considered an extremist. Was not Jesus an extremist in love – 'Love your enemies, bless them that curse you, pray for them that despitefully use you.' Was not Amos an extremist for justice – 'Let justice roll down like waters and righteousness like a mighty stream.' Was not Paul an extremist for the gospel of Jesus Christ – 'I bear in my body the marks of the Lord Jesus.' Was not Martin Luther an extremist – 'Here I stand; I can do none other so help me God.' Was not John Bunyan an extremist – 'I will stay in jail to the end of my days before I make a butchery of my conscience.' Was not Abraham Lincoln an extremist – 'This nation cannot survive half slave and half free.' Was not Thomas Jefferson an extremist – 'We hold these truths to be self-evident, that all men are created equal.' So the question is not whether we will be extremist but what kind of extremist will we be. Will we be extremists for hate or will we be extremists for love? Will we be extremists for the preservation of injustice – or will we be extremists for the cause of justice? In that dramatic scene on Calvary's hill, three men were crucified. We must not forget that all three were crucified for the same crime –

the crime of extremism. Two were extremists for immorality, and thusly fell below their environment. The other, Jesus Christ, was an extremist for love, truth and goodness, and thereby rose above his environment. So, after all, maybe the South, the nation and the world are in dire need of creative extremists.

I had hoped that the white moderate would see this. Maybe I was too optimistic. Maybe I expected too much. I guess I should have realized that few members of a race that has oppressed another race can understand or appreciate the deep groans and passionate yearnings of those that have been oppressed and still fewer have the vision to see that injustice must be rooted out by strong, persistent and determined action. I am thankful, however, that some of our white brothers have grasped the meaning of this social revolution and committed themselves to it. They are still all too small in quantity, but they are big in quality. Some like Ralph McGill, Lillian Smith, Harry Golden and James Dabbs have written about our struggle in eloquent, prophetic and understanding terms. Others have marched with us down nameless streets of the South. They have languished in filthy roach-infested jails, suffering the abuse and brutality of angry policemen who see them as 'dirty nigger-lovers.' They, unlike so many of their moderate brothers and sisters, have recognized the urgency of the moment and sensed the need for powerful 'action' antidotes to combat the disease of segregation.

Let me rush on to mention my other disappointment. I have been so greatly disappointed with the white church and its leadership. Of course, there are some notable exceptions. I am not unmindful of the fact that each of you has taken some significant stands on this issue. I commend you, Rev. Stallings, for your Christian stand on this past Sunday, in welcoming Negroes to your worship service on a non-segregated basis. I commend the Catholic leaders of this state for integrating Springhill College several years ago.

But despite these notable exceptions I must honestly reiterate that I have been disappointed with the church. I do not say that as one of the negative critics who can always find something wrong with the church. I say it as a minister of the gospel, who loves the church; who was nurtured in its bosom; who has been sustained by its spiritual blessings and who will remain true to it as long as the cord of life shall lengthen.

I had the strange feeling when I was suddenly catapulted into the leadership of the bus protest in Montgomery several years ago that we would have the support of the white church. I felt that the white ministers, priests and rabbis of the South would be some of our strongest allies. Instead, some have been outright opponents, refusing to understand the freedom movement and misrepresenting its leaders; all too many others have been more cautious than courageous and have remained silent behind the anesthetizing security of the stained-glass windows.

In spite of my shattered dreams of the past, I came to Birmingham with the hope that the white religious leadership of this community would see the justice of our cause, and with deep moral concern, serve as the channel through which our just grievances would get to the power structure. I had hoped that each of you would understand. But again I have been disappointed. I have heard numerous religious leaders of the South call upon their worshippers to comply with a desegregation decision because it is the *law*, but I have longed to hear white ministers say, 'Follow this decree because integration is morally *right* and the Negro is your brother.' In the midst of blatant injustices inflicted upon the Negro, I have watched white churches stand on the sideline and merely mouth pious irrelevancies and sanctimonious trivialities. In the midst of a mighty struggle to rid our nation of racial and economic injustice, I have heard so many ministers say, 'Those are social issues with which the gospel has no real concern,' and I have watched so many churches commit themselves to a completely other-worldly religion which made a strange distinction between body and soul, the sacred and the secular.

So here we are moving toward the exit of the twentieth century with a religious community largely adjusted to the status quo, standing as a tail-light behind other community agencies rather than a headlight leading men to higher levels of justice.

I have traveled the length and breadth of Alabama, Mississippi and all the other southern states. On sweltering summer days and crisp autumn mornings I have looked at her beautiful churches with their lofty spires pointing heavenward. I have beheld the impressive outlay of her massive religious education buildings. Over and over again I have found myself asking: 'What kind of people worship here? Who is their God? Where were their voices when the lips of Governor Barnett dripped with words of interposition and nullification? Where were they when Governor

Wallace gave the clarion call for defiance and hatred? Where were their voices of support when tired, bruised and weary Negro men and women decided to rise from the dark dungeons of complacency to the bright hills of creative protest?'

Yes, these questions are still in my mind. In deep disappointment, I have wept over the laxity of the church. But be assured that my tears have been tears of love. There can be no deep disappointment where there is not deep love. Yes, I love the church; I love her sacred walls. How could I do otherwise? I am in the rather unique position of being the son, the grandson and the great-grandson of preachers. Yes, I see the church as the body of Christ. But, oh! How we have blemished and scarred that body through social neglect and fear of being nonconformists.

There was a time when the church was very powerful. It was during that period when the early Christians rejoiced when they were deemed worthy to suffer for what they believed. In those days the church was not merely a thermometer that recorded the ideas and principles of popular opinion; it was a thermostat that transformed the mores of society. Wherever the early Christians entered a town the power structure got disturbed and immediately sought to convict them for being 'disturbers of the peace' and 'outside agitators.' But they went on with the conviction that they were 'a colony of heaven,' and had to obey God rather than man. They were small in number but big in commitment. They were too God-intoxicated to be 'astronomically intimidated.' They brought an end to such ancient evils as infanticide and gladiatorial contest.

Things are different now. The contemporary church is often a weak, ineffectual voice with an uncertain sound. It is so often the arch supporter of the status quo. Far from being disturbed by the presence of the church, the power structure of the average community is consoled by the church's silent and often vocal sanction of things as they are.

But the judgment of God is upon the church as never before. If the church of today does not recapture the sacrificial spirit of the early church, it will lose its authentic ring, forfeit the loyalty of millions, and be dismissed as an irrelevant social club with no meaning for the twentieth century. I am meeting young people every day whose disappointment with the church has risen to outright disgust.

Maybe again, I have been too optimistic. Is organized religion too inextricably bound to the status quo to save our nation and the world? Maybe I must turn my faith to the inner spiritual church, the church within the church, as the true *ecclesia* and the hope of the world. But again I am thankful to God that some noble souls from the ranks of organized religion have broken loose from the paralyzing chains of conformity and joined us as active partners in the struggle for freedom. They have left their secure congregations and walked the streets of Albany, Georgia, with us. They have gone through the highways of the South on tortuous rides for freedom. Yes, they have gone to jail with us. Some have been kicked out of their churches, and lost support of their bishops and fellow ministers. But they have gone with the faith that right defeated is stronger than evil triumphant. These men have been the leaven in the lump of the race. Their witness has been the spiritual salt that has preserved the true meaning of the Gospel in these troubled times. They have carved a tunnel of hope through the dark mountain of disappointment.

I hope the church as a whole will meet the challenge of this decisive hour. But even if the church does not come to the aid of justice, I have no despair about the future. I have no fear about the outcome of our struggle in Birmingham, even if our motives are presently misunderstood. We will reach the goal of freedom in Birmingham and all over the nation, because the goal of America is freedom. Abused and scorned though we may be, our destiny is tied up with the destiny of America. Before the pilgrims landed at Plymouth we were here. Before the pen of Jefferson etched across the pages of history the majestic words of the Declaration of Independence, we were here. For more than two centuries our foreparents labored in this country without wages; they made cotton king; and they built the homes of their masters in the midst of brutal injustice and shameful humiliation – and yet out of a bottomless vitality they continued to thrive and develop. If the inexpressible cruelties of slavery could not stop us, the opposition we now face will surely fail. We will win our freedom because the sacred heritage of our nation and the eternal will of God are embodied in our echoing demands.

I must close now. But before closing I am impelled to mention one other point in your statement that troubled me profoundly. You warmly commended the Birmingham police force for keeping 'order' and 'preventing violence.' I don't believe you would have so warmly commended the police force if you had seen its

82

angry violent dogs literally biting six unarmed, nonviolent Negroes. I don't believe you would so quickly commend the policemen if you would observe their ugly and inhuman treatment of Negroes here in the city jail; if you would watch them push and curse old Negro women and young Negro girls; if you would see them slap and kick old Negro men and young boys; if you will observe them, as they did on two occasions, refuse to give us food because we wanted to sing our grace together. I'm sorry that I can't join you in your praise for the police department.

It is true that they have been rather disciplined in their public handling of the demonstrators. In this sense they have been rather publicly 'nonviolent.' But for what purpose? To preserve the evil system of segregation. Over the last few years I have consistently preached that nonviolence demands that the means we use must be as pure as the ends we seek. So I have tried to make it clear that it is wrong to use immoral means to attain moral ends. But now I must affirm that it is just as wrong, or even more so, to use moral means to preserve immoral ends. Maybe Mr. Connor and his policemen have been rather publicly nonviolent, as Chief Pritchett was in Albany, Georgia, but they have used the moral means of nonviolence to maintain the immoral end of flagrant racial injustice. T. S. Eliot has said that there is no greater treason than to do the right deed for the wrong reason.

I wish you had commended the Negro sit-inners and demonstrators of Birmingham for their sublime courage, their willingness to suffer and their amazing discipline in the midst of the most inhuman provocation. One day the South will recognize its real heroes. They will be the James Merediths, courageously and with a majestic sense of purpose facing jeering and hostile mobs and the agonizing loneliness that characterizes the life of the pioneer. They will be old, oppressed, battered Negro women, symbolized in a seventy-two year old woman of Montgomery, Alabama, who rose up with a sense of dignity and with her people decided not to ride the segregated buses, and responded to one who inquired about her tiredness with ungrammatical profundity: 'My feet is tired, but my soul is rested.' They will be the young high school and college students, young ministers of the Gospel and a host of their elders courageously and nonviolently sitting-in at lunch counters and willingly going to jail for conscience's sake. One day the South will know that when these disinherited children of God sat down at lunch counters they were in reality standing up for the best in the American dream and the most sacred values in our Judeo-Christian heritage, and thusly, carrying our whole nation back to those great wells of democracy which were dug deep by the founding fathers in the formulation of the Constitution and the Declaration of Independence.

Never before have I written a letter this long (or should I say a book?). I'm afraid that it is much too long to take your precious time. I can assure you that it would have been much shorter if I had been writing from a comfortable desk, but what else is there to do when you are alone for days in the dull monotony of a narrow jail cell other than write long letters, think strange thoughts, and pray long prayers?

If I have said anything in this letter that is an overstatement of the truth and is indicative of an unreasonable impatience, I beg you to forgive me. If I have said anything in this letter that is an understatement of the truth and is indicative of my having a patience that makes me patient with anything less than brotherhood, I beg God to forgive me.

I hope this letter finds you strong in the faith. I also hope that circumstances will soon make it possible for me to meet each of you, not as an integrationist or a civil-rights leader, but as a fellow clergyman and a Christian brother. Let us all hope that the dark clouds of racial prejudice will soon pass away and the deep fog of misunderstanding will be lifted from our fear-drenched communities and in some not too distant tomorrow the radiant stars of love and brotherhood will shine over our great nation with all of their scintillating beauty.

> Yours for the cause of Peace and Brotherhood,
> Martin Luther King, Jr

5

THE CASE AGAINST CIVIL DISOBEDIENCE

Herbert J. Storing

In this essay, which was completed a few days before the assassination of Martin Luther King, I examine and criticize, among other matters, King's philosophy of nonviolent resistance. There is a bitter sorrow in seeing part of my argument underlined with the blood of this American leader and the consequent civil disorder. While I find some personal satisfaction in what I believe was King's growing understanding of the limits of civil disobedience, this only increases my sense of the loss to the nation. We have lost not only an eloquent advocate of civil disobedience but a leader who was in the course of transcending civil disobedience in the direction of statesmanship. We may pay heavily for the loss.

As a teacher, however, Martin Luther King is not lost to us. He still speaks; we may listen and think. I have no better way of paying him honor and respect than to seek instruction in a critical examination of his principles, and that is what I have tried to do here.

The most striking characteristic of civil disobedience is its irrelevance to the problems of today. The fashion in civil disobedience seems likely to die out as quickly as it burst into flame with the actions of the Montgomery bus boycotters and the words of Martin Luther King. Moreover, today's rejection of civil disobedience comes not mainly from right-wing defenders of law, order, and the status quo, but from the very sources of radical

From: H. J. Storing, 'The Case Against Civil Disobedience,' in Robert A. Goldwin (ed.), *On Civil Disobedience: Essays Old and News* (Chicago, IL: Rand McNally, 1969), pp. 95–106, 114–20.

reform and protest from which the advocates of civil disobedience have drawn their principles and programs. Disobedience abounds, but it has thrust civility aside. We take up the question of civil disobedience, then, at a time when there is a good deal of agreement from all sides of the political compass that civil disobedience is obsolete or irrelevant. Nor should this be surprising. Civil disobedience, however important it seemed a short time ago, is an altogether secondary and derivative matter, scarcely capable of being put in a form that is not contradictory, shallow, and a feeble guide to action. It deserves, nevertheless, serious consideration, for it is remarkable in its capacity to point to far more fundamental, timely, and relevant political questions.

Civil disobedience, I shall argue, is an unsuccessful attempt to combine, on the level of principle, revolution and conventional political action. The fundamental choice lies, as Malcolm X often said, between bullets and ballots. In both revolution and conventional political action something that could be called civil disobedience may play a part, but that part is altogether contingent, subject to prudential considerations, and subordinate to the greater principles of political action. Civil disobedience is the resort – always a theoretically and practically weak resort – of the *subject* of law, exercised because the subject cannot or will not take up the rights and duties of the citizen.

I will consider civil disobedience in the context of the Negro movement. This has, in recent years, been the main locus of civil disobedience and the area in which it has received its most thorough articulation. I will rely primarily, although not entirely, on the principles enunciated by Martin Luther King, who has stood since the Montgomery bus boycott in 1956 as the most authoritative and best spokesman of civil disobedience in the Negro movement. According to King, civil disobedience is the open, nonviolent, even loving breaking of law with a willingness to accept the punishment. It will be helpful to bear in mind two closely related distinctions. First, nonviolent resistance, as King taught and practiced it, does not always involve civil disobedience. The Montgomery bus boycott, at least in its early stages, was not illegal, but it was a form of nonviolent resistance. Nonviolent resistance may take the form of massive but legal protest. However, as King clearly saw, the heart of nonviolent resistance is disobeying a law or lawful authority in protest against injustice. Second, civil disobedience is to be distinguished from testing the constitutionality of law. This distinction is often obscured because what starts out as the former may end as the latter, and very often in practice the two kinds of activities are pressed forward at the same time. But the distinction in principle is clear. If a Negro makes use of facilities reserved by local law for whites and if upon being arrested and fined he appeals and secures a decision from the Supreme Court that the local law is unconstitutional, he has not committed an illegal act. (If, on the other hand, he loses his appeal but by his action persuades the federal or state government to legislate against the segregation, he has committed an illegal act, despite the subsequent change in the law.) The institution of judicial review, in which the acts of governmental authorities are tested in the light of the higher law of the Constitution, provides for a kind of tamed or civilized 'civil disobedience.' One of the practical consequences of this institution is to divert disobedience and even revolution into the channel of law. Judicial review mediates between the positive claims of the legislature or official of initial jurisdiction and the universal claims of justice, through the higher positive law of the Constitution. But it is only a mediation; and the distinction remains between 'breaking' a 'law' that is invalid under the Constitution, which involves no unlawful behavior, and breaking a valid law because it is claimed to be unjust, which does of course involve unlawful behavior – even if the claim of injustice is sound and even if it is recognized as sound by a subsequent amendment of the law.

According to King, the Negro found in the doctrine of nonviolent resistance a practical and a moral answer to his centuries-old cry for justice. Decades of patient submission had produced no acceptable results; yet a resort to violence was practically and morally out of the question. Direct nonviolent resistance permits the Negro to move positively to foster a crisis and thus to expose a cleavage which his former passivity had helped to conceal.[1] By actively refusing to cooperate with an unjust system – the injustice, say, of segregated lunch counters – and at the same time

1 Martin Luther King, Jr *Stride Toward Freedom* (New York: Harper & Brothers, 1958), pp. 193-4; *Why We Can't Wait* (New York: New American Library Signet Book, 1964), p. 79.

by turning the other cheek to the violence that his resistance stimulates, the Negro wields a sword far more effective than violence could ever be. Large-scale non-cooperation calls attention to the unjust system and strains its facilities. The demonstrators' failure to resist the billy club and the fire hose underlines the difference between oppressor and oppressed. Nonviolent resistance is the sword that heals. It ennobles its user and cuts without wounding. Loving the oppressor while standing nonviolently against the unjust system of segregation, the demonstrator turns his enemy into a friend, thus doubly contributing to the ultimate end, integration, which is 'genuine intergroup and interpersonal living' or 'total interrelatedness.' [2]

One of the sharpest and most penetrating attacks on King's nonviolent resistance was made by Malcolm X: 'Just as the slavemaster of that day used Tom, the house Negro, to keep the field Negroes in check, the same old slavemaster today has Negroes who are nothing but modern Uncle Toms, twentieth-century Uncle Toms, to keep you and me in check, to keep us under control, keep us passive and peaceful and nonviolent. That's Tom making you nonviolent.' It's like the dentist deadening the pain with novocaine: 'Blood running all down your jaw, and you don't know what's happening. Because someone has taught you to suffer – peacefully.' [3] 'I don't mean go out and get violent; but at the same time you should never be nonviolent unless you run into some nonviolence. I'm not responsible for what I do. And that's the way every Negro should get.' [4]

Many moderates in the Civil Rights Movement, while rejecting the most extreme statements of men like Malcolm X and Stokely Carmichael, also find themselves increasingly unwilling to defend the doctrine of nonviolent resistance. There has consequently been much discussion lately – often rather shallow discussion – about the limits of nonviolence and the forms, effectiveness, and justifiability of violence. But at a deeper level the tendency to reject the nonviolent part of King's teaching derives from a taking seriously of the revolutionary part of that teaching.

King frequently spoke of the Negro Revolution, the third

2 *Stride Toward Freedom*, p. 220; *Why We Can't Wait*, p. 152.
3 George Brietman (ed.), *Malcolm X Speaks* (New York: Grove Press, Inc., 1966), p. 12.
4 ibid., pp. 33-4.

American revolution; and in former times, at least, he adopted the revolutionary's uncompromising rejection of politics as usual. Scorning 'moderate' contentions that the Negro demonstrations in Birmingham in 1963 were ill-timed, King asserted 'that it was ridiculous to speak of timing when the clock of history showed that the Negro had already suffered one hundred years of delay.' 'Gradualism and moderation are not the answer to the great moral indictment which, in the Revolution of 1963, finally came to stand in the center of our national stage.' The Negro wants 'absolute and immediate freedom and equality . . . right here in this land today. . . . Negroes no longer are tolerant of or interested in compromise. . . . In the bursting mood that has overtaken the Negro in 1963, the word "compromise" is profane and pernicious.' [5] In the words of SNCC chairman, John Lewis, in 1963, 'the revolution is at hand, and we must free ourselves of the chains of political and economic slavery. . . . To those who have said "Be Patient and Wait," we must say that "Patience is a dirty and nasty word." ' [6]

Perhaps all this is only the exaggeration of the partisan, legitimate in times when 'gradualism' and 'moderation' have been soiled by use as disguises for repression and injustice. Uncompromising talk is not necessarily incompatible with prudent action. A relatively small group of followers may be more or less successfully turned from righteous indignation to political prudence, as conditions require. But King spoke not to the few but to the many; and a mass is much less easily maneuvered, much more likely to crush its leaders' prudence with its leaders' extremism. King said of cautious moderates in 1964 that 'the breath of the new movement chilled them.' [7] Very soon King felt the full storm he had helped to create.

Malcolm X rejected nonviolence in the name of the truly revolutionary character of the Negro movement: 'There's no such thing as a nonviolent revolution. . . .' 'Revolution is bloody, revolution is hostile, revolution knows no compromise, revolution overturns and destroys everything that gets in its way.' 'These Negroes aren't asking for any nation – they're trying to

5 *Why We Can't Wait*, pp. 66, 128, 131.
6 John Lewis, 'Speech at March on Washington, 1963,' Staughton Lynd (ed.), *Nonviolence in America: A Documentary History* (Indianapolis: Bobbs-Merrill, 1966), p. 484.
7 *Why We Can't Wait*, p. 119.

crawl back on the plantation.' 'Revolution is always based on land. Revolution is never based on begging somebody for an integrated cup of coffee. Revolutions are never fought by turning the other cheek. Revolutions are never based upon love-your-enemy and pray-for-those-who-spitefully-use-you. And revolutions are never waged singing "We Shall Overcome." Revolutions are based upon bloodshed. Revolutions are never compromising. Revolutions are never based upon negotiations. Revolutions are never based upon any kind of tokenism whatsoever. Revolutions are never based upon that which is begging a corrupt society or a corrupt system to accept us into it. Revolutions overturn systems. And there is no system on this earth which has proven itself more corrupt, more criminal, than this system that in 1964 still colonizes 22 million African-Americans, still enslaves 22 million Africo-Americans.' [8]

Malcolm urged that Negroes take seriously the idea of revolution, so loosely used by King. He tested King's moderation against King's extremism; and he found that moderation weak, false, and untenable. Although the assassin's bullet prevented Malcolm from concluding his reflections on the character of the Negro revolution and on the means open to the Negro to overturn the American system or abandon it, he was remarkably successful in exposing the revolutionary side – the system-overturning, violent side – of nonviolent resistance. It will be part of the business of the immediate future to explore the fundamental questions raised by the radical versions of black power and black nationalism. There are questions of ends. Is the problem simply that whites have power and blacks do not? Or is there some fundamental and ineradicable injustice in the American system? If the latter, is that injustice essentially the 'racism' now officially acknowledged, or is it a deeper defect, such as a preoccupation with material comfort and a lessening of concern for the 'human values'? What are the valued and valuable characteristics of the Negro? Have they grown out of his heroic resistance to and survival under oppression? Are they of African derivation? What will be the character of the new society? There are also questions of means. Is the future to be sought in separation? In some form of internal 'separation'? What are the possible modes and outcomes of revolutionary action by Negroes within the United

8 *Malcolm X Speaks*, pp. 9–10, 50.

States? Of violent confrontation? There are many fundamental questions raised if a Negro revolution is taken seriously, but civil disobedience is not one of them. If what is called for is revolution, civil disobedience is at most a mere tactic, of no more independent significance as a principle and of no greater moral or political stature than the tactics of guerrilla warfare, boycott, and sabotage.

Granting, however, that the most strident voices of the Negro movement today reject the American system radically and thus reject civil disobedience as anything but a mere tactic, is there not another view which remains fundamentally committed to the American system, which seeks to hold that system to its avowed principles so far as its behavior toward Negroes is concerned? And is this not the true ground of justification of the espousal and practice of civil disobedience by American Negroes? Is there not a fundamental distinction to be made between the reform of a political system that is fundamentally sound, although unjust in some very important particulars, and the overturning of one that is corrupt at heart?

One of the striking characteristics of Martin Luther King's doctrine, a characteristic that it seems to share with other versions of civil disobedience, is the extent to which this crucial distinction is obscured. In *Stride Toward Freedom*, King described his concern when the impending 1955 boycott against segregated busses in Montgomery, Alabama, was likened to the White Citizens' Councils' resistance to school desegregation. Reflecting on the differences between these cases and on the teachings of Thoreau, King said, 'Something began to say to me, "He who passively accepts evil is as much involved in it as he who helps to perpetrate it. He who accepts evil without protesting against it is really cooperating with it." '[9] King's major statement of civil disobedience is his famous 'Letter from Birmingham City Jail,' written in 1963, in which he replies to those who ask how Negroes can urge others to obey the 1954 school desegregation decision while themselves breaking laws.[10] 'The answer lies in the fact that there are two types of laws; just and unjust. I would

9 *Stride Toward Freedom*, p. 51; cf. p. 212.
10 The 'Letter from Birmingham City Jail' is printed in *Why We Can't Wait*, pp. 76-95; [it is reprinted in this volume, pp. 68-84].

be the first to advocate obeying just laws.' King goes on to provide some rules of thumb for distinguishing just from unjust laws (to which we shall return), and he concedes that some respect is due to law *per se*. 'In no sense do I advocate evading or defying the law, as would the rabid segregationist. That would lead to anarchy. One who breaks an unjust law must do so openly, lovingly, and with a willingness to accept the penalty.' He argues 'that an individual who breaks a law that conscience tells him is unjust, and who willingly accepts the penalty of imprisonment in order to arouse the conscience of the community over its injustice, is in reality expressing the highest respect for law.' Indeed, such behavior is not only permitted but demanded. 'We must learn that passively to accept an unjust system is to cooperate with that system, and thereby to become a participant in its evil.' 'To cooperate passively with an unjust system makes the oppressed as evil as the oppressor.'[11]

There are several issues here that deserve to be sorted out and considered. First is the problem of discovering justice, which is the aim and the test of law. King, unlike some other advocates of nonviolent resistance, adheres to the view that there *are* just and unjust laws, and that this distinction is not merely a matter of personal preference. Individual 'conscience' is, for him, not merely personal but directed by a cosmic guide towards the truly just. The foundation of civil disobedience must be, in King's view, not mere 'feeling' or 'commitment', but justice. Yet King's discussion of justice is exceedingly loose. The heart of his definition is that 'Any law that uplifts human personality is just. Any law that degrades human personality is unjust. All segregation statutes are unjust because segregation distorts the soul and damages the personality.'[12] As John Lewis said, 'segregation is evil and . . . it must be destroyed in all forms.'[13] Now it is

11 ibid., pp. 61–77; Martin Luther King, *Strength To Love* (New York: Harper & Row, 1963), pp. 6, 83; cf. *Stride Toward Freedom*, p. 212.
12 In his 'Letter from Birmingham City Jail,' King suggests two other 'examples' of unjust laws – when a majority inflicts on a minority a code that is not binding on itself, or when a code is inflicted on a minority which the minority had no part in enacting because not permitted to vote. The latter is important but insufficient, since King would not confine unjust laws to those adopted without the participation of some minority. The former is a simple statement of the extremely complex 'equal protection' problem that has so vexed the courts and takes on substance only when seen in the light of King's view of the injustice of racial segregation.
13 Lynd (ed.), *Nonviolence in America*, p. 483.

becoming increasingly clear to growing numbers of people that segregation is not always and under all circumstances unjust, that the assimilationist test by which King judged race relations is inadequate if not false, and that the questions of what it *means* to 'uplift the human personality' and how that can be done are a good deal more complicated than they appeared to King in the context of legally segregated southern cities. The growing reaction against nonviolent resistance includes a more or less emphatic rejection of the assimilationist *end*. For our present purpose, however, the important point is that to the extent that the demands of justice are obscure the ground for civil disobedience is weakened and the need for political deliberation and political working out of the answers is strengthened.

A second issue is whether even an open and loving breaking of the law with a willingness to accept the penalty does not constitute or lead to a defiance of the law and whether it would not on any substantial scale lead to anarchy.[14] An open refusal to obey an unjust law shows the highest respect for law in the same way that an open insult to a degraded woman, with a willingness to be slapped for the insult, shows the highest respect for womanhood. Our usual view, however, is that we owe respect to the law as law, to women as women, even when they do *not* in fact exhibit the traits we respect them for. We think that those traits are strengthened by our acting on the presumption of their presence, even when they are not present. This is not the whole story, obviously, and there are circumstances where the rule does not apply. But do we not treat the respectable qualities as the rule because we want to maintain them as the rule, and do we not carefully identify and circumscribe the exceptions in order to help maintain their exceptional character? Do we not, as beneficiaries of the law, have an interest in having the law obeyed even where there is disagreement about its justice? Do we not benefit from a community of law-abiding men? Are we seriously prepared to say, with Thoreau, 'For my own part, I should not

---

14 Consider the reasonable, if perhaps rather strict, rule of CORE: 'When in an action project, a CORE member will obey the order issued by the authorized leader or spokesman of the project, whether these orders please him or not. If he does not approve of such orders, he shall later refer the criticism back to the group or to the committee which was the source of the project plan.' Francis Broderick and August Meier (eds.), *Negro Protest Thought in the Twentieth Century* (Indianapolis: Bobbs-Merrill Co., 1965), p. 302.

like to think that I ever rely on the protection of the State'?[15] The advocates of civil disobedience contend that we are protected from these dangers to the law by the practical and moral consequences of the rule that the lawbreaker must act openly and with a willingness to accept the punishment. But are we so sure that we can enforce this rule, as the teaching of disobedience extends through the populace, especially the desperately poor, the degraded, and the bitter? Despite some outstanding successes in limited areas under special circumstances, I think it is now clear – as it should have been from the beginning – that the broad result of the propagation of civil disobedience is disobedience. The question then becomes whether the encouragement of disobedience endangers law and civil society, and the answer seems clear enough today, if it was ever in doubt, that it does.

Indeed, why *should* the breaker of an unjust law do so 'openly, lovingly and with a willingness to accept the penalty'? The reason, King suggests, is to show his respect for law. It is not clear, in the first place, why if he need not obey the law to show respect for law, he needs to accept the punishment to show respect for law. It is not surprising that the subtlety of this distinction tends to get lost in its application. Moreover, accepting the punishment for breaking an unjust law is not always necessary to show respect for law. Revolution need not be in disrespect of law, as the American Revolution surely was not. Nor, on the other hand, is civil disobedience – open and loving breaking of law with a willingness to accept the punishment – always the way to show respect for law. King says:

> We should never forget that everything Adolf Hitler did in Germany was 'legal' and everything the Hungarian freedom fighters did in Hungary was 'illegal'. It was 'illegal' to aid and comfort a Jew in Hitler's Germany. Even so, I am sure that, had I lived in Germany at the time, I would have aided and comforted my Jewish brothers. If today I lived in a Communist country where certain principles dear to the Christian faith are suppressed, I would openly advocate disobeying that country's antireligious laws.[16]

But would King have openly aided and comforted Jews in

15 Henry David Thoreau, 'Civil Disobedience', this volume, p. 39.
16 King, 'Letter', this volume, p. 75.

Hitler's Germany? Precious few Jews he would have aided! Would he openly advocate disobeying the antireligious laws of a Communist country at the price of leaving his and other Christian flocks untended? And would he - ought he to? - disobey the laws of Hitler's Germany lovingly? Is he obliged to show his respect for 'law' in general by willingly accepting the punishment imposed by the 'laws' of that regime? The extension of the principles of civil disobedience to such cases makes a mockery of law and justice.

A more tenable argument would be that the breaking of an unjust law *in a fundamentally just regime* must be done in an open, loving manner and with a willingness to accept the punishment, not to show respect for law in the abstract but to show respect for and concede the legitimacy of this system of law, of which this unjust law is a part. The laws of segregation deserve to be broken, this argument runs; but their breaking ought to be done in a way that shows respect for and helps to support the broader legal principles of the American government which, unlike the segregation laws, deserve the respect of a just man. The distinction, which King fails to make, between regimes like that of the United States and regimes like that of Nazi Germany is at the foundation of the political action of all decent, to say nothing of just, men, precisely because it is the distinction between those political systems to which decent men can and cannot lend their cooperation. Obviously this does not settle questions of political action. It is only the beginning. If the regime is fundamentally unjust it must be changed, brought down, endured, or deserted - whichever seems most likely to result in something better. If the regime is fundamentally just, there remains the substance of politics, involving all of the heavy and difficult judgments about where justice can be done and injustice avoided consistently with the overall aim of maintaining and strengthening the capacity of the system to act well.

There is another side of this issue to which King also appears to have given little attention. Sometimes he speaks of just and unjust laws, sometimes of just and unjust systems. Where does the duty not to cooperate with injustice end? Must the conscientious man refuse his cooperation with every unjust law? with every system of which an unjust law is a part? The preeminence of the issue of legally sanctioned or supported racial discrimination in the South provided a focus for civil disobedience there which did not force questions like this to the surface, but they quickly arise as less clear-cut injustices are confronted. It seems likely that King would have accepted the well-known rule provided by Thoreau:

> If the injustice is part of the necessary friction of the machine of government, let it go, let it go: perchance it will wear smooth – certainly the machine will wear out. If the injustice has a spring, or a pulley, or a rope, or a crank, exclusively for itself, then perhaps you may consider whether the remedy will not be worse than the evil; but if it is of such a nature that it requires you to be the agent of injustice to another, then, I say, break the law. Let your life be a counter friction to stop the machine. What I have to do is to see, at any rate, that I do not lend myself to the wrong which I condemn.[17]

But the distinction manifestly breaks down (as Thoreau virtually concedes later in the essay)[18] once one recognizes the obvious fact of the interdependence of the parts of a political system. The nexus of taxes, the specific ground of Thoreau's disobedience, connects every man with every wrong (as well as every right) done by the state. And if a man pays no tax – and is so consistent as to permit no one to pay it for him – he would still be connected by commerce or civil intercourse. If the lesson of civil disobedience is to become *in nowise* the agent of injustice, the result is revolution against this government, both in Thoreau's time and ours, and against every government I have read of or heard of. That does indeed seem to be the drift of this hero of civil disobedience, who milked so much out of one night in jail. 'Under a government which imprisons any unjustly, the true place for a just man is also in prison.' King never expressed himself quite so foolishly. But if, on the other hand, the advocates of civil disobedience are to be understood to say not that one must never in any way contribute to injustice but that one should consider whether he is, through his cooperation or compromise with a given political system, the instrument of *too much* injustice in comparison with the good that his cooperation

17 Thoreau, 'Civil Disobedience' this volume, p. 39.
18 'In fact, I quietly declare war with the State, after my fashion, though I will still make what use and get what advantage of her as I can, as is usual in such cases.'

does, then he has begun – barely begun – to think and act *politically*, which is to say, beyond civil disobedience. [. . .]

There is one further argument that needs to be considered, which is that, contrary to what I have contended, civil disobedience is not only a mode of politics but a subtle and profound support of law. The argument is an extension of the command that the unjust law be disobeyed openly and lovingly and with a willingness to accept the punishment. Civil disobedience implies, in this view, not merely a passive respect for law but an active participation with the law in a dialogue about justice. Harris Wofford, Jr., for example, takes one of the arguments often made by opponents of civil disobedience and turns it to a defense of civil disobedience. The law does not merely regulate; it also teaches. But whereas it is often argued that the teaching function of law is weakened by disobedience, Wofford contends that 'the law will play its full role as a teacher only when we look upon it as a question.' The law is 'the voice of our body politic with which we must remain in dialogue.' Each law should be looked upon by the free man 'not as a command but as a question, for implicit in each law is the alternative of obedience or of respectful civil disobedience and full acceptance of the consequences.'[19] Once each man is freed from the belief that he must obey the law just because it is law, he will ask, shall I obey this law? Is it just? Wofford suggests that it is this choice that makes men free and also that this choice will lead to a fruitful dialogue, the result of which will be an improved understanding of the ends of law. 'I am presenting civil disobedience as a natural and necessary part of the great Due Process of our law, that process of persuasion through which we govern ourselves.'[20]

This is obviously an attractive idea. Civil disobedience may at

19 The Journal of Religious Thought, Autumn–Winter, 1957–8, p. 31.
20 Harris Wofford, Jr., 'The Law and Civil Disobedience,' *The Presbyterian Outlook*, vol. 142, no. 34, p. 5. [. . .]
  While the free-choice argument does not appear to be basic, its tendency is suggested by the following. Wofford says that while we all engage in such forms of 'civil disobedience' as jaywalking or speeding, we hesitate to resist unjust laws. 'Instead of taking Socrates straight, we seem to prefer the comic version. I am referring to Aristophanes' portrayal in *The Clouds*, where the student of Socrates says 'But I wish to succeed, just enough for my need, and to slip through the clutches of law.' But there again we are free to choose which Socrates – which inner light or higher law – to follow, and it is the choice that makes us free.' Better, it would seem, to disobey a just law than to disobey no law at all.

last find solid ground if it can be shown to be part of our great 'due process' of law, the dialogue through which the law teaches and thereby learns. There are, however, some problems. Wofford seems to think of civil society as a great seminar on justice, with the law as discussion leader. This is not an altogether false view, but it passes over too quickly the primary functions of law. This is not the place for any extended discussion of this matter, but if the law teaches, surely it also commands, punishes, and habituates.

Law – our law at any rate – is not merely command, but is it not that in the first place? Wofford argues that 'implicit in each law is the alternative of obedience or of respectful civil disobedience and full acceptance of the consequences.'[21] It is difficult to take seriously the suggestion that the law intends to offer the 'option' of civil disobedience. The law does not present itself in the form of an either-or proposition. It is in the form of a command that men behave in a certain way, with a penalty attached as punishment if the command is disobeyed. If, on the other hand, Wofford means merely to describe the alternatives that are 'implicit' in the sense of logically consistent, then the statement is too narrow, for secretive disobedience, avoidance, and violent rejection are also implicit in this sense. So far as enforcement is concerned, we may recall that the American Founders had experienced, under the Articles of Confederation, a system of law that attempted to dispense with sanctions, penalties, or punishments for disobedience; and they learned that such laws amount in fact 'to nothing more than advice or recommendation.' Law does not address itself merely to the reason. It is precisely 'because the passions of men will not conform to the dictates of reason and justice without constraint' that government is necessary.[22] Moreover, the law rests on and encourages habitual law-abidingness, the 'taking for granted' of the justice of the law and its title to obedience. If mere habituation threatens freedom, sound habituation provides its necessary foundation. The man who seeks his freedom in a resistance to law as law will find instead anarchy or, more likely, paralysis. It is only through command, enforcement, and habituation that the law of the liberal regime performs one of its most admired

21 *The Journal of Religious Thought*, Autumn–Winter, 1957–8, p. 31.
22 *The Federalist*, no. 15.

functions, to provide the basis for political deliberation and political education.

Unquestionably the law does teach. It gives reasons and thereby invites an inspection of the validity of these reasons. Thoreau was wrong when he denied that the state ever 'intentionally confronts a man's sense, intellectual or moral.' The state confronts men's intellectual and moral sense every day in the public deliberations and addresses of the officers of the state, in the law courts, and in the laws themselves, with their preambles, 'whereas' clauses, and explanatory notes and provisions. But while it is true that the giving of reasons implies a willingness to have those reasons and thus the foundation of the law questioned, the primary teaching lies in the reasons, not in the response. Admit that the reason of law may be regarded as a question to its subjects; admit that this is an invitation to a dialogue; admit that the subject takes a necessary part; admit that there is mutual instruction in the dialogue. Yet it is, after all, Socrates who asks the questions, who teaches. The 'education' that is involved in civil disobedience is, in the very best case, the responsive, subordinate, learning part of the dialogue. The guiding question of political education is, after all, not, shall I obey? but, what shall be done?

Civil disobedience is part of the subject's view, as distinguished from the citizen's view, of law and government. It is the subject for whom the first question is obedience or disobedience. It is the subject who is restricted in his political participation to those modes that are connected with his power to obey or not obey. It is the subject whose question is not, what shall be done? but, shall I obey? For people whose only role is that of subject, civil disobedience may indeed be the only available form of political participation. It may sometimes help to secure an excluded people a place among the governors of this self-governing community. But it is always a feeble instrument; because its principles are contradictory, its effects are dubious, it tends to undermine respect for the law, and above all its foundation is the role and point of view of the recipient of law, the subject. Civil disobedience is not rule, and it will be the resort of those who cannot or will not share in rule. Civil disobedience may be necessary and at least partly successful in removing restrictions on the registration of Negro voters in the South. It is neither necessary nor successful in dealing with the problems of northern slums – as Martin Luther King seemed to learn. Civil disobedience is a response to initiatives from elsewhere, an appeal to someone else to do something – or, more often, to stop doing something. It is inherently subordinate, responsive, dependent, and – for the citizen of a democracy – degrading.

There is a good deal of evidence that many Negro leaders today, having, like Frederick Douglass, pursued civil disobedience through its false morality to its political dead end, and rejecting the revolutionary demands of separation or destruction, are turning to a sober assessment of their political alternatives and political tasks. Bayard Rustin has described the beginning of this change in his well-known essay, 'From Protest to Politics': 'What began as a protest movement is being challenged to translate itself into a political movement.'[23] In his last book, King, while defending nonviolent resistance against radical attack, conceded its inadequacy. 'We found a method in nonviolent protest that worked, and we employed it enthusiastically. We did not have leisure to probe for a deeper understanding of its laws and lines of development.'[24] We shall never know how far this probing might have gone, but it is clear that King looked increasingly to political power. Negroes need, he wrote in 1967, 'to generate the kind of power that shapes basic decisions.' There is a need to develop leaders and to enroll Negroes, formerly confined to the school of protest, in the school of citizenship.

> How shall we turn the ghettos into a vast school? How shall we make every street corner a forum, not a lounging place for trivial gossip and petty gambling, where life is wasted and human experience withers to trivial sensations? How shall we make every houseworker and every laborer a demonstrator, a voter, a canvasser and a student? The dignity their jobs may deny them is waiting for them in political social action.[25]

This political and social action by the Negro will be, in the first place, in pursuit of his own immediate needs and interests.

23 *Commentary*, February, 1965; in Broderick and Meier (eds.), *Negro Protest Thought in the Twentieth Century*, p. 407.
24 Martin Luther King, *Where Do We Go From Here, Chaos or Community?* (Boston: Beacon Press, 1967), p. 137.
25 ibid., pp. 138, 156.

'We can no longer rely on pressuring and cajoling political units toward desired actions,' James Farmer has said. 'We must be in a position of power, a position to change these political units when they are not responsive. The only way to achieve political objectives is through power, political power.'[26] This is the beginning of democratic politics. There is not yet much evidence among major Negro leaders of the understanding that a Frederick Douglass had of an Abraham Lincoln. (There may, it must be conceded, be more than one reason for that.) The emphasis that even the moderates place upon power is a sign, not only of their rhetorical problem in the face of a radical challenge, but also of the relatively narrow view they take of citizenship and political leadership. But the decent pursuit of self-interest through politics is, in the American system of ruling and being ruled, the beginning from which the subject of the law is stimulated and guided, through alliances and bargaining and compromises, to something like the comprehensive view of the true citizen. In such citizenship, as King suggests, lies not only a power but a dignity surpassing anything accessible through the mere subject's tactics of civil disobedience.

The circumstances of the Negro in America, under slavery and after the Civil War, taught Frederick Douglass a lesson which many whites at that time and many whites and blacks today have forgotten: that a fundamentally decent and just civil society, in which men are protected and encouraged in the pursuit of happiness, is a rare and precious thing. Not so rare and precious that it cannot be vigorously used, changed, and improved. American civil society is robust enough to take a good deal of mauling – that is one of its rare and precious qualities. The advocates of civil disobedience are surely right in asserting that American society can tolerate and be improved by vigorous criticism and dissent. Accepting the fundamental soundness of the American political system, its *capacity* to do justice, does not require any lessening in the energy directed toward the huge imperfections that this system suffers. It does require that that

26 James Farmer, 'Annual Report to the CORE National Convention,' July 1, 1965; Broderick and Meier (eds.) *Negro Protest Thought in the Twentieth Century*, p. 425. See also James Farmer, 'Civil Disobedience and Beyond,' in Robert A. Goldwin (ed.), *On Civil Disobedience: Essays Old and New*, (Chicago, IL.: Rand McNally, 1969), pp. 133–45.

soundness, that capacity to do justice, be taken as the first principle of political reason and political action. No action can be well taken, no words wisely spoken, except in reference to that first principle.

Let it be granted that the injunction to 'obey the law merely because it is a law' is not a sufficient principle of political action or of political duty – though, in all conscience, it seems to come closer than an injunction *not* to obey the law merely because it is a law. Injustice can be protested and private conscience gratified from a protest march or a jail cell, but the positive demands of justice cannot be served there. What Frederick Douglass once said of the uncompromising abolitionism of men like Garrison and Thoreau may be said today of civil disobedience: 'As a mere expression of abhorrence' of injustice, 'the sentiment is a good one; but it expresses no intelligible principle of action, and throws no light on the pathway of duty.'[27]

27 *Life and Writings of Frederick Douglass*, Philip S. Foner (ed.) (New York: International Publishers, 1950), Vol. II, p. 351.

6

DEFINITION AND JUSTIFICATION OF CIVIL DISOBEDIENCE

John Rawls

THE DEFINITION OF CIVIL DISOBEDIENCE

I now wish to illustrate the content of the principles of natural duty and obligation by sketching a theory of civil disobedience. As I have already indicated, this theory is designed only for the special case of a nearly just society, one that is well-ordered for the most part but in which some serious violations of justice nevertheless do occur. Since I assume that a state of near justice requires a democratic regime, the theory concerns the role and the appropriateness of civil disobedience to legitimately established democratic authority. It does not apply to the other forms of government nor, except incidentally, to other kinds of dissent or resistance. I shall not discuss this mode of protest, along with militant action and resistance, as a tactic for transforming or even overturning an unjust and corrupt system. There is no difficulty about such action in this case. If any means to this end are justified, then surely nonviolent opposition is justified. The problem of civil disobedience, as I shall interpret it, arises only within a more or less just democratic state for those citizens who recognize and accept the legitimacy of the constitution. The difficulty is one of a conflict of duties. At what point does the duty to comply with laws enacted by a legislative majority (or with executive acts supported by such a majority) cease to be binding in view of the right to defend one's liberties and the duty to oppose injustice? This question involves the nature and limits of majority rule. For this reason the problem of

From: John Rawls, *A Theory of Justice* (Cambridge MA: Harvard University Press, 1971), secs. 55, 57, 59. The footnotes have been renumbered.

civil disobedience is a crucial test case for any theory of the moral basis of democracy.

A constitutional theory of civil disobedience has three parts. First, it defines this kind of dissent and separates it from other forms of opposition to democratic authority. These range from legal demonstrations and infractions of law designed to raise test cases before the courts to militant action and organized resistance. A theory specifies the place of civil disobedience in this spectrum of possibilities. Next, it sets out the grounds of civil disobedience and the conditions under which such action is justified in a (more or less) just democratic regime. And finally, a theory should explain the role of civil disobedience within a constitutional system and account for the appropriateness of this mode of protest within a free society.

Before I take up these matters, a word of caution. We should not expect too much of a theory of civil disobedience, even one framed for special circumstances. Precise principles that straightaway decide actual cases are clearly out of the question. Instead, a useful theory defines a perspective within which the problem of civil disobedience can be approached; it identifies the relevant considerations and helps us to assign them their correct weights in the more important instances. If a theory about these matters appears to us, on reflection, to have cleared our vision and to have made our considered judgments more coherent, then it has been worthwhile. The theory has done what, for the present, one may reasonably expect it to do: namely, to narrow the disparity between the conscientious convictions of those who accept the basic principles of a democratic society.

I shall begin by defining civil disobedience as a public, nonviolent, conscientious yet political act contrary to law usually done with the aim of bringing about a change in the law or policies of the government.[1] By acting in this way one

1 Here I follow H. A. Bedau's definition of civil disobedience. See his 'On Civil Disobedience,' *Journal of Philosophy*, vol. 58 (1961), pp. 653-61. It should be noted that this definition is narrower than the meaning suggested by Thoreau's essay [. . .]. A statement of a similar view is found in Martin Luther King's 'Letter from Birmingham City Jail' (1963), reprinted in H. A. Bedau (ed.), *Civil Disobedience* (New York: Pegasus, 1969), pp. 72-89. The theory of civil disobedience in the text tries to set this sort of conception into a wider framework. Some recent writers have also defined civil disobedience more broadly. For example, Howard Zinn, *Disobedience and Democracy* (New York: Random House, 1968), pp. 119f, defines it as 'the deliberate, discriminate violation of law for a vital social purpose.' I am concerned with a more restricted notion. I do not

addresses the sense of justice of the majority of the community and declares that in one's considered opinion the principles of social cooperation among free and equal men are not being respected. A preliminary gloss on this definition is that it does not require that the civilly disobedient act breach the same law that is being protested.[2] It allows for what some have called indirect as well as direct civil disobedience. And this a definition should do, as there are sometimes strong reasons for not infringing on the law or policy held to be unjust. Instead, one may disobey traffic ordinances or laws of trespass as a way of presenting one's case. Thus, if the government enacts a vague and harsh statute against treason, it would not be appropriate to commit treason as a way of objecting to it, and in any event, the penalty might be far more than one should reasonably be ready to accept. In other cases there is no way to violate the government's policy directly, as when it concerns foreign affairs, or affects another part of the country. A second gloss is that the civilly disobedient act is indeed thought to be contrary to law, at least in the sense that those engaged in it are not simply presenting a test case for a constitutional decision; they are prepared to oppose the statute even if it should be upheld. To be sure, in a constitutional regime, the courts may finally side with the dissenters and declare the law or policy objected to unconstitutional. It often happens, then, that there is some uncertainty as to whether the dissenters' action will be held illegal or not. But this is merely a complicating element. Those who use civil disobedience to protest unjust laws are not prepared to desist should the courts eventually disagree with them, however pleased they might have been with the opposite decision.

It should also be noted that civil disobedience is a political act not only in the sense that it is addressed to the majority that holds political power, but also because it is an act guided and justified by political principles, that is, by the principles of justice which regulate the constitution and social institutions generally. In justifying civil disobedience one does not appeal to principles of personal morality or to religious doctrines, though these may

at all mean to say that only this form of dissent is ever justified in a democratic state.
2 This and the following gloss are from Marshall Cohen, 'Civil Disobedience in a Constitutional Democracy,' *The Massachusetts Review*, vol. 10 (1969), pp. 224-6, 218-21, respectively.

coincide with and support one's claims; and it goes without saying that civil disobedience cannot be grounded solely on group or self-interest. Instead one invokes the commonly shared conception of justice that underlies the political order. It is assumed that in a reasonably just democratic regime there is a public conception of justice by reference to which citizens regulate their political affairs and interpret the constitution. The persistent and deliberate violation of the basic principles of this conception over any extended period of time, especially the infringement of the fundamental equal liberties, invites either submission or resistance. By engaging in civil disobedience a minority forces the majority to consider whether it wishes to have its actions construed in this way, or whether, in view of the common sense of justice, it wishes to acknowledge the legitimate claims of the minority.

A further point is that civil disobedience is a public act. Not only is it addressed to public principles, it is done in public. It is engaged in openly with fair notice; it is not covert or secretive. One may compare it to public speech, and being a form of address, an expression of profound and conscientious political conviction, it takes place in the public forum. For this reason, among others, civil disobedience is nonviolent. It tries to avoid the use of violence, especially against persons, not from the abhorrence of the use of force in principle, but because it is a final expression of one's case. To engage in violent acts likely to injure and to hurt is incompatible with civil disobedience as a mode of address. Indeed, any interference with the civil liberties of others tends to obscure the civilly disobedient quality of one's act. Sometimes if the appeal fails in its purpose, forceful resistance may later be entertained. Yet civil disobedience is giving voice to conscientious and deeply held convictions; while it may warn and admonish, it is not itself a threat.

Civil disobedience is nonviolent for another reason. It expresses disobedience to law within the limits of fidelity to law, although it is at the outer edge thereof.[3] The law is broken, but fidelity to law is expressed by the public and nonviolent nature of the act, by the willingness to accept the legal consequences of

3 For a fuller discussion of this point, see Charles Fried, 'Moral Causation,' *Harvard Law Review*, vol. 77 (1964), pp. 1268f. For clarification below of the notion of militant action, I am indebted to Gerald Loev.

one's conduct.[4] This fidelity to law helps to establish to the majority that the act is indeed politically conscientious and sincere, and that it is intended to address the public's sense of justice. To be completely open and nonviolent is to give bond of one's sincerity, for it is not easy to convince another that one's acts are conscientious, or even to be sure of this before oneself. No doubt it is possible to imagine a legal system in which conscientious belief that the law is unjust is accepted as a defense for noncompliance. Men of great honesty with full confidence in one another might make such a system work. But as things are, such a scheme would presumably be unstable even in a state of near justice. We must pay a certain price to convince others that our actions have, in our carefully considered view, a sufficient moral basis in the political convictions of the community.

Civil disobedience has been defined so that it falls between legal protest and the raising of test cases on the one side, and conscientious refusal and the various forms of resistance on the other. In this range of possibilities it stands for that form of dissent at the boundary of fidelity to law. Civil disobedience, so understood, is clearly distinct from militant action and obstruction; it is far removed from organized forcible resistance. The militant, for example, is much more deeply opposed to the existing political system. He does not accept it as one which is nearly just or reasonably so; he believes either that it departs widely from its professed principles or that it pursues a mistaken conception of justice altogether. While his action is conscientious in its own terms, he does not appeal to the sense of justice of the majority (or those having effective political power), since he thinks that their sense of justice is erroneous, or else without effect. Instead, he seeks by well-framed militant acts of disruption and resistance, and the like, to attack the prevalent view of justice or to force a movement in the desired direction. Thus the militant may try to evade the penalty, since he is not

---

4 Those who define civil disobedience more broadly might not accept this description. See, for example, Zinn, *Disobedience and Democracy*, pp. 27–31, 39, 119f. Moreover he denies that civil disobedience need be nonviolent. Certainly one does not accept the punishment as right, that is, as deserved for an unjustified act. Rather one is willing to undergo the legal consequences for the sake of fidelity to law, which is a different matter. There is room for latitude here in that the definition allows that the charge may be contested in court, should this prove appropriate. But there comes a point beyond which dissent ceases to be civil disobedience as defined here.

prepared to accept the legal consequences of his violation of the law; this would not only be to play into the hands of forces that he believes cannot be trusted, but also to express a recognition of the legitimacy of the constitution to which he is opposed. In this sense militant action is not within the bounds of fidelity to law, but represents a more profound opposition to the legal order. The basic structure is thought to be so unjust or else to depart so widely from its own professed ideals that one must try to prepare the way for radical or even revolutionary change. And this is to be done by trying to arouse the public to an awareness of the fundamental reforms that need to be made. Now in certain circumstances militant action and other kinds of resistance are surely justified. I shall not, however, consider these cases. As I have said, my aim here is the limited one of defining a concept of civil disobedience and understanding its role in a nearly just constitutional regime.

THE JUSTIFICATION OF CIVIL DISOBEDIENCE

With these various distinctions in mind, I shall consider the circumstances under which civil disobedience is justified. For simplicity I shall limit the discussion to domestic institutions and so to injustices internal to a given society. The somewhat narrow nature of this restriction will be mitigated a bit by taking up the contrasting problem of conscientious refusal in connection with the moral law as it applies to war. I shall begin by setting out what seem to be reasonable conditions for engaging in civil disobedience, and then later connect these conditions more systematically with the place of civil disobedience in a state of near justice. Of course, the conditions enumerated should be taken as presumptions; no doubt there will be situations when they do not hold, and other arguments could be given for civil disobedience.

The first point concerns the kinds of wrongs that are appropriate objects of civil disobedience. Now if one views such disobedience as a political act addressed to the sense of justice of the community, then it seems reasonable, other things equal, to limit it to instances of substantial and clear injustice, and preferably to those which obstruct the path to removing other injustices. For this reason there is a presumption in favor of restricting civil disobedience to serious infringements of the first principle of justice, the principle of equal liberty, and to blatant violations of the second part of the second principle, the principle of fair equality of opportunity. Of course, it is not always easy to tell whether these principles are satisfied. Still, if we think of them as guaranteeing the basic liberties, it is often clear that these freedoms are not being honored. After all, they impose certain strict requirements that must be visibly expressed in institutions. Thus when certain minorities are denied the right to vote or to hold office, or to own property and to move from place to place, or when certain religious groups are repressed and others denied various opportunities, these injustices may be obvious to all. They are publicly incorporated into the recognized practice, if not the letter, of social arrangements. The establishment of these wrongs does not presuppose an informed examination of institutional effects.

By contrast infractions of the difference principle are more difficult to ascertain. There is usually a wide range of conflicting yet rational opinion as to whether this principle is satisfied. The reason for this is that it applies primarily to economic and social institutions and policies. A choice among these depends upon theoretical and speculative beliefs as well as upon a wealth of statistical and other information, all of this seasoned with shrewd judgment and plain hunch. In view of the complexities of these questions, it is difficult to check the influence of self-interest and prejudice; and even if we can do this in our own case, it is another matter to convince others of our good faith. Thus unless tax laws, for example, are clearly designed to attack or to abridge a basic equal liberty, they should not normally be protested by civil disobedience. The appeal to the public's conception of justice is not sufficiently clear. The resolution of these issues is best left to the political process provided that the requisite equal liberties are secure. In this case a reasonable compromise can presumably be reached. The violation of the principle of equal liberty is, then, the more appropriate object of civil disobedience. This principle defines the common status of equal citizenship in a constitutional regime and lies at the basis of the political order. When it is fully honored the presumption is that other injustices, while possibly persistent and significant, will not get out of hand.

A further condition for civil disobedience is the following. We may suppose that the normal appeals to the political majority have already been made in good faith and that they have failed. The legal means of redress have proved of no avail. Thus, for example, the existing political parties have shown themselves indifferent to the claims of the minority or have proved unwilling to accommodate them. Attempts to have the laws repealed have been ignored and legal protests and demonstrations have had no success. Since civil disobedience is a last resort, we should be sure that it is necessary. Note that it has not been said, however, that legal means have been exhausted. At any rate, further normal appeals can be repeated; free speech is always possible. But if past actions have shown the majority immovable or apathetic, further attempts may reasonably be thought fruitless, and a second condition for justified civil disobedience is met. This condition is, however, a presumption. Some cases may be so extreme that there may be no duty to use first only legal means of political opposition. If, for example, the legislature were to enact some outrageous violation of equal liberty, say by forbidding the religion of a weak and defenseless minority, we surely could not expect that sect to oppose the law by normal political procedures. Indeed, even civil disobedience might be much too mild, the majority having already convicted itself of wantonly unjust and overtly hostile aims.

The third and last condition I shall discuss can be rather complicated. It arises from the fact that while the two preceding conditions are often sufficient to justify civil disobedience, this is not always the case. In certain circumstances the natural duty of justice may require a certain restraint. We can see this as follows. If a certain minority is justified in engaging in civil disobedience, then any other minority in relevantly similar circumstances is likewise justified. Using the two previous conditions as the criteria of relevantly similar circumstances, we can say that, other things equal, two minorities are similarly justified in resorting to civil disobedience if they have suffered for the same length of time from the same degree of injustice and if their equally sincere and normal political appeals have likewise been to no avail. It is conceivable, however, even if it is unlikely, that there should be many groups with an equally sound case (in the sense just defined) for being civilly disobedient; but that, if they were all to act in this way, serious disorder would follow which might well undermine the efficacy of the just constitution. I assume here that there is a limit on the extent to which civil disobedience can be engaged in without leading to a breakdown in the respect for law and the constitution, thereby setting in motion consequences unfortunate for all. There is also an upper bound on the ability of the public forum to handle such forms of dissent; the appeal that civilly disobedient groups wish to make can be distorted and their intention to appeal to the sense of justice of the majority lost sight of. For one or both of these reasons, the effectiveness of civil disobedience as a form of protest declines beyond a certain point; and those contemplating it must consider these constraints.

The ideal solution from a theoretical point of view calls for a cooperative political alliance of the minorities to regulate the overall level of dissent. For consider the nature of the situation: there are many groups each equally entitled to engage in civil disobedience. Moreover they all wish to exercise this right, equally strong in each case; but if they all do so, lasting injury may result to the just constitution to which they each recognize a natural duty of justice. Now, when there are many equally strong claims which if taken together exceed what can be granted, some fair plan should be adopted so that all are equitably considered. In simple cases of claims to goods that are indivisible and fixed in number, some rotation or lottery scheme may be the fair solution when the number of equally valid claims is too great.[5] But this sort of device is completely unrealistic here. What seems called for is a political understanding among the minorities suffering from injustice. They can meet their duty to democratic institutions by coordinating their actions so that while each has an opportunity to exercise its right, the limits on the degree of civil disobedience are not exceeded. To be sure, an alliance of this sort is difficult to arrange; but, with perceptive leadership, it does not appear impossible.

Certainly the situation envisaged is a special one, and it is quite possible that these sorts of considerations will not be a bar

5 For a discussion of the conditions when some fair arrangement is called for, see Kurt Baier, *The Moral Point of View* (Ithaca, NY: Cornell University Press, 1958), pp. 207–13; and David Lyons, *Forms and Limits of Utilitarianism* (Oxford: The Clarendon Press, 1965), pp. 160–76. Lyons gives an example of a fair rotation scheme and he also observes that (waiving costs of setting them up) such fair procedures may be reasonably efficient. See pp. 169–71. I accept the conclusions of his account, including his contention that the notion of fairness cannot be explained by assimilating it to utility, pp. 176f. The earlier discussion by C. D. Broad, 'On the Function of False Hypotheses in Ethics,' *International Journal of Ethics*, vol. 26 (1916), esp. pp. 385–90, should also be noted here.

to justified civil disobedience. There are not likely to be many groups similarly entitled to engage in this form of dissent while at the same time recognizing a duty to a just constitution. One should note, however, that an injured minority is tempted to believe its claims as strong as those of any other; and therefore even if the reasons that different groups have for engaging in civil disobedience are not equally compelling, it is often wise to presume that their claims are indistinguishable. Adopting this maxim, the circumstance imagined seems more likely to happen. This kind of case is also instructive in showing that the exercise of the right to dissent, like the exercise of rights generally, is sometimes limited by others having the very same right. Everyone's exercising this right would have deleterious consequences for all, and some equitable plan is called for.

Suppose that in the light of the three conditions, one has a right to appeal one's case by civil disobedience. The injustice one protests is a clear violation of the liberties of equal citizenship, or of equality of opportunity, this violation having been more or less deliberate over an extended period of time in the face of normal political opposition, and any complications raised by the question of fairness are met. These conditions are not exhaustive; some allowance still has to be made for the possibility of injury to third parties, to the innocent, so to speak. But I assume that they cover the main points. There is still, of course, the question whether it is wise or prudent to exercise this right. Having established the right, one is now free, as one is not before, to let these matters decide the issue. We may be acting within our rights but nevertheless unwisely if our conduct only serves to provoke the harsh retaliation of the majority. To be sure, in a state of near justice, vindictive repression of legitimate dissent is unlikely, but it is important that the action be properly designed to make an effective appeal to the wider community. Since civil disobedience is a mode of address taking place in the public forum, care must be taken to see that it is understood. Thus the exercise of the right to civil disobedience should, like any other right, be rationally framed to advance one's ends or the ends of those one wishes to assist. The theory of justice has nothing specific to say about these practical considerations. In any event questions of strategy and tactics depend upon the circumstances of each case. But the theory of justice should say at what point these matters are properly raised.

Now in this account of the justification of civil disobedience I have not mentioned the principle of fairness. The natural duty of justice is the primary basis of our political ties to a constitutional regime. . . . Only the more favored members of society are likely to have a clear political obligation as opposed to a political duty. They are better situated to win public office and find it easier to take advantage of the political system. And having done so, they have acquired an obligation owed to citizens generally to uphold the just constitution. But members of subjected minorities, say, who have a strong case for civil disobedience will not generally have a political obligation of this sort. This does not mean, however, that the principle of fairness will not give rise to important obligations in their case.[6] For not only do many of the requirements of private life derive from this principle, but it comes into force when persons or groups come together for common political purposes. Just as we acquire obligations to others with whom we have joined in various private associations, those who engage in political action assume obligatory ties to one another. Thus while the political obligation of dissenters to citizens generally is problematical, bonds of loyalty and fidelity still develop between them as they seek to advance their cause. In general, free association under a just constitution gives rise to obligations provided that the ends of the group are legitimate and its arrangements fair. This is as true of political as it is of other associations. These obligations are of immense significance and they constrain in many ways what individuals can do. But they are distinct from an obligation to comply with a just constitution. My discussion of civil disobedience is in terms of the duty of justice alone; a fuller view would note the place of these other requirements.

THE ROLE OF CIVIL DISOBEDIENCE

The third aim of a theory of civil disobedience is to explain its role within a constitutional system and to account for its connection with a democratic polity. As always, I assume that the society in question is one that is nearly just; and this implies that

6 For a discussion of these obligations, see Michael Walzer, *Obligations: Essays on Disobedience, War, and Citizenship* (Cambridge MA: Harvard University Press, 1970), ch. III.

it has some form of democratic government, although serious injustices may nevertheless exist. In such a society I assume that the principles of justice are for the most part publicly recognized as the fundamental terms of willing cooperation among free and equal persons. By engaging in civil disobedience one intends, then, to address the sense of justice of the majority and to serve fair notice that in one's sincere and considered opinion the conditions of free cooperation are being violated. We are appealing to others to reconsider, to put themselves in our position, and to recognize that they cannot expect us to acquiesce indefinitely in the terms they impose upon us.

Now the force of this appeal depends upon the democratic conception of society as a system of cooperation among equal persons. If one thinks of society in another way, this form of protest may be out of place. For example, if the basic law is thought to reflect the order of nature and if the sovereign is held to govern by divine right as God's chosen lieutenant, then his subjects have only the right of suppliants. They can plead their cause but they cannot disobey should their appeal be denied. To do this would be to rebel against the final legitimate moral (and not simply legal) authority. This is not to say that the sovereign cannot be in error but only that the situation is not one for his subjects to correct. But once society is interpreted as a scheme of cooperation among equals, those injured by serious injustice need not submit. Indeed, civil disobedience (and conscientious refusal as well) is one of the stabilizing devices of a constitutional system, although by definition an illegal one. Along with such things as free and regular elections and an independent judiciary empowered to interpret the constitution (not necessarily written), civil disobedience used with due restraint and sound judgment helps to maintain and strengthen just institutions. By resisting injustice within the limits of fidelity to law, it serves to inhibit departures from justice and to correct them when they occur. A general disposition to engage in justified civil disobedience introduces stability into a well-ordered society, or one that is nearly just.

It is necessary to look at this doctrine from the standpoint of the persons in the original position. There are two related problems which they must consider. The first is that, having chosen principles for individuals, they must work out guidelines for assessing the strength of the natural duties and obligations, and, in particular, the strength of the duty to comply with a just constitution and one of its basic procedures, that of majority rule. The second problem is that of finding reasonable principles for dealing with unjust situations, or with circumstances in which the compliance with just principles is only partial. Now it seems that, given the assumptions characterizing a nearly just society, the parties would agree to the presumptions (previously discussed) that specify when civil disobedience is justified. They would acknowledge these criteria as spelling out when this form of dissent is appropriate. Doing this would indicate the weight of the natural duty of justice in one important special case. It would also tend to enhance the realization of justice throughout the society by strengthening men's self-esteem as well as their respect for one another. As the contract doctrine emphasizes, the principles of justice are the principles of willing cooperation among equals. To deny justice to another is either to refuse to recognize him as an equal (one in regard to whom we are prepared to constrain our actions by principles that we would choose in a situation of equality that is fair), or to manifest a willingness to exploit the contingencies of natural fortune and happenstance for our own advantage. In either case deliberate injustice invites submission or resistance. Submission arouses the contempt of those who perpetuate injustice and confirms their intention, whereas resistance cuts the ties of community. If after a decent period of time to allow for reasonable political appeals in the normal way, citizens were to dissent by civil disobedience when infractions of the basic liberties occurred, these liberties would, it seems, be more rather than less secure. For these reasons, then, the parties would adopt the conditions defining justified civil disobedience as a way of setting up, within the limits of fidelity to law, a final device to maintain the stability of a just constitution. Although this mode of action is, strictly speaking, contrary to law, it is nevertheless a morally correct way of maintaining a constitutional regime.

In a fuller account the same kind of explanation could presumably be given for the justifying conditions of conscientious refusal (again assuming the context of a nearly just state). I shall not, however, discuss these conditions here. I should like to emphasize instead that the constitutional theory of civil disobedience rests solely upon a conception of justice. Even the features of publicity and nonviolence are explained on this basis. And the same is true of the account of conscientious refusal, although it requires a further elaboration of the contract doctrine. At no point has a reference been made to other than political principles; religious or pacifist conceptions are not essential. While those engaging in civil disobedience have often been moved by convictions of this kind, there is no necessary connection between them and civil disobedience. For this form of political action can be understood as a way of addressing the sense of justice of the community, an invocation of the recognized principles of cooperation among equals. Being an appeal to the moral basis of civic life, it is a political and not a religious act. It relies upon common-sense principles of justice that men can require one another to follow and not upon the affirmations of religious faith and love which they cannot demand that everyone accept. I do not mean, of course, that non-political conceptions have no validity. They may, in fact, confirm our judgment and support our acting in ways known on other grounds to be just. Nevertheless, it is not these principles but the principles of justice, the fundamental terms of social cooperation between free and equal persons, that underlie the constitution. Civil disobedience as defined does not require a sectarian foundation but is derived from the public conception of justice that characterizes a democratic society. So understood, a conception of civil disobedience is part of the theory of free government.

One distinction between medieval and modern constitutionalism is that in the former the supremacy of law was not secured by established institutional controls. The check to the ruler who in his judgments and edicts opposed the sense of justice of the community was limited for the most part to the right of resistance by the whole society, or any part. Even this right seems not to have been interpreted as a corporate act; an unjust king was simply put aside.[7] Thus the Middle Ages lacked the basic ideas of modern constitutional government, the idea of the sovereign people who have final authority and the institutionalizing of this authority by means of elections and parliaments, and other constitutional forms. Now, in much the same way that the modern conception of constitutional government builds

7 See J. H. Franklin (ed.), *Constitutionalism and Resistance in the Sixteenth Century* (New York: Pegasus, 1969), in the introduction, pp. 11-15.

upon the medieval, the theory of civil disobedience supplements the purely legal conception of constitutional democracy. It attempts to formulate the grounds upon which legitimate democratic authority may be dissented from in ways that while admittedly contrary to law nevertheless express a fidelity to law and appeal to the fundamental political principles of a democratic regime. Thus to the legal forms of constitutionalism one may adjoin certain modes of illegal protest that do not violate the aims of a democratic constitution in view of the principles by which such dissent is guided. I have tried to show how these principles can be accounted for by the contract doctrine.

Some may object to this theory of civil disobedience that it is unrealistic. It presupposes that the majority has a sense of justice, and one might reply that moral sentiments are not a significant political force. What moves men are various interests, the desires for power, prestige, wealth, and the like. Although they are clever at producing moral arguments to support their claims, between one situation and another their opinions do not fit into a coherent conception of justice. Rather their views at any given time are occasional pieces calculated to advance certain interests. Unquestionably there is much truth in this contention, and in some societies it is more true than in others. But the essential question is the relative strength of the tendencies that oppose the sense of justice and whether the latter is ever strong enough so that it can be invoked to some significant effect.

A few comments may make the account presented more plausible. First of all, I have assumed throughout that we have to do with a nearly just society. This implies that there exists a constitutional regime and a publicly recognized conception of justice. Of course, in any particular situation certain individuals and groups may be tempted to violate its principles but the collective sentiment in their behalf has considerable strength when properly addressed. These principles are affirmed as the necessary terms of cooperation between free and equal persons. If those who perpetrate injustice can be clearly identified and isolated from the larger community, the convictions of the greater part of society may be of sufficient weight. Or if the contending parties are roughly equal, the sentiment of justice of those not engaged can be the deciding factor. In any case, should circumstances of this kind not obtain, the wisdom of civil disobedience is highly problematic. For unless one can appeal to the sense of justice of the larger society, the majority may simply be aroused to more repressive measures if the calculation of advantages points in this direction. Courts should take into account the civilly disobedient nature of the protester's act, and the fact that it is justifiable (or may seem so) by the political principles underlying the constitution, and on these grounds reduce and in some cases suspend the legal sanction.[8] Yet quite the opposite may happen when the necessary background is lacking. We have to recognize then that justifiable civil disobedience is normally a reasonable and effective form of dissent only in a society regulated to some considerable degree by a sense of justice.

There may be some misapprehension about the manner in which the sense of justice is said to work. One may think that this sentiment expresses itself in sincere professions of principle and in actions requiring a considerable degree of self-sacrifice. But this supposition asks too much. A community's sense of justice is more likely to be revealed in the fact that the majority cannot bring itself to take the steps necessary to suppress the minority and to punish acts of civil disobedience as the law allows. Ruthless tactics that might be contemplated in other societies are not entertained as real alternatives. Thus the sense of justice affects, in ways we are often unaware of, our interpretation of political life, our perception of the possible courses of action, our will to resist the justified protests of others, and so on. In spite of its superior power, the majority may abandon its position and acquiesce in the proposals of the dissenters; its desire to give justice weakens its capacity to defend its unjust advantages. The sentiment of justice will be seen as a more vital political force once the subtle forms in which it exerts its influence are recognized, and in particular its role in rendering certain social positions indefensible.

In these remarks I have assumed that in a nearly just society there is a public acceptance of the same principles of justice. Fortunately this assumption is stronger than necessary. There can, in fact, be considerable differences in citizens' conceptions of justice provided that these conceptions lead to similar political

8 For a general discussion, see Ronald Dworkin, 'On Not Prosecuting Civil Disobedience,' *The New York Review of Books,* June 6, 1968.

judgments. And this is possible, since different premises can yield the same conclusion. In this case there exists what we may refer to as overlapping rather than strict consensus. In general, the overlapping of professed conceptions of justice suffices for civil disobedience to be a reasonable and prudent form of political dissent. Of course, this overlapping need not be perfect; it is enough that a condition of reciprocity is satisfied. Both sides must believe that however much their conceptions of justice differ, their views support the same judgment in the situation at hand, and would do so even should their respective positions be interchanged. Eventually, though, there comes a point beyond which the requisite agreement in judgment breaks down and society splits into more or less distinct parts that hold diverse opinions on fundamental political questions. In this case of strictly partitioned consensus, the basis for civil disobedience no longer obtains. For example, suppose those who do not believe in toleration, and who would not tolerate others had they the power, wish to protest their lesser liberty by appealing to the sense of justice of the majority which holds the principle of equal liberty. While those who accept this principle should, as we have seen, tolerate the intolerant as far as the safety of free institutions permits, they are likely to resent being reminded of this duty by the intolerant who would, if positions were switched, establish their own dominion. The majority is bound to feel that their allegiance to equal liberty is being exploited by others for unjust ends. This situation illustrates once again the fact that a common sense of justice is a great collective asset which requires the cooperation of many to maintain. The intolerant can be viewed as free-riders, as persons who seek the advantages of just institutions while not doing their share to uphold them. Although those who acknowledge the principles of justice should always be guided by them, in a fragmented society as well as in one moved by group egoisms, the conditions for civil disobedience do not exist. Still, it is not necessary to have strict consensus, for often a degree of overlapping consensus allows the reciprocity condition to be fulfilled.

There are, to be sure, definite risks in the resort to civil disobedience. One reason for constitutional forms and their judicial interpretation is to establish a public reading of the political conception of justice and an explanation of the application of its principles to social questions. Up to a certain point it is better that the law and its interpretation be settled than that it be settled rightly. Therefore it may be protested that the preceding account does not determine who is to say when circumstances are such as to justify civil disobedience. It invites anarchy by encouraging everyone to decide for himself, and to abandon the public rendering of political principles. The reply to this is that each person must indeed make his own decision. Even though men normally seek advice and counsel, and accept the injunctions of those in authority when these seem reasonable to them, they are always accountable for their deeds. We cannot divest ourselves of our responsibility and transfer the burden of blame to others. This is true on any theory of political duty and obligation that is compatible with the principles of a democratic constitution. The citizen is autonomous yet he is held responsible for what he does. [. . .] If we ordinarily think that we should comply with the law, this is because our political principles normally lead to this conclusion. The many free and reasoned decisions of individuals fit together into an orderly political regime.

But while each person must decide for himself whether the circumstances justify civil disobedience, it does not follow that one is to decide as one pleases. It is not by looking to our personal interests, or to our political allegiances narrowly construed, that we should make up our minds. To act autonomously and responsibly a citizen must look to the political principles that underlie and guide the interpretation of the constitution. He must try to assess how these principles should be applied in the existing circumstances. If he comes to the conclusion after due consideration that civil disobedience is justified and conducts himself accordingly, he acts conscientiously. And though he may be mistaken, he has not done as he pleased. The theory of political duty and obligation enables us to draw these distinctions.

There are parallels with the common understandings and conclusions reached in the sciences. Here, too, everyone is autonomous yet responsible. We are to assess theories and hypotheses in the light of the evidence by publicly recognized principles. It is true that there are authoritative works, but these sum up the consensus of many persons each deciding for himself. The absence of a final authority to decide, and so of an official interpretation that all must accept, does not lead to confusion, but is rather a condition of theoretical advance. Equals accepting and applying reasonable principles need have no established superior. To the question, who is to decide? the answer is: all are to decide, everyone taking counsel with himself, and with reasonableness, comity, and good fortune, it often works out well enough.

In a democratic society, then, it is recognized that each citizen is responsible for his interpretation of the principles of justice and for his conduct in the light of them. There can be no legal or socially approved rendering of these principles that we are always morally bound to accept, not even when it is given by a supreme court or legislature. Indeed, each constitutional agency, the legislature, the executive, and the court, puts forward its interpretation of the constitution and the political ideals that inform it.[9] Although the court may have the last say in settling any particular case, it is not immune from powerful political influences that may force a revision of its reading of the constitution. The court presents its doctrine by reason and argument; its conception of the constitution must, if it is to endure, persuade the major part of the citizens of its soundness. The final court of appeal is not the court, nor the executive, nor the legislature, but the electorate as a whole. The civilly disobedient appeal in a special way to this body. There is no danger of anarchy so long as there is a sufficient working agreement in citizens' conceptions of justice and the conditions for resorting to civil disobedience are respected. That men can achieve such an understanding and honor these limits when the basic political liberties are maintained is an assumption implicit in a democratic polity. There is no way to avoid entirely the danger of divisive strife, any more than one can rule out the possibility of profound scientific controversy. Yet if justified civil disobedience seems to threaten civil concord, the responsibility falls not upon those who protest but upon those whose abuse of authority and power justifies such opposition. For to employ the coercive apparatus of the state in order to maintain manifestly unjust institutions is itself a form of illegitimate force that men in due course have a right to resist. [. . .]

9 For a presentation of this view to which I am indebted, see A. M. Bickel, *The Least Dangerous Branch* (New York: Bobbs-Merrill, 1962), esp. chs. V and VI.

7

DISOBEDIENCE AS A PLEA FOR RECONSIDERATION

Peter Singer

A form of disobedience [. . .] aims, not at presenting a view to the public, but at prodding the majority into reconsidering a decision it has taken. A majority may act, or fail to act, without realizing that there are truly significant issues at stake, or the majority may not have considered the interests of all parties, and its decision may cause suffering in a way that was not foreseen. Disobedience, and especially disobedience followed by acceptance of punishment, may make the majority realize that what is for it a matter of indifference is of great importance to others. Disobedience which aims to make the majority reconsider in this way is not an attempt to coerce them, and within limits broadly similar to those just discussed in connection with disobedience for publicity, it is compatible with acceptance of a fair compromise as a means of settling issues. Once it becomes apparent that the majority are not willing to reconsider, however, this sort of disobedience must be abandoned. One way of ascertaining whether the majority are willing to reconsider is to hold a referendum. This is one argument in favour of a provision in a democratic system for referenda to be held at the request of a minority group, as in Switzerland.

Disobedience of this sort – by a minority who feel very strongly about an issue, against a decision taken by a majority to whom the matter is of no great importance – can help to mitigate one of the stock weaknesses of democratic theory. It has long been recognized that there is a danger of injustice in democracy because the democratic system takes no account of the intensity with which views are held, so that a majority which does not care

From: Peter Singer, *Democracy and Disobedience* (Oxford University Press, 1973), pp. 84–92.

very much about an issue can out-vote a minority for which the issue is of vital concern. By civil disobedience the minority can demonstrate the intensity of its feelings to the majority. If the majority did in fact make its decision through short-sightedness, and not because the hardship to the minority is an unavoidable evil, justified by a far greater good on the whole, it will have the opportunity of altering its decision. Where there is reason to believe that the majority does not feel strongly about a matter, disobedience causing a certain amount of inconvenience can be justified in order to test the strength of feeling of the majority. If minor inconvenience will cause the majority to alter its decision, this indicates that the original decision was one of those in which a largely apathetic majority imposes its will on a deeply concerned minority. Since, in theory, weighting votes according to intensity of feeling would give rise to a still fairer compromise than is achieved by giving everyone an equal vote, to cause such inconvenience to the majority would be compatible with fair compromise. If the majority makes it clear, however, that it is prepared to put up with inconvenience, it must be assumed that it is not, after all, apathetic about the issue.

It is of course possible that a decision by a majority causing hardship to a minority results neither from oversight, nor from a regrettable necessity, but is part of a policy of deliberate exploitation of the minority by a majority which does not have equal concern for the welfare of all its citizens. This kind of situation has been discussed earlier.

This is an appropriate point at which to consider the theory of civil disobedience proposed by John Rawls in his much-discussed book, *A Theory of Justice*,[1] for Rawls's conception of the proper role of disobedience in a constitutional democracy has much in common with the kind of disobedience we have just been discussing. According to Rawls, civil disobedience is an act which 'addresses the sense of justice of the community and declares that in one's considered opinion the principles of social co-operation among free and equal men are not being respected'.[2] Civil disobedience is here regarded as a form of address, or an appeal. Accordingly, Rawls comes to conclusions

1 Clarendon Press, Oxford, 1972. The theory of civil disobedience is to be found in ch. 6, mostly in sects. 55, 57 and 59 [this volume, pp. 103–21].
2 ibid., p. 364.

similar to those I have reached about the form which such disobedience should take. It should, he says, be non-violent and refrain from hurting or interfering with others because violence or interference tends to obscure the fact that what is being done is a form of address. While civil disobedience may 'warn and admonish, it is not itself a threat'. Similarly, to show sincerity and general fidelity to law, one should be completely open about what one is doing, willing to accept the legal consequences of one's act.

I am therefore in agreement with Rawls on the main point: limited disobedience, far from being incompatible with a genuinely democratic form of government, can have an important part to play as a justifiable form of protest. There are, however, some features of Rawls's position which I cannot accept. These features derive from the theory of justice which is the core of the book. The reader may have noticed that the sentence I quoted above contains a reference to 'the sense of justice of the community' and to the 'principles of social co-operation among free and equal men'. Rawls's justification of civil disobedience depends heavily on the idea that a community has a sense of justice which is a single sense of justice on which all can agree, at least in practice if not in all theoretical details. It is the violation of this accepted basis of society which legitimates disobedience. To be fair to Rawls, it must be said that he is not maintaining that men ever do or did get together and agree on a sense of justice, and on the principles of social co-operation. Rather the idea is that a basically just society will have a sense of justice that corresponds to the principles that free and equal men would have chosen, had they met together to agree, under conditions designed to ensure impartiality, to abide by the basic principles necessary for social co-operation. It should also be said that Rawls does not maintain that every society in fact has such a sense of justice, but he intends his theory of disobedience to apply only to those that do. (As an aside, he suggests that the wisdom of civil disobedience will be problematic when there is no common conception of justice, since disobedience may serve only to rouse the majority to more repressive measures.)[3]

This is not the place to discuss Rawls's theory of justice as a whole. I want to discuss only its application to our topic. From

3 ibid., pp. 386–7 [Ed: this and subsequent footnotes have been renumbered].

his view that civil disobedience is justified by 'the principles of justice which regulate the constitution and social institutions generally', Rawls draws the consequence that 'in justifying civil disobedience one does not appeal to principles of personal morality or to religious doctrines. . . . Instead one invokes the commonly shared conception of justice which underlies the political order.'[4]

Even bearing in mind that this is intended to apply only to societies in which there is a common conception of justice, one can see that this is a serious limitation on the grounds on which disobedience can be justified. I shall suggest two ways in which this limitation could be unreasonable.

First, if disobedience is an appeal to the community, why can it only be an appeal which invokes principles which the community already accepts? Why could one not be justified in disobeying in order to ask the majority to alter or extend the shared conception of justice? Rawls might think that it could never be necessary to go beyond this shared conception, for the shared conception is broad enough to contain all the principles necessary for a just society. Disobedience, he would say, can be useful to ensure that society does not depart too seriously from this shared conception, but the conception itself is unimpeachable. The just society, on this view, may be likened to a good piece of machinery: there may occasionally be a little friction, and some lubrication will then be necessary, but the basic design needs no alteration.

Now Rawls can, of course, make this true by definition. We have already seen that he intends his theory of disobedience to apply only to societies which have a common conception of justice. If Rawls means by this that his theory applies only when the shared conception of justice encompasses all the legitimate claims that anyone in the society can possibly make, then it follows that no disobedience which seeks to extend or go beyond the shared conception of justice can be legitimate. Since this would follow simply in virtue of how Rawls had chosen to use the notion of a shared conception of justice, however, it would be true in a trivial way, and would be utterly unhelpful for anyone wondering whether he would be justified in disobeying in an actual society.

4 ibid., p. 365.

If Rawls is to avoid this trivializing of his position it would seem that he must be able to point to at least some societies which he thinks have an adequate sense of justice. This course would invite our original question: why will disobedience be justified only if it invokes this particular conception of justice? This version of the theory elevates the conception of justice at present held by some society or societies into a standard valid for all time. Does any existing society have a shared conception of justice which cannot conceivably be improved? Maybe we cannot ourselves see improvements in a particular society's conception of justice, but we surely cannot rule out the possibility that in time it may appear defective, not only in its application, but in the fundamentals of the conception itself. In this case, disobedience designed to induce the majority to rethink its conception of justice might be justified.

I cannot see any way in which Rawls can avoid one or other of these difficulties. Either his conception of justice is a pure ideal, in which case it does not assist our real problems, or it unjustifiably excludes the use of disobedience as a way of making a radical objection to the conception of justice shared by some actual society.

Rawls's theory of civil disobedience contains a second and distinct restriction on the grounds of legitimate disobedience. As we have seen, he says that the justification of disobedience must be in terms of justice, and not in terms of 'principles of personal morality or religious doctrine'. It is not clear exactly what this phrase means, but since Rawls opposes it to 'the commonly shared conception of justice which underlies the political order' we may take it to include all views that are not part of this shared conception. This makes it a substantial restriction, since according to Rawls there are important areas of morality which are outside the scope of justice. The theory of justice is, he says, 'but one part of a moral view'.[5] As an example of an area of morality to which justice is inapplicable, Rawls instances our relations with animals. It is, he says, wrong to be cruel to animals, although we do not owe them justice. If we combine this view with the idea that the justification of civil disobedience must be in terms of justice, we can see that Rawls is committed to holding that no amount of cruelty to animals can justify disobedience.

5 ibid., p. 512.

Rawls would no doubt admit that severe and widespread cruelty to animals would be a great moral evil, but his position requires him to say that the licensing, or even the promotion of such cruelty by a government (perhaps to amuse the public, or, as is more likely nowadays, for experimental purposes) could not possibly justify civil disobedience, whereas something less serious would justify disobedience if it were contrary to the shared conception of justice. This is a surprising and I think implausible conclusion. A similar objection could be made in respect of any other area of morality which is not included under the conception of justice. Rawls does not give any other examples, although he suggests (and it is implied by his theory of justice) that our dealings with permanent mental defectives do not come under the ambit of justice.[6]

So far I have criticized Rawls's theory of disobedience because of certain restrictions it places on the kind of reason which can justify disobedience. My final comment is different. Rawls frequently writes as if it were a relatively simple matter to determine whether a majority decision is just or unjust. This, coupled with his view that the community has a common conception of justice, leads him to underestimate the importance of a settled, peaceful method of resolving disputes. It could also lead one to the view that there are cases in which the majority is clearly acting beyond its powers, that is, that there are areas of life in which the decision-procedure is entirely without weight; for instance, if it tries to restrict certain freedoms. (This view is similar to that discussed earlier in connection with rights.) Consider the following passage:

> It is assumed that in a reasonably just democratic regime there is a public conception of justice by reference to which citizens regulate their political affairs and interpret the constitution. The persistent and deliberate violation of the basic principles of this conception over any extended period of time, especially the infringement of the fundamental equal liberties, invites either submission or resistance. By engaging in civil disobedience a minority forces the majority to consider whether it wishes to have its actions construed in this way, or whether, in view of the common sense

6 ibid., p. 510.

127

of justice, it wishes to acknowledge the legitimate claims of the minority.[7]

There will, of course, be some instances in a society when the actions of the majority can be seen only as a deliberate violation for selfish ends of basic principles of justice. Such actions do 'invite submission or resistance'. It is a mistake, though, to see these cases as in any way typical of those disputes which lead people to ask whether disobedience would be justified. Even when a society shares a common conception of justice, it is not likely to agree on the application of this conception to particular cases. Rawls admits that it is not always clear when the principles of justice have been violated, but he thinks it is often clear, especially when the principle of equal liberty (for Rawls the first principle of justice) is involved. As examples, he suggests that a violation of this principle can clearly be seen when 'certain religious groups are repressed' and when 'certain minorities are denied the right to vote or to hold office. . . .'[8] These cases appear straightforward, but are they? Timothy Leary's League for Spiritual Discovery claimed to be a religious group using the drug LSD as a means of exploring ultimate spiritual reality. At least three other groups – the Neo-American Church, the Church of the Awakening, and the Native American Church – have used hallucinogenic drugs as part of religious ceremonies. Of these groups, only the last has legal permission to do so. Is freedom of worship being denied to the others? When is a group a religious group? There are similar problems about denying minorities the vote. Is the denial of the vote to children a violation of equal liberty? Or to convicted prisoners? It may seem obvious to us that these are legitimate exceptions, but then it seemed obvious to many respectable citizens a hundred years ago that blacks and women should not have the vote, and it seemed obvious to Locke that the suppression of atheism and Roman Catholicism were quite compatible with the principle of religious toleration.

When we go beyond religious persecution and the denial of voting rights, it is even easier to find complex disputes on which sincere disagreement over the justice of an action is likely to occur. Many of the issues which have led to civil disobedience in recent years have been of this more complex kind. This is why I

7 ibid., p. 365–6.
8 ibid., p. 372.

do not think it helpful to assume that most issues arise from deliberate disregard of some common principles, or to try to specify limits, whether in the form of rights or of principles of justice, on what the majority can legitimately do.

8

THE JUSTIFIABILITY OF VIOLENT CIVIL DISOBEDIENCE

John Morreall

I

In most discussions of civil disobedience, certain characteristics are offered as essential to an act of justifiable civil disobedience, or sometimes to any act of civil disobedience. Among these one of the most frequently mentioned is nonviolence. Some thinkers, like Bedau and Wasserstrom, require an act to be nonviolent before they will even count it as an act of civil disobedience; the very concept for them includes the notion of nonviolence.[1] Others, like Stuart Brown, Rex Martin and Michael Bayles, admit the possibility of a violent act of civil disobedience; but hold that, though nonviolent civil disobedience is justifiable, violent civil disobedience is not justifiable.[2]

It is not our aim to argue about how words are or should be used, and so it is not our central concern to counter positions like Bedau's, which make civil disobedience nonviolent *by definition*. For Bedau's use of the term is harmless as long as we do not let it beg the question of the justifiability of violent political disobedience of the kind which, except for the violence, would

From: John Morreall, 'The Justifiability of Violent Civil Disobedience,' *Canadian Journal of Philosophy*, 6 (1976), pp. 35–47.

1 Though, curiously, Bedau admits that taking 'civil' disobedience as *nonviolent* disobedience involves a pun. See Hugo Adam Bedau, 'On Civil Disobedience,' *Journal of Philosophy*, LVII (1961), p. 656. Also Richard Wasserstrom, in H.A. Freeman *et al.*, *Civil Disobedience* (Santa Barbara: Center for the Study of Democratic Institutions, 1966), p. 18.

2 Stuart M. Brown Jr., 'Civil Disobedience,' *Journal of Philosophy*, LVII (1961), p. 678; Rex Martin, 'Civil Disobedience,' *Ethics*, LXXX (January, 1970); Michael Bayles, 'The Justifiability of Civil Disobedience,' *Review of Metaphysics*, XXIV, No. 1 (1970), pp. 17–18.

count for Bedau as civil disobedience.[3] Our concern is rather to see whether selective political disobedience directed against certain immoral laws or policies can be violent and still be justifiable. And because we cannot hope to establish everything in one paper, we shall be assuming that some acts of *nonviolent* civil disobedience are justifiable. Here we have in mind such things as sit-ins, illegal boycotts, illegal blocking of automobile or rail traffic, etc., the justifiability of which has, I think, been sufficiently well established.

Our first task, then, is to find the significant difference between a violent act of civil disobedience (we'll use the term to apply to both violent and nonviolent acts, as Brown, Martin and Bayles do, simply for convenience), which many have taken to be unjustifiable, and a nonviolent act of civil disobedience, which is usually accepted as justifiable. Many writers on the topic, especially Bedau, assume that we all know just what violence is, and just why it could have no place in civil disobedience. As examples of violence he offers 'sabotage, assassination, street fighting'; in simplistic fashion he seems to think that 'deliberately destroying property, endangering life and limb, [and] inciting to riot' are instances which pretty well sum up the essence of violence.[4]

But to think of violence only in terms of the unlimited violence found in riots and revolutions not only prejudices the issue of whether violence could ever be deliberately limited in scope to achieve limited ends (which, as we shall argue, is the kind of violence used in justifiably violent civil disobedience): this kind of thinking also gives us an extremely narrow view of what it is that is objectionable about violence. Now we grant that Bedau's

3 We should mention that Bedau cannot claim anything near universal agreement on his calling only nonviolent acts, acts of civil disobedience. See, for example, Berel Lang, 'Civil Disobedience and Nonviolence: A Distinction with a Difference,' *Ethics*, LXXX (January, 1970); Christian Bay, 'Civil Disobedience: Prerequisite for Democracy in Mass Society,' in David Spitz (ed.), *Political Theory and Social Change* (New York: Atherton Press, 1967), p. 169; and the articles by Brown, Martin and Bayles. Nor could Bedau claim that nonviolence was analytically tied to the notion of civil disobedience by the most outstanding proponents of civil disobedience; for as he admits on p. 656, Thoreau, the man who coined the term 'civil disobedience,' did not consider nonviolence a necessary part of what he meant by that term. A reasonable case can be made, moreover, for saying that Mohandas Gandhi and Martin Luther King saw nonviolence as one *tactic* of civil disobedience, but not necessarily the *only* one.
4 Bedau, op. cit. p. 656.

examples are examples of violence – but only of overt physical violence. And the essence of violence does not lie in the use of great physical force, as Bedau and others[5] seem to assume. Not only are there instances of great physical force being used which are not acts of violence, but, more importantly, there are many acts of violence done to people in which no physical contact is ever made.

Here Holmes' discussion of what it is to 'do violence' to a person or a thing, and Garver's linking of violence in human affairs with the concept of violation are helpful.[6] Ultimately violence, as it has implications for human beings living in society, must have a direct or indirect reference to *persons.* 'What is fundamental about violence,' says Garver, 'is that a person is violated.' Holmes expresses the core notion of 'doing violence' this way: 'Something having value, integrity, dignity, sacredness, or generally some claim to respect is treated in a manner that is contemptuous of this claim.'[7]

The reason that a person can be violated, that we can be contemptuous of his claim to our respect, is that as a person he has certain *prima facie* rights; the claim to respect he makes is made in virtue of his being the kind of thing he is. First, he has a right to his body. It is up to him to decide what will be done with and to his body. When we do physical violence to a person, it is this *prima facie* right that we are not respecting.

Obviously, too, there are other ways of doing violence to a person than by physically harming him. For a person not only has a *prima facie* right to his body, but also, in virtue of the kind of thing he is, a *prima facie* right to make his own free decisions and to carry them out. It is this kind of right that is referred to when mention is made of man's rights to 'life, liberty, and the pursuit of happiness.' We can do violence to a person not only by harming his body, but also by physically or psychologically eliminating or diminishing his autonomy; under this heading would come all kinds of psychological violence and coercion. The parents who, in order to get their children to be passive and obey commands mechanically, constantly berate and scream at

5 See, e.g., Ronald B. Miller, 'Violence, Force, and Coercion,' in Jerome A. Shaffer (ed.), *Violence* (New York: David McKay, 1971), pp. 11-26.
6 Robert L. Holmes, 'Violence and Nonviolence,' in Shaffer, op. cit., pp. 110-13; and Newton Garver, 'What Violence Is,' *The Nation* (June 24, 1968), p. 819.
7 Holmes, op. cit., p. 110.

them, can do much more violence to their children in not respecting them as free persons, than would be done by even a considerable amount of physical violence. Psychological violence is often far more damaging than mere physical injury.

Consider the case Garver mentions of the parents who, when they learned that their teenage daughter had spent the night with a married man, took the girl and her pet dog into a field and told her to dig a shallow grave. Then they gave her a pistol and told her to kill the dog and bury it.[8] When she turned the gun to her own head and fired, she was not acting under physical coercion, and the law could not touch the parents because they had committed no *physical* violence against her. But quite obviously the gravest violence had been done to the girl.

There is another basic right that arises from the nature of human autonomy. Since human action is not only free but purposive, and since the carrying out of many human purposes involves appropriating and using things from the environment,[9] persons also have a *prima facie* right to the products of their labor, the right to private property. We can do violence to a person, then, not only by doing him bodily harm or by diminishing his autonomy through coercion, but also by not respecting his right to own and control property. The connection of this right to property to the nature of human action is one which is often glossed over or ignored, in saying that we can inflict violence upon persons or upon property, as if in the one case we were mistreating a *person* and in the other mistreating a *thing*. Ultimately, as we have tried to argue, violence is done, directly or indirectly, only to persons. We cannot, literally speaking, mistreat a car: whatever sense it makes to speak of mistreating an inanimate object[10] comes from the relation of that object to some person.

Acts of violence are always acts which 'get at' *persons*. Unless the destruction of some physical object will 'get at' a person, it is not an act of violence. Throwing rocks through the windows of my neighbor's new car would be an act of violence: throwing

8 Garver, op. cit., p. 820.
9 Consider, e.g., the basic and universal activities of gathering food and building shelters.
10 We are leaving aside here, as outside the scope of political philosophy, a consideration of whether any 'respect' is due to animals or even to plans merely in virtue of what they are, and not as the property of persons.

rocks through the windows of a junked car at the city dump (assuming that this has no ecological overtones nor makes it harder for dump personnel to dispose of the car) would not be an act of violence.

Before concluding our discussion of the nature of violence we should add that although all acts of violence involve the treatment of a person in a manner contemptuous of his *prima facie* rights as a human being, not all acts which disrespect persons are of sufficient magnitude or intensity to be labelled acts of violence. If I pinch your arm lightly, or destroy a single match out of your matchbook, such acts would not normally qualify as violent. Punching your arm hard enough to leave a bruise, however, or destroying your whole winter supply of firewood would be acts of violence. As persons we have a certain 'threshold of injury'; we do not consider the light pinch or the destruction of the match wrongs committed against us under normal circumstances (though, of course, if a person is in a highly emotional state, and we knew that the slightest annoyance would send him into a blind rage, such actions could easily be acts of violence).

II

With this understanding of the nature of violence, it becomes difficult to defend a theory in which civil disobedience is justifiable but violence is not. If the position is taken that the nonviolence requirement in civil disobedience rules out physical violence because such violence would violate the rights people have to their own bodies, rights, it is usually stressed, which are protected *by law*; then it would seem that the same requirement would also have to rule out psychological violence, including any kind of coercion; inasmuch as this also violates the (law-protected[11]) rights of persons, especially their right to autonomy. Indeed, it would seem that the rights which are not respected in cases of psychological violence should be even more sacred than the right to own property, the latter being one which many writers on civil disobedience insist should never be violated in acts of civil disobedience. To say that only *physical* violence is to be ruled out in civil disobedience seems an arbitrary stipula-

11 E.g., laws against making loud noise at night, laws against harassment, laws against blackmail.

tion. Why should getting at people by making physical contact with them, or by damaging their property, be singled out as in principle unjustifiable, while other violent means of getting at people, including, incidentally, their right to control over their own property through illegal trespassing, are accepted as justifiable? If acts like sitting in large groups on railroad tracks in order to stop troop trains can sometimes be justified, the *prima facie* right of the railroad to control over its property somehow being justifiably violated; how is it that destroying a few feet of the track before assembling the crowd on the track, in order to prolong the inconvenience and insure more publicity, cannot be justified?

If civil disobedience is to be truly nonviolent, then it seems that not only must *prima facie* rights to control over one's own body and the ownership of property be respected; the rights one has to autonomy and to *control* over his property must also be respected. And if civil disobedience is to be nonviolent in the latter ways, it seems doubtful that forcing people to stop troop trains because you are on the track, or forcing someone to change a policy because you and six hundred of your comrades refuse to leave his office building until he does 'agree' to accept your demands, can be justifiable. As Harry Prosch comments, when we consider what the two are trying to accomplish, a so-called 'nonviolent' coercive tactic and a physically violent coercive one differ little.[12] 'In terms of its practical impact, therefore, your tactic [the physically nonviolent one] is basically a military one rather than a morally persuasive one – or even a political one. It is a contest of force, even though the only force *you* may be resorting to is that of the inertia of your own body.' After all, blocking a railroad train has much more in common with a physically violent protest than with a letter-writing campaign.

The line is usually drawn between physically violent means of changing laws and physically nonviolent means of doing so (a distinction which is supposed to give us a way of separating justifiable from unjustifiable acts); when in reality the important distinction to be made (though it does not give us a test of justifiability) is between tactics which achieve change by forcing those in power to change the law or policy, and tactics which

12 'Limits to the Moral Claim in Civil Disobedience,' *Ethics*, LXXV (1965), pp. 104–5.

work by *changing people's minds.* The significant line to be drawn here is between *coercion* – physical or psychological – and *persuasion.*

Now some have claimed that civil disobedience is nonviolent in all respects, and that its efficacy lies only in the moral persuasion which it exercises. We can see the reason for this claim by merely extending the reason for banning *physical* violence, as we have tried to do, to its logical end. According to Robert Audi, 'Civil disobedience requires that those practising it be making a reasoned attempt to appeal to the conscience of others; they must not be attempting to impose their will on others through the use of force, which they certainly would be doing if violence were a calculated part of civil disobedience.' [13] To understand the claim that civil disobedience must rely on persuasion and never resort to any form of coercion, we need only take Audi's word 'violence' here as referring to all types of violence – physical and psychological. For not only is physical violence incompatible with persuasion; *any* form of coercion is.

If we do rule out *any* coercion in acts of civil disobedience, however, it seems that we have gone too far; for we have ruled out the greater share of what has traditionally been called civil disobedience, on the grounds that practically all of it has involved some form of coercion. In ruling out all coercion, moreover, it becomes unclear why any law would have to be broken in order to carry out the moral persuasion to which we have limited ourselves. If we are going to respect all the *prima facie* rights of persons to their bodies, to their autonomy and to their property, and merely try to *convince* others of the rightness of our cause, then it would seem the rare situation in which we could ever break a law in carrying out this persuasion.

A position which begins by saying that physical violence cannot be justified in acts of civil disobedience, then, because it violates people's *prima facie* rights, must ultimately conclude that no form of coercion is justifiable in acts of civil disobedience. That few theories of civil disobedience would want to go this far, however, is obvious. But how can we avoid going this far and still remain consistent?

The answer to this question is a relatively simple one, but one which will no longer rule out physical violence in acts of civil

13 'On the Meaning and Justification of Violence,' in Shaffer, op. cit., p. 94.

disobedience. In reality, though a good deal of the effectiveness of civil disobedience springs from its persuasiveness, there is also an element of coercion in practically all acts of civil disobedience. When a group of students (presumably justifiably) takes over an administration building in attempts to get certain policies changed which were not changed through rational appeals to the administration, they are usually attempting to get as large an audience as possible to listen to the rationality of their proposals. But this is not *all* they are doing, for they could get just as large an audience through completely legal means. They are also trying to apply pressure upon the administration, they are adding the force of coercion to the reasonableness of their demands. Now if coercion is *all* that is being used, we would probably not call such an act civil disobedience. If people are presenting their demands not as reasonable and just, but simply as *demands* – whether backed up by physically nonviolent or physically violent coercion – then we say that these people are trying to *impose* their will on everyone else. The unacceptability of such 'naked coercion' is obvious.

But what about the coercion that *is* present in civil disobedience? Doesn't it violate people's *prima facie* rights to autonomy, as physical violence violates their rights to their own bodies and property? In the answer to this question lies the reason why coercion is sometimes justifiable, and also the reason why physical violence is sometimes justifiable. For the rights which physical violence or coercion violate, the rights which laws are set up to protect, are not absolute rights, but only, as we have been saying, *prima facie* rights. Under normal circumstances I have a right to determine what is done to my body, and you would be unjustified in, say, firing a bullet into my leg. But if I am coming at you with a knife, obviously intent on harming you, and you have a loaded gun in your pocket, it is obvious that I no longer have a claim to bodily security. My right not to be shot by you has been forfeited or superseded by my intent to murder you and your corresponding right to preserve our own life by defending yourself with the gun. This is why we say that to harm a person, or even to kill him, in self-defence is justifiable.

The same would hold true for the slaveowner chasing a runaway slave in the United States of the 1850s. If he has almost caught up with the slave, and my engaging him in a fistfight would give the slave the few precious minutes he needs to get away again, then I would be perfectly justified in grabbing the man and knocking him to the ground to give the slave the time he needs. The law says that I must help slaveowners capture their runaway slaves, the slaveowner may claim; he may also claim that he has a right to his own bodily security. But, obviously, both the law, because it is immoral, and his right to bodily security, because it has been superseded by the slave's right to be free, are not morally binding on me.

Nor need the person whose *prima facie* rights are being superseded by a guilty party. If I have the only well in my town that has not gone dry, and my neighbors will die if they don't get drinking water, my right to exclusive use of that well has been superseded by their need of my water to stay alive – at least until they can get water elsewhere.

And we can apply these same principles to acts of civil disobedience. If it is obvious that the claim which a law makes upon me is an immoral one, then my public disobedience of that law can be justified, because my *prima facie* obligation to obey the law has been superseded by a higher moral obligation.

In a case such as that of the master chasing the slave, moreover, I not only can be justified in publicly breaking the law requiring me to assist in the capture of runaway slaves, in order to publicize the immorality of *that* law: I can also be justified in breaking the law which protects the master's *prima facie* right against being assaulted.

Just as my rights can be superseded though I have done nothing wrong, as in the case of the well, furthermore, so too the rights of innocent people can be superseded in the execution of acts of civil disobedience. If a grossly immoral and un-constitutional war is being waged, for example, the right of railway engineers on troop trains to carry out their job without interference from protesters on the tracks, may be superseded by the more important right of the people in the country to which the troops are headed, to life itself. If an anti-war demonstration which shows reasonable promise of helping to end the war is taking place, then the man whose drive to the office is impeded by demonstrators in the street handing out leaflets makes a faulty objection when he says, 'These people can't be justified, because they're violating my right to drive down the street without illegal obstructions.'

The slaveowner case, I think, is one wherein civil disobedience can be physically violent and still justifiable. A more recent example might be the case of civil disobedients' pouring blood on draft files in protest of the Vietnam War. The government's right not to have its records damaged, though it may hold in most cases, has simply been superseded in this case. The right which people in Vietnam have to life takes precedence over the U.S. government's right to property.

Now, obviously, we must have a good reason for ever violating a *prima facie* right, just as we need a good reason for violating a law. And we must have a stronger claim in order to, say, seriously injure a man than to merely damage a possession of his which has little value. At times it may be extremely difficult to decide which of the two *prima facie* rights takes precedence in particular situations, especially in a case of civil disobedience where the connection of the *prima facie* rights to be violated and laws to be broken, with the immoral law being protested against, is only an indirect connection. We might wonder further if cases ever occur in which physically injuring an innocent party could be justified as part of an act of civil disobedience. But all these contingent requirements and contingent difficulties do not obscure the main point which we have tried to make: an act of civil disobedience can be justifiable when it violates the *prima facie* rights – or perhaps we should have been saying '*prime facie*-ly violates the rights' – of persons, because these rights are not absolute and can be superseded by higher moral claims.

And in justifying acts of civil disobedience, though a stronger claim may be required to justify damaging draft files than is required to justify inflicting serious inconvenience upon the draft board by the criminal trespass of a sit-in, there is nothing which makes acts of physical violence any more *unjustifiable in principle* than acts of interfering with another's control over his property, or acts of coercion. If what has traditionally passed as civil disobedience can be justified at all, I submit, there is nothing which rules out justifying acts of civil disobedience that involve physical violence.

III

At the beginning of this paper we noted that some theorists admitted the possibility of violent acts of civil disobedience, but held that such acts could never be justified. Having discussed in detail, then, how acts of physically violent civil disobedience can in fact be justified, it might be enlightening to consider a few of the arguments which were supposed to prove that this is impossible. And because the reasoning Stuart Brown uses is fairly representative of these arguments as a group, I would like to take his three arguments one at a time to see what is wrong with them.

The first reason which Brown advances for the unjustifiability of violent civil disobedience is that 'the use of force and violence, being evil in itself and being no less evil for being used in a good cause, can be morally justified only in circumstances where the alternative is an even greater evil and cannot, therefore, be justified in cases of civil disobedience.' [14] And, according to Brown, if the alternative to violent civil disobedience were to become a greater evil than the violence would involve, then what is justified is no longer justified on the grounds of civil disobedience, but on the grounds of *revolution*. Unless we would be justified in overthrowing the whole political–legal system, we could not be justified in using any kind of violence. 'If one cannot justify civil rebellion, then one cannot justify the use of force and violence.' [15]

Brown's claims here are patently false. First of all, in at least some cases of violent civil disobedience, the alternative to the act of civil disobedience (which act is seen, of course, as part of a campaign to eliminate an immoral law or policy) is 'an even greater evil' than the violence inflicted by the act. In the slaveowner case, for example, not only would my helping him capture the slave be a greater evil than my tackling him to give the slave a chance to get away; but my just standing back in 'nonparticipation,' which Brown suggests could not be evil because it is merely negative, would also be a greater evil than tackling him.[16] We can often commit such sins of omission, doing evil by merely 'doing nothing'. The act of tackling the slaveowner, furthermore, need not be a revolutionary act, for we can consistently both endorse the government on the whole and wish to change certain of its laws which are immoral.

14 Brown, op. cit., pp. 678–9.
15 ibid., p. 679.
16 Leslie MacFarlane, in 'Justifying Political Disobedience,' *Ethics*, LXXIX (1968), considers the case of the railway clerks who arranged the transit of Jews to the Nazi extermination camps. These men not only had the negative duty of not participating in such evil acts, he argues: they had 'a positive duty to resist, sabotage, and frustrate the evil,' p. 44.

Brown's contention that unless a rebellion overthrowing the government is justifiable, the use of any violence is not justifiable, would need a great deal of fleshing out even to sound superficially plausible. The state uses violence all the time – in wars, police action, executions – and presumably, does so justifiably. As private citizens we corporally punish our children. And if we are being attacked on the street with no policeman in sight, we use violence to defend ourselves. Part of Brown's misunderstanding of the whole issue of violence and its justification stems from his failure to distinguish between limited violence designed to achieve selective particular ends, as is found in the above examples and in cases of justifiable violent civil disobedience, and the all-out violence of a total revolution. Not all acts of violence threaten the existence of the government; many of them do not even threaten our lives or bodily security (e.g. the pouring of blood on draft files). We grant that a situation justifying revolution would be necessary to justify starting mass fires and throwing grenades into restaurants, for these are the *means* of a revolution. But we insist that the justifiability of a revolution is not a prerequisite for justifying the *limited* use of violent means to achieve selective ends in acts of civil disobedience.

At this point it is sometimes argued that even the carefully limited violence which we have appealed to is always unjustifiable. Rex Martin, for example, says that the sovereignty of a democratic state 'resides largely in its ability to proscribe individual violence by law on the one hand, and to monopolize coercive force, at least in principle, on the other.' [17] If we have given our allegiance to a government, then, we would be acting inconsistently and wrongly if we ever used violence against democratic laws and policies. In holding that the democrat *qua* democrat has an unconditional obligation never to use such violence, however, Martin is wrong. The democrat's endorsement of a democratic state no more entails this kind of obligation than it entails the obligation to always obey democratic law. [18] For just as we can justifiably break immoral democratic laws and not act inconsistently with our endorsement of the democracy as a decision-making procedure, we can also sometimes use justifiable violence in an act of civil disobedience against an immoral

17 Martin, op. cit., p. 132.
18 On this latter non-entailment see Marvin Schiller, 'On the Logic of Being a Democrat,' *Philosophy*, XLIV (1969).

law or policy, without acting inconsistently without endorsement of the democracy as a whole.

Brown's second argument for the unjustifiability of violent civil disobedience is an appeal to 'the need to maintain a clear, sharp distinction between justified acts of civil disobedience and justified acts of civil rebellion.' [19] 'There is a *logical* relationship between civil disobedience and civil rebellion,' [20] he asserts; in fact 'one can imagine a program of civil disobedience designed to confuse and weaken a community to the point at which a revolution could be launched and succeed. In this case civil disobedience would be an essential part of a carefully planned conspiracy to revolt.' [21] And since revolution and civil disobedience would otherwise be indistinguishable, Brown feels that we must insist upon the criterion of violence to distinguish them.

What Brown has failed to take into account, leaving aside the issue of whether his reasoning here could show anything to be justifiable or unjustifiable, is that there already is a major difference between revolution and civil disobedience, viz. the selective and limited nature of the latter. The person committing an act of civil disobedience is not intending to overthrow the whole political-legal system; he is rather trying to change certain specific laws or policies *within* that system, which system, on the whole, he endorses.[22] And because his proclaimed ends are limited, furthermore, his means - be they violent or nonviolent - are also limited.

Brown's claim that acts of civil disobedience could be used to start off a revolution shows just how thoroughly he misunderstands the nature of civil disobedience. For, as Bayles points out, the person who objects morally to the *entire* political-legal system and is working for a *complete* change of the existing structure, is a revolutionary, not a civil disobedient.[23] The mere fact that some of a revolutionary's acts may be physically nonviolent, or even the fact that he may break only a few laws at a time, does not make his acts any less revolutionary, and certainly could not make them acts of civil disobedience, the prerequisite

19 Brown, op. cit., p. 679.
20 ibid., p. 678, emphasis mine.
21 ibid., p. 677.
22 Bayles, op. cit., p. 5.
23 ibid., p. 4.

for which is that the person performing the act endorse, on the whole, the system within which he is trying to make specific changes.[24]

The third reason Brown offers is that we must 'preserve civil disobedience as a tolerable, ritualized form of public protest in which lawbreaking is minimal and for the most part formal.' [25] If physically violent civil disobedience were permitted, then it might not have the effect that it should have, because people would get it confused with other kinds of law-breaking.

Here we need only note that this is not really an argument against the *possibility* of a justifiable violent act of civil disobedience. It can at most be a warning that more thought and attention to how the public will react must go into a violent act of civil disobedience than into a nonviolent one, or into a physically violent act than into one involving only, say, illegal trespass. People in general, it seems, tend to disapprove of violence in general; and so the limited scope of any violence used in an act of civil disobedience, as well as the specific goals of that act, must be clearly set out in order for the act to have the proper effect on the public. I myself found some violent acts used against the U.S. involvement in Vietnam, the destruction of draft files, for example, more acceptable – because more effective in achieving their ends – than some nonviolent acts, e.g. the overdone 'peace march'. The point, however, is simply that unless Brown could show that no violent act of civil disobedience *could* include the necessary safeguards or *could* achieve its ends, then mere contingent facts about who happens to respond better to which forms of civil disobedience cannot invalidate the claim that violent acts of civil disobedience are in principle justifiable.

24 Even if we were to stretch the notion of civil disobedience to cover certain physically nonviolent acts used to start off a revolution, the selected and limited nature of those acts would still distinguish them from the acts of a full-scale revolution.
25 Brown, op. cit., p. 680.

9

CIVIL DISOBEDIENCE AND NON-COOPERATION

Vinit Haksar

In the previous chapter I rejected the view that unless the aim of
the protesters is to coerce the authorities it is irrational to break
the law. I appealed to some of Gandhi's ideas to show that even if
your aim is to convert (without coercing) the authorities, it
makes sense to break the law under certain conditions. I now
want to appeal to some other Gandhian ideas to show yet another
way in which law-breaking makes sense within a non-coercive
model. In some cases, law-breaking can be justified as a part of a
non-coercive non-cooperative movement. I shall attempt to show
that such non-cooperation may be non-coercive even when it
results in the state being unable to implement its evil laws or
policies.

Gandhi thought that under certain conditions non-cooperation with an evil state is the duty of a citizen. And he believed
that, at any rate when certain conditions are fulfilled, non-
cooperation with an evil state commits one to civil disobedience.

> You assist an administration most effectively by obeying its
> orders and decrees. An evil system never deserves such
> allegiance. Allegiance to it means partaking of the evil. A
> good man will therefore resist an evil system or administ-
> ration with his whole soul. Disobedience of the laws of the
> evil State is therefore a duty. (*N.V.R.*, p. 238)*

He also believed that the breaking of the laws of an evil state
should not take violent or coercive form, so he maintained that

---

From: Vinit Haksar, *Civil Disobedience, Threats and Offers: Gandhi and
Rawls* (Delhi: Oxford University Press, 1986), pp. 29–41.
*[The reference is to M. K. Gandhi, *Nonviolent Resistance* (New York: Schocken
Books, 1961)].

'civil disobedience is a necessary part of non-cooperation' (*N.V.R.*, p. 238). This is quite consistent with his earlier belief that non-cooperation is not necessarily involved in civil disobedience (*N.V.R.*, pp. 214–15), though it is inconsistent with his earlier belief that non-cooperation is possible and often desirable without civil disobedience (*N.V.R.*, pp. 3–4). What is common to his earlier and later positions is the view that civil disobedience is at least one important method of non-cooperating with the régime.

There are two positions that Gandhi takes regarding why we should not be a party to a wrong. Sometimes he appears to take a non-consequentialist line, arguing that it is simply one's duty to dissociate oneself from evil: 'cooperation must be withdrawn because the people must not be a party to a wrong' (*N.V.R.*, p. 116). But at other times he appears to accept a consequentialist justification for his position: 'if a government does a grave injustice the subjects must withdraw cooperation wholly or partially sufficiently to wean the ruler from his wickedness' (*N.V.R.*, p. 115). There are similar complications with regard to Gandhi's views on nonviolence in general. Sometimes he thinks one ought to do what is right, irrespective of consequences (*N.V.R.*, p. 113). At others he seems to give a consequentialist justification, commending non-violence by appealing to its good results, e.g. that it 'results in the long run in the least loss of life.' [1] His argument that evil means should never be used in pursuit of good ends, because if they are so used the ends will become distorted and corrupted, is also a consequentialist argument.

Perhaps one can attempt to reconcile these two sorts of justifications by making a distinction of levels. If the problem is, for instance, why we should refrain from participating in *x* on a particular occasion, the answer would be that *x*-ing is wrong. But if we ask, why is the practice of *x*-ing wrong, his answer would be a consequentialist one.

Peter Singer, in his valuable book,[2] is unfair to the person who breaks the law because he does not want to co-operate with evil. He considers Thoreau's view, 'I do not lend myself to the

---

1 'Non-violence' in J. G. Murphy (ed.), *Civil Disobedience and Violence* (Belmont CA: Wadsworth Publishing Company, 1971), p. 100.
2 Peter Singer, *Democracy and Disobedience* (Oxford: The Clarendon Press, 1973).

wrong which I condemn', and criticizes it for being more concerned with preserving one's moral purity than with removing the evil. I think Singer is unfair to Thoreau. Thoreau argued that by going to prison the protester not only preserves his honour but also increases his power of influencing the evil state. Those who believe that in jail the protester loses his influence:

> do not know by how much truth is stronger than error, nor how much more eloquently and effectively he can combat injustice who has experienced a little in his own person. . . . If the alternative is to keep all just men in prison or give up war and slavery, the State will not hesitate which to choose.[3]

Moreover, Thoreau claimed that by refusing to pay taxes the resister would make it more difficult for the state to finance its evil policies.

Both Rawls and Singer regard civil disobedience as a non-coercive plea to the authorities and the public on the part of the protesters. True, Singer, unlike Rawls, contends that the civil disobedients can not only appeal to the existing sense of justice of the public and the authorities, but also try to reform and improve that sense of justice. But Singer is still content only to appeal to that sense of justice, existing or potential; he, too, is willing to wait patiently until the authorities are converted. Neither Rawls nor Singer do justice to the view that allows civil disobedients to non-cooperate in order to make it difficult for the state to carry out its evil policies.

I want to show that Gandhian non-cooperation can be, at the same time, both non-coercive and effective in frustrating the state in carrying out its will. But first I shall examine some of the reasons Rawls and Singer give for rejecting a coercive model of civil disobedience; later it will, I hope, become clear that their arguments have little, if any, force against Gandhian non-co-operation.

Now I think Rawls and Singer would not deny that sometimes coercion and even violence may be justified (*T. of J.*, p. 368). They do not imply that coercion and violence should never be used as a form of disobedience; what they maintain is that coercion and violence must not be used as a form of *civil*

3 'On the Duty of Civil Disobedience,' in *Civil Disobedience and Violence*, p. 28.

disobedience. I think they rule out coercive civil disobedience on the grounds that it blurs the distinction between publicity and addressing the authorities on the one hand, and coercion and intimidation on the other. But what does it matter if this distinction is blurred? It may be replied that this would make civil disobedience pointless, for if one of the objects of civil disobedience is to function as a mode of address, then how can it achieve this if the public begins to think of it as coercive and intimidating? Now, I think obstructive and coercive devices are not necessarily incompatible with the goal of publicity. It is quite possible that in some circumstances the protesters could get even more publicity by resorting to such tactics, however deplorable such tactics may be on other grounds. Theoretically, it is also possible to imagine circumstances where such tactics may promote the goal of rational persuasion of one's opponent. For instance, suppose the opponent refuses to listen to the protesters' case, then the protesters could forcibly surround the opponent and force the opponent into entering a rational discussion about the grievances of the protesters. Theoretically, it is possible to imagine situations where, though coercive tactics are used to get the discussions started, they are not used once the discussions have begun. But, of course, in practice it is highly likely that if the protesters use coercive (or violent) tactics to get the discussions started, they may attempt to continue using such tactics even after the discussions have begun. The temptation to do so may be too strong. The same point applies to the goal of publicity. The protesters may achieve more publicity by the use of coercive tactics, but then they will be strongly tempted to use such tactics to extract concessions from the authorities forcibly. Such considerations show that coercive or violent tactics may in practice be incompatible with the aim of getting the authorities to accede freely to the protesters' demands. But they do not show that the aim of publicity for one's cause is inconsistent with the use of coercive tactics.

Gandhi's views on civil disobedience and non-cooperation are highly interesting and fall somewhere between the Rawls–Singer non-coercive position and the coercive kind of civil disobedience advocated by others. Gandhi seems to present an alternative that is not mentioned by the other theorists under discussion. One of the recurring themes in Gandhi's writings is that civil disobedients should never resort to coercive tactics. He says of his movement that 'it's a movement of conversion, not of compulsion even of the tyrant' (*N.V.R.*, p. 331); again: 'The *Satyagrahi's* object is to convert, not to coerce the wrong-doer' (*N.V.R.*, p. 87). And he allows civil disobedience against one's enemies, but not fasts against one's enemies on the grounds that such fasts are likely to be coercive (*N.V.R.*, pp. 181–2). That he is opposed to coercion can also be inferred from his doctrine that good ends do not justify the use of evil means. This doctrine would imply that since coercion is evil it must not be used as a means to the removal of even grave injustices.

It can be seen from the above that Gandhi would be opposed to coercive civil disobedience, not only of the violent kind advocated by Zinn but even of the 'nonviolent' kind advocated by Barry. But Gandhi's position is also different from the Rawls–Singer position; thus he says the civil disobedients should not just wait for:

> wrong to be righted till the wrong-doer has been roused to his sense of his iniquity. We must not, for fear of ourselves or others having to suffer, remain participators in it. But we must combat the wrong by ceasing to assist the wrong-doer directly or indirectly . . . if a Government does a grave injustice the subjects must withdraw cooperation wholly or partially, sufficiently to wean the ruler from his wickedness. (*N.V.R.*, p. 115)

And we saw earlier that Gandhi commended resistance 'in order to bend the unjust Government to the will of the people' (*N.V.R.*, p. 21).

Now, it may be asked, is Gandhi not being inconsistent in professing to be anti-coercive and yet recommending non-cooperation that can make it difficult for the state to carry out its policies? I shall now offer a reconstruction of the Gandhian theory which will save Gandhi from this charge of inconsistency. This reconstructed version will be in harmony with the spirit of a good deal of what he said, if not with the letter of everything he said.

Civil disobedience and non-cooperation, when conducted according to Gandhian principles, do not constitute a threat or coercion *in any evil sense*. Rather, they involve a refusal to co-operate with or assist an evil policy, and an offer to co-operate on honourable and just terms; according to Gandhi:

although non-cooperation is the main weapon in the armoury of *Satyagraha*, it should not be forgotten that it is after all only a means to secure the cooperation of the opponent consistently with truth and justice.[4]

Non-cooperation is no more coercive than the ordinary shop-keeper's raising of his prices (e.g. because his costs have gone up substantially). And just as the ordinary shopkeeper is not necessarily using evil means, nor is the non-cooperator necessarily evil. It may be objected that there is a difference; the shopkeeper is making an offer, whereas the non-cooperator is withdrawing co-operation in order to change the policies of his opponent. But I think the shopkeeper when he charges a price can be seen as doing two things: refusing to sell it at a price below the stated price, and offering to sell it at the stated price. If he has raised his price then he, too, has *withdrawn* his previous offer. None of this entails that he is using any evil means, such as coercion, in some evil sense. So why should the case be different with the civil disobedient non-cooperator?

Is there perhaps this difference, that the civil disobedient non-cooperator is non-cooperating in order to change the policy of the opponent, while the shopkeeper charges prices in order to make a reasonable income or profit from the sale of his goods? But the shopkeeper, too, is in a sense putting pressure on the customer; he is in effect saying, 'you won't get my goods unless you pay me the stated price'. Many customers may want to buy his goods at less than his stated price, even when the stated price is a fair one; and when he refuses to sell it at a price lower than the fair one, he is doing something more than just appealing to the sense of justice (actual or potential) of the customer. The seller does not give the goods and then request the customer to give the fair price, leaving the customer free to decide after he has taken the goods whether or not to pay the fair price. Yet it cannot be inferred that the seller is therefore using evil means, or that he is coercing in some evil sense. Similarly, when the civil disobedient non-cooperates with the authorities and refuses simply to wait patiently until the authorities have had a change of heart; it is true that he does not merely appeal to the sense of justice (actual or potential) of the authorities, but it does follow that he

4 *Harijan*, 29 April 1939, p. 101.

is using evil means, such as coercion in any evil sense, in order to promote his legitimate goals. True, sometimes civil disobedient non-cooperators can use their great powers to exploit the authorities. The same is true of sellers: a monopolist can exploit the customer. But one cannot infer that, wherever civil disobedients non-cooperate with the authorities, they are using evil means such as being coercive in some evil sense – just as one cannot infer that the ordinary seller is using evil means from the fact that the monopolist is doing so. Indeed, even the monopolist who has the power to coerce (in an evil sense) the customer may not exercise this power; he may just charge the fair price. Similarly, even civil disobedient non-cooperators who are very powerful may not coerce the authorities when they refuse to co-operate on unjust terms, or when they refuse to assist the régime in its wicked policies; they could be willing to co-operate on just and honourable terms.

Although there are coercive and evil forms of non-cooperation, this does not make the non-coercive forms of civil disobedient non-cooperation morally unacceptable. Of course, some people may take the line that in liberal democracies it is always evil to resort to law-breaking, and if so it would follow that the Gandhian non-cooperator who resorts to civil disobedience will be involved in the use of evil means, and so in such régimes there will be no room for Gandhian civil disobedience, for it does not permit the use of evil means. But this argument is so strong that it would rule out the Rawlsian kind of civil disobedience as well. Rawls cannot use this kind of argument against Gandhian civil disobedience, for he clearly does not treat all law-breaking as involving the use of evil means. The Rawlsian civil disobedient, too, breaks the law, and yet according to Rawls he is not using evil means to achieve his goal. Where the régime does not honour the terms of social co-operation, Rawls thinks that, provided certain conditions are satisfied, the citizens may break the law without doing any moral wrong, for even in near-just societies the citizen does not have the duty to obey the law in all circumstances.

The problem, then, for Rawls and Singer is this. If they are willing to commend civil disobedience under certain conditions, why do they not, as Gandhi does, allow civil disobedience as a means towards non-cooperation? They have arguments to show why we should not resort to coercion, but such arguments at best show why we should not resort to violent, or even nonviolent but coercive, kinds of civil disobedience; they do not show what is wrong with the nonviolent and non-coercive forms of non-cooperative movements of the Gandhian kind, which by withdrawing support make it difficult for the state to carry out its evil policies. Rawls thinks that the civil disobedients should be willing to submit to the penalty, thus establishing their sincerity to themselves and to others. But Gandhian civil disobedience, even when it is used as a form of non-cooperation, certainly satisfies this condition; indeed it seems to do so even better than Rawlsian civil disobedience, since, as we saw earlier, Gandhian civil disobedients are willing to suffer much more than are the Rawlsian civil disobedients. Rawls would be against the coercive kinds of civil disobedience (e.g. the kind recommended by Barry or by Zinn) [5] on the grounds that 'any interference with the civil liberties of others tends to obscure the civilly disobedient character of one's act' (*T. of J.*, p. 366). But Gandhian non-cooperators insist on ruling out the use of evil means for the pursuit of their goals, and this fact, coupled with the willingness of the Gandhian resister to suffer substantial penalties, can prevent the civil disobedient character of their act from being obscured. Why must the fact that you refuse to assist a régime in its evil policies obscure your appeal to the régime to give up its evil ways? Singer believes that coercive civil disobedience, in addition to blurring the distinction between intimidation and publicity, is liable to encourage a breakdown of the system by encouraging anarchical tendencies. It is on such grounds that he criticizes the non-cooperators who tried to 'fuck the draft' in the USA by submitting false registration forms, etc. But such arguments have much less force against Gandhian non-cooperation, for Gandhi insisted on not using evil means, and so in the example just referred to he would not have permitted the submission of false forms.

Of course, the danger of chaos and anarchy must not be dismissed lightly. Gandhi himself stressed such dangers, and that is why he insisted that very stringent conditions must be satisfied before civil disobedience can be justified; moreover [. . .] he insisted that individuals must have the appropriate personal

5 'A Fallacy on Law and Order: That Civil Disobedience Must be Absolutely Nonviolent,' in *Civil Disobedience and Violence*, pp. 103–11.

qualifications before they can acquire the right to embark on civil disobedience. Without such precautions things can get out of hand and nonviolence can give way to violence. Indeed, even Gandhian movements sometimes degenerated in this fashion, and Gandhi has admitted to his own 'Himalayan blunder', which he attributed to the neglect of such precautions.

Some risk of violence is often there even when reasonable precautions have been taken before embarking on civil disobedience. Now, such risk has to be balanced against the danger of violence arising from not doing anything substantial:

> the risk of supineness in the face of a grave issue is infinitely greater . . . to do nothing is to invite violence for a certainty. (*N.V.R.*, p. 116)

> it is no easy task to restrain the fury of a people incensed by a deep sense of wrong. I urge those who talk or work against non-cooperation to . . . go down to the people, learn their feelings . . . they will find, as I have found, that the only way to avoid violence is to enable them to give such expression to their feelings as to compel redress. (*N.V.R.*, p. 117)

This can be called the safety-valve argument in favour of civil disobedience; Gandhian civil disobedience helps to prevent greater violence, and to channel protests into non-evil forms. What has Rawls to offer when his patient appeals to the authorities fail? He envisages abandonment of civil disobedience and the use of militancy and violence! (*T. of J.*, p. 368).

When he used the safety-valve argument, Gandhi did not threaten violence; he was really giving a non-threatening warning of worse things to come if the legitimate demands of the resistors were not met, and he was defending his movement against the charge that it is likely to lead to violence. Gandhi's warning is an excellent illustration of Rawls's point that civil disobedience, 'while it may warn and admonish . . . is not itself a threat' (*T. of J.*, p. 366). But now it may be protested: are Gandhi and Rawls not being hypocritical in dissociating themselves from violence yet making use of such potential violence in their arguments with the authorities? Is there really such a moral difference between the man who says, 'Meet my demands, otherwise I shall hit you', and the man who says, 'Meet my demands,

otherwise someone, not acting on my authority, will hit you' ?
Are Gandhi and Rawls not being like that regular meat-eater
who, before sitting down for his meals, utters the prayer, 'Oh
Lord, forgive the butcher who killed this lovely animal.' ? For,
just as the meat-eater enjoys the fruits of the butcher's doings and
so does not have the right to dissociate himself from what the
butcher does, so similarly do Gandhi and Rawls not have the
right to dissociate themselves from the violent men, for they are
both willing to use the future behaviour of violent men in their
argument to persuade the authorities to give in to the demands of
the protesters. But this criticism of Gandhi (and of Rawls) is not
quite fair. For Gandhi could claim to dissociate himself from
violence because he commended and practised various ways of
reducing violence, whereas the smug meat-eater in our example
was doing nothing to prevent the killing of animals, and was if
anything contributing to such killings by paying the butcher for
meat.

There is still a residual problem for Gandhi. Suppose the
authorities in the Brave New World have almost eliminated the
danger of physical violence, by a system of falsehood, drugs,
conditioning, etc. Suppose Gandhians then come along and start
launching a non-cooperation movement. It may now be objected
against this movement that it may well upset the apple cart and
degenerate into physical violence. Now Gandhi would be against
using physical violence as a *means* to the attainment of his
legitimate goals, but it does not follow that he would be against
the using of means such as non-cooperation that may as a
consequence lead to some physical violence on the part of others.
Of course, he would agree that we should never neglect such
possible consequences. But he could argue that although such
consequences have to be taken into account, they have to be
balanced against other consequences and values, such as the
danger to liberties or truth, and non-physical violence – what
Gandhi sometimes called psychological violence. Taking all
these considerations into account, it may well be that even from a
consequentialist standpoint, Gandhian civil disobedience may be
justified in some situations, even where it may result in a net
increase in physical violence.

The safety-valve argument has only a small part to play in the
Gandhian case for civil disobedience; its function at best is to try,
when possible, to rebut the suggestion that the non-cooperation

movement results in the increase in physical violence. But we have seen that even when this suggestion cannot be rebutted there may be a case for civil disobedience. The positive case for civil disobedience has to be built in a way different from that used in the safety-valve argument. Thus Gandhi would argue that we have a right not to assist the authorities in carrying out a policy of grave injustice, and so forth. And once we realize that there are values besides the net reduction of physical violence, we could give a consequentialist justification of civil disobedience even in the Brave New World of the kind we referred to in the previous paragraph.

The safety-valve argument can also be used by those who resort to coercive civil disobedience. It *may* be that in some situations the coercive kind of civil disobedience recommended by Barry will provide a better safety-valve than Gandhian civil disobedience does. Whether burning cricket pitches provides a better safety-valve than the self-sufferings of the Gandhian civil disobedients is an empirical matter. No a priori safety-valve argument can show why we should always, or even normally, prefer Gandhian civil disobedience to coercive civil disobedience. To justify this preference we would have to appeal to other considerations as well, namely, that good ends do not justify the use of evil means or the violation of our moral duties, that in any case the (net) reduction of physical violence is not the only end to be taken into account, that it is better if we can promote and protect the various values without resorting to coercion in an evil sense. Also, as we saw earlier, some of the Rawls and Singer arguments are perhaps more effective against coercive civil disobedience than against Gandhian civil disobedience.

One of the criticisms made against Gandhi is that he relies too much on the significance of the act–omission distinction. Thus it has been said that he condemns positive acts of violence but neglects the fact that violence can result from omissions, from failure to act. For instance, if you withhold labour in a vital industry, this omission to work, too, can cause violence. Now I think that Gandhian non-cooperation can be constructed in a way that does not rely too heavily on this distinction. Let us admit that omissions, too, can cause violence. But they do so only if there has been a violation of a duty – not necessarily of a legal duty, but of a moral duty; nor necessarily of a moral duty recognized by society, but of a moral duty that ought to be recognized by society.[6] Thus if you think that by their going on strike certain labourers are responsible for the death of certain citizens who were dependent on their services, then you are committed to the view that the labourers broke some duty, such as their duty to provide their labour. Or again, if you believe that the wealthy in Britain are causing the deaths of the starving in famine-stricken areas, then you are committed to the view that the wealthy in Britain have a moral duty (which society ought to recognize) to give aid to the starving. Now similarly, if people start a non-cooperative civil disobedience movement and some few people suffer as a consequence, then the non-cooperators can only be held (morally) responsible if they have broken some moral duty. Then if you believe in Gandhian non-cooperation, you will not go in for non-cooperation as long as doing so would involve your violating your (moral) duty. Gandhian non-cooperation relies less heavily on the significance of the act–omission distinction and more on the distinction between conduct (whether act or omission) that violates a moral duty and conduct (whether act or omission) that does not violate any moral duty.

It would be wrong to characterize the Gandhian non-cooperative civil disobedience movement as one that permits only omissions against the authorities and not also actions against the authorities. Marching, breaking the law, advocating others to break the law, etc., are positive actions. So the difference

6 John Harris ('Marxist Conception of Violence,' *Philosophy and Public Affairs*, vol. 3, no. 2 [Winter 1974], pp. 208–9) believes that for *A* to cause *Y* by his failure to do *X* the following conditions are sufficient (though not necessary): *A* should have done *X*, *X* would have prevented *Y*, and *Y* involves harm to human beings. If Harris is right, then the milk drivers in Gandhi's example would have caused the deaths of the babies. But Harris's test is clearly insufficient. Suppose there are people living in the slums of New York who are suffering from malnutrition and lack of medicine; and suppose the Indian government by cutting down its five-year plan and letting its own citizens starve, could send the resources to New York that would remove the sufferings of the slum-dwellers of New York. It surely would not follow that the Indian government, by its failure to send the relevant resources, is causing harm to the slum-dwellers of New York. It is also relevant to ask whether the Indian government is violating any relevant duty. But to make the analogy with the milk drivers case closer, suppose the Indian government had in the past been supplying resources to the slum-dwellers in New York, and then decided to stop doing so. Would it not then be causing harm to the slum-dwellers? I think the answer would still be in the negative unless the Indian government was violating a relevant duty, e.g., if one takes the view that it had a duty to supply resources to those who had been accustomed to its help.

between Gandhi and the coercive civil disobedients is not to be explained by saying that the former allows only omissions against the authorities. The difference is to be explained by appealing to the principle that Gandhi allows only non-cooperation and civil disobedience when there is no violation of moral duty; or, in other words, Gandhi does not allow evil means (whether through action or through omissions) to be used in order to promote the goals of the civil disobedients. It is on such grounds that he would condemn violent civil disobedience, as well as 'nonviolent' civil disobedience which interferes with civil liberties of the citizens, or which uses falsehoods, etc. I suspect Gandhi is committed to something like the doctrine of double effect, and quite a lot of discussion of that doctrine would apply, *mutatis mutandis*, to Gandhi's theories.

That Gandhi subscribed to the view that there can be no violence (in an evil sense) without infraction of duty can be seen from the following:

> If the milk drivers of New York have a grievance against the municipality from criminal mismanagement of its trust and if, in order to bend it, they decide to cut off the milk supply, they would be guilty of a crime against humanity. But suppose that the milk drivers were underpaid by their employers, that they were consequently starving, they would be justified if they had tried every other available and proper method of securing better wages, in refusing to drive the milk carts even though their action resulted in the deaths of the babies of New York. . . . It was no part of their duties as employees under every circumstance to supply milk to babies. There is no violence when there is no infraction of duty. (*N.V.R.*, p. 167)

He then goes on to apply such ideas to the Indian non-cooperation movement – which involved the boycott of foreign goods:

> If the people in Lancashire . . . suffer thereby, non-cooperation cannot by any law of morals be held to be an act of violence. India never bound herself to maintain Lancashire. (*N.V.R.*, p. 168)

Since Gandhi believed that coercion was a species of violence, he was committed to the view that coercion presupposes a violation of duty.

Rawls is aware of the anarchical dangers of civil disobedience, but he is also impressed by the fact that civil disobedience can work as a stabilizing device. One of his chief concerns is that his near-just society should not be allowed to degenerate. I suspect that he believes that one of the main advantages his society has over a hierarchical Utopia is that his Utopia is, if properly constructed, likely to be more stable over time. According to Rawls, in his near-just society one of the chief safeguards against degeneration is the devotion to the principles of justice that the citizens have, their natural duty to justice and just institutions. Civil disobedience, when properly conducted, may convert the authorities and help to bring them back to the just path; on the other hand, submission to substantial injustice can sometimes make the perpetrators of injustice feel contempt for their victims, and confirm them (the perpetrators) in their unjust ways. So civil disobedience can sometimes make civil liberties more rather than less secure (*T. of J.*, p. 384). There are, I think, two kinds of stability worth distinguishing. A hierarchical society or a Brave New World may be stable in the sense that it may manage to preserve itself for long periods; but even if it does so it will, from the point of view of the lover of equality and autonomy, be a degenerate system. Now Rawls, when he talks of stability, must be taken to mean not just absence of change, but absence of degeneration and decadence.

So we can make several replies to the person who is ultra-cautious about embarking on civil disobedience. First . . . the state can reduce the danger of anarchy by stepping up the penalties for disobedience. Second, there is the Gandhian safety-valve argument. And third, there is the Rawlsian argument that if you do not resort to civil disobedience this may confirm and encourage the authorities in their unjust ways, thus leading to degeneration of the system.

Rawls also has the argument that if legitimate civil disobedience leads to untoward consequences, the responsibility lies with the perpetrators of the injustice rather than with the disobedients. This argument is similar to Gandhi's argument mentioned earlier about Indian non-cooperators not being responsible for what happens to Lancashire. I think there is considerable force in such arguments, but they have to be used with care. When Nixon was in power, towards the end of his period in office there was a rumour that if he was impeached something terrible might happen, e.g. he might in a fit of lunacy start a nuclear war. Now it was rightly felt by most congressmen that the chances of such a catastrophe were too small to outweigh the evil of putting up with a corrupt president. But *suppose* the chances of a catastrophe were much higher. In that event surely it would have been the height of irresponsibility to neglect such probabilities by arguing that if the catastrophe takes place the responsibility will be Nixon's, not ours. Surely, if the chances of a catastrophe had been high enough, it would have been the duty of congressmen to put up with a wicked president, assuming that there really was no third way out. Similarly, suppose the civil disobedients insisted on getting their injustice redressed, and that their demands (along with other similar demands which are in fact likely to be made) are likely to lead to a social catastrophe much greater than the initial injustice. The civil disobedients must not neglect such consequences. But when the consequences are not so grave, or not sufficiently probable, the civil disobedients can more plausibly argue that they should not be held responsible for any untoward consequences. Even from the consequentialist point of view one must take into account the suffering of those upon whom the initial injustice was imposed. Often such sufferings, if not redressed, are of a worse order than any evil that may result from the civil disobedience movement.

10

CIVIL DISOBEDIENCE

Joseph Raz

COMMON PHILOSOPHICAL ATTITUDES TO CIVIL DISOBEDIENCE

It is common ground to most discussions of the subject, and one which I share, that civil disobedience is sometimes justified or even obligatory. Many authors do tend to favour a stronger view which they often fail clearly to separate from this one, namely that one has, under certain conditions, a right to civil disobedience. It is, therefore, necessary to clarify the difference between these claims.

Consider an analogous case. People have, let us assume, a moral right to freedom of expression. That right extends to cases in which one should not exercise it. One should not repeat stories about people which one does not believe to be true. But one has a right to do so. The right to free expression is not recognized in the law of the Soviet Union despite the fact that it is permissible there to express views agreeable to the Soviet Communist Party. The reason one says that the right is there denied is not because the views of the Communist Party are wrong and should not be expressed. Even one who accepts their truth will have to admit that there is no freedom of expression in the Soviet Union, though he may find no fault in this. Freedom of expression is denied there not because one cannot express true beliefs but because one cannot express false ones, beliefs which one should not have nor express. This and nothing less is implied by the common observation that the freedom is to express any view one

From: Joseph Raz, *The Authority of Law* (Oxford: The Clarendon Press, 1979), pp. 266–75.

wishes (subject to a certain small number of restrictions such as that against libel).

At first blush it may be thought surprising that one should have a right to do that which one ought not. Is it not better to confine rights to that which it is right or at least permissible to do? But to say this is to misunderstand the nature of rights. One needs no right to be entitled to do the right thing. That it is right gives one all the title one needs. But one needs a right to be entitled to do that which one should not. It is an essential element of rights to action that they entitle one to do that which one should not. To say this is not, of course, to say that the purpose or justification of rights of action is to increase wrong-doing. Their purpose is to develop and protect the autonomy of the agent. They entitle him to choose for himself rightly or wrongly. But they cannot do that unless they entitle him to choose wrongly.[1]

Herein lies the difference between asserting that civil disobedience is sometimes right and claiming that one has, under certain conditions, a right to civil disobedience. The latter claim entails, as the first does not, that one is, under those conditions, entitled civilly to disobey even though one should not do so.

I have said that more writers than those who openly endorse such a right gravitate towards supporting its existence. This tendency is manifested in their concern with setting formal limits on the permissible forms of civil disobedience. Consider one often discussed limitation: civil disobedience, it is often said, must be non-violent. It is clear that, other things being equal, non-violent disobedience is much to be preferred to violent disobedience. First, the direct harm caused by the violence is avoided. Secondly, the possible encouragement to resort to violence in cases where this would be wrong, which even an otherwise justified use of violence provides, is avoided. Thirdly, the use of violence is a highly emotional and explosive issue in many countries and in turning to violence one is likely to antagonize potential allies and confirm in their opposition many of one's opponents. All these considerations, and others, suggest

1 These comments on rights to act are in keeping with the general analysis of rights developed in several articles by H. L. A. Hart, even though they do not commit me to all the details of his views. Cf., for example, 'Bentham on Legal Rights,' in A. W. B. Simpson (ed.), *Oxford Essays in Jurisprudence*, 2nd series (Oxford, 1973).

great reluctance to turn to the use of violence, most particularly violence against the person. But do they justify the total proscription of violence as a means to achieving a political aim? They do not. The evil the disobedience is designed to rectify may be so great, may indeed itself involve violence against innocent persons (such as the imprisonment of dissidents in labour camps in the Soviet Union), that it may be right to use violence to bring it to an end. It may be relevant here to draw attention to the fact that certain non-violent acts, indeed some lawful acts, may well have much more severe consequences than many an act of violence: consider the possible effects of a strike by ambulance drivers.

Some people do of course reject the use of violence absolutely regardless of any other considerations. Pacifists take such a view. But on any other basis violence for political gains cannot be rejected absolutely.[2] Many writers have argued for similar conclusions. My aim is not to vindicate the use of violence, which I would hope to see used only very rarely and with great caution. My aim is to point to the (often silent) presuppositions of the argument to condemn all violent civil disobedience by people who are not pacifists and do not reject all violence as wrong absolutely. This rejection of violence is due no doubt to a certain extent to a somewhat confused apprehension of the various considerations mitigating against violence mentioned above, but to a certain extent they are inspired by a feeling that if civil disobedience is justified then there is a right to it.

To say that there is a right to civil disobedience is to allow the legitimacy of resorting to this form of political action to one's political opponents. It is to allow that the legitimacy of civil disobedience does not depend on the rightness of one's cause. The comments above make clear that by all accounts the rightness of the cause it is meant to support. There is always the question of the appropriateness of the means. Will they not contribute to an even greater evil, are there not less harmful or less risky ways of supporting the same cause, etc.? Those who hold that there is a right to civil disobedience are committed to the view that in general[3] the rightness of the cause contributes

2 Some will say that violent action cannot be considered civil disobedience because by its meaning civil disobedience does not apply to such action. But even if right this is irrelevant. Such a linguistic point cannot prove the wrongness of my action.

3 Many if not all political theories rule out certain political goals as altogether illegitimate and do not extend to them any toleration.

not at all to the justification of civil disobedience. Such a view leads quite naturally to a consideration of formal limits on the forms such disobedience may take.

The logic of such reasoning becomes transparent once one considers the similar line of reasoning concerning lawful political action. Liberal states do not make the legitimacy of political action dependent on the cause it is meant to serve. People may support political aims of all complexions.[4] But the right to political action is circumscribed in such states by limitations as to the form of the permissible actions. Given that we are used to thinking in this way of lawful political action, it is only natural to extend the same approach to unlawful political activity. Such an attitude regards pursuit of political goals of all kinds – good as well as bad – through civil disobedience as justified provided one observes the forms of permissible action.

Considered against this background it is understandable that so much intellectual effort has been invested in an attempt to articulate and justify a doctrine of the permissible forms of civil disobedience. It must be used as a measure of last resort after all other means have failed to obtain one's desired goal; it must be non-violent; it must be openly undertaken; and its perpetrators must submit to prosecution and punishment; such acts must be confined to those designed to publicize certain wrongs and to convince the public and the authorities of the justice of one's claims; it should not be used to intimidate or coerce. Such and similar conditions have been much discussed and often favoured. All of them are open to objections similar to those deployed above against the non-violence requirements. Why, for example, should civil disobedience be always thought of as a measure of last resort? True, other things being equal, it has by-products (setting a bad example even if the act is justified in the instant case) which lawful political action does not have. But other things are rarely equal and sometimes civil disobedience should be preferred to lawful action even when that action will be effective. Which is worse: a miners' march in London which perpetrates various offences such as obstruction to the highway, or a lawful lengthy miners' strike?

Such objections are correct. But to be completely successful they must tackle directly the reasoning which leads to such

4 Subject to the proviso above.

apparently arbitrary restrictions on legitimate civil disobedience. It is necessary to examine the question of the right to civil disobedience.

A RIGHT TO POLITICAL PARTICIPATION

There are some bad arguments for a right to civil disobedience:

(1) It could be argued that since one's own acts of civil disobedience may well encourage others to break the law in pursuit of their wrong political objectives one is not entitled to engage in such activities unless they are similarly entitled. This is a *non sequitur.* If one's otherwise justified disobedience may lead others to disobey in circumstances where it is wrong to do so, then one's own disobedience is permissible only if it is justified to run the risk of this happening, that is only if the advantages of one's disobedience are sufficient to outweigh this as well as all the other resulting disadvantages. It does not follow that others have a right to disobey for wrong objectives, only that one should be cautious in considering disobedience for it may lead others to do so.

(2) It could be argued that there is a right to civil disobedience, for the contrary is conceivable only if there is a moral authority to judge which causes are right and which are wrong. Since there are no such moral authorities, since everyone has an equal right to judge for himself what is right and what is wrong, it follows that everyone has a right to civil disobedience in support of a cause which he finds to be right, even if it is in fact wrong. But this argument is valid only if it follows from the admitted fact that there are no general moral authorities, that each person is an ultimate and unchallengeable authority concerning the morality of his own actions. But in fact all that follows is that nobody is. Therefore, moral disagreements cannot be resolved by appeal to authority – not even that of the individual concerning his own actions – but, if at all, only by resort to substantive rational argument. Therefore, it does not follow that there is a right to disobedience, though it is true that there are no moral authorities who can judge whether the disobedience is justified or not.

(3) It could be argued that since it is unfair to deny to others

what one allows oneself, it follows that if one allows oneself to resort to civil disobedience in support of one's political goals one should allow others the right to use civil disobedience to support theirs. But this is at best an argument *ad hominem*. People who defend their own disobedience by reference to their right to pursue their political goals by such means cannot in fairness deny a similar right to their political opponents. But a person who supports his action by argument to show that it is in defence of a just cause can without unfairness deny a right to civil disobedience. He allows others to perform similar actions in pursuit of similarly just aims. He denies both himself and others the right to disobey in support of morally wrong aims.

(4) Some may argue from relativism. Since there is no rationally conclusive proof of moral right and wrong, one could not defend civil disobedience by relying on the rightness of one's cause. It cannot be proved and hence if one is justified in acting on one's beliefs one must, to be consistent, allow others the right to act in support of their beliefs. This argument is flawed. If interpreted in the spirit of radical scepticism it leads to the conclusion that no moral conclusions can ever be rationally held or defended and therefore it is rationally impossible to hold or defend the view that there is a right to civil disobedience. Interpreted as an argument for relativism rather than scepticism, it means that though one can rationally hold moral views one cannot conclusively prove their validity so that people presented with the evidence will be irrational not to endorse the conclusion. But then if one rationally believes a certain political ideal to be invalid, the fact that others are not irrational to reject this view does not entail that one cannot hold them immoral for acting on it. On the contrary, by one's very (rational) commitment to the view that the ideal is wrong, one is committed to the view that so is action based on it. No right to civil disobedience can be established in this way.[5]

We need to make a new beginning, to find a way of relating the general principles governing the right to lawful political activity

5 This argument shows that nothing in this essay presupposes either the truth or falsity of relativism.

to the question of civil disobedience. But it is not possible to return here to first principles. Instead I shall take it for granted that every person has a right to political participation in his society. Let me call this the liberal principle. I do not call it the democratic principle for in itself it does not commit one to a democratic government, only to a right to a certain degree of political participation. Nothing in the argument that follows depends on one's assessment of the precise limits of the right and I shall not attempt to specify them. It is clear, nevertheless, that the right to political participation is limited. It is limited because of the need to respect the same right in others and because the right to political participation is neither the only nor an absolute value and it has to be limited in order to safeguard other values. It is further clear that, subject to certain limited possible objections, the limitations on the scope of the right are independent of the political objective sought. The right means nothing if it does not mean the right of every member of a society to try to get his society to endorse, at least to some degree, political objectives which he supports, be they what they may. Given that by and large the limitations on the right are independent of the political objectives the right is used to support, they must inevitably turn on the means used to support such objectives. It must be a right confined to certain forms of action and not to others.

The most direct implication of the limited right to political participation is that it is binding on law-makers. It should be recognized and defended by the law. In other words the law should set limits to one's legal right to political activity and these should coincide with those which are right on moral and political grounds. To say this is not to imply that the extent of the moral right should affect but not itself be affected by legal rules. Many alternative determinations of the precise boundaries of the right may be largely equivalent in value and many more possible determinations are better or worse than the optimum by small margins. Furthermore, it is greatly desirable to have the limits declared in an open and public way by a generally accepted authority. Therefore, if the legally declared boundaries of the right of political action fall within the area of reasonable potential determinations the fact that they are legally declared makes them morally binding. An argument in favour of an otherwise slightly superior potential solution will not succeed in undermining the morally binding force of an otherwise slightly inferior but legally endorsed boundary. In this way the law affects one's moral right to political action. But principally it should be moulded by it.

All states can accordingly be divided into those in which the liberal principle is adequately recognized and protected in law and those in which it is not. Let states of the first kind be called 'liberal states' and the others 'illiberal states'. The main presupposition of this essay is that all states ought to be liberal states. The two main conclusions entailed by this view are that (1) there is no moral right to civil disobedience in liberal states; (2) normally there is such a right in illiberal states.

CIVIL DISOBEDIENCE IN A LIBERAL STATE

Given that the illiberal state violates its members' right of political participation, individuals whose rights are violated are entitled, other things being equal, to disregard the offending laws and exercise their moral right as if it were recognized by law. Of course, other things are rarely equal. In the illiberal state, to exercise one's right may involve breaking the law and such action will sometimes have undesirable consequences, which would have been avoided had the action been lawful. Therefore, the illiberality of the illiberal state may have the effect of narrowing down the *moral* right to political action of its members. However, subject to this reservation, members of the illiberal state do have a right to civil disobedience which is roughly that part of their moral right to political participation which is not recognized in law.

The case is reversed in a liberal state. Here there can be no right to civil disobedience which derives from a general right to political participation. One's right to political activity is, by hypothesis, adequately protected by law. It can never justify breaking it. Put it another way: every claim that one's right to political participation entitles one to take a certain action in support of one's political aims (be they what they may), even though it is against the law, is *ipso facto* a criticism of the law for outlawing this action. For if one has a right to perform it its performance should not be civil disobedience but a lawful political act. Since by hypothesis no such criticism can be directed against the liberal state there can be no right to civil disobedience in it.

166

This conclusion does not mean that civil disobedience in a liberal state is never justified. A liberal state was defined in a rather technical and narrow sense. It is simply one which respects the right to political participation. It may contain any number of bad and iniquitous laws. Sometimes it will be right to engage in civil disobedience to protest against them or against bad public policies. The practical implications of the argument above concerning disobedience in a liberal state are as follows:

Generally two kinds of argument are relevant for judging another person's action, two kinds of argument that a man can use to convince another rationally that he is entitled to perform a certain act. He can show that the act is right (or that there is reason to think that it is) or he can show that he has (or that there is reason to think that he has) a right to perform it. To show that the act is right is to get the other person to approve its performance. To show that one has a right to it is to show that even if it is wrong he is entitled to perform it. In a liberal state the second argument is not available in defence of civil disobedience. It can be rationally supported by people who approve its aims, but it has no claim to the toleration of those who do not. There could, for example, be no claim that the general public or public authorities shall not take action to prevent the disobedience or to punish its commission (provided such action is proportionate to the offence, etc.) which is based on a right to toleration.[6] The only moral claim for support or non-interference must be based on the rightness of the political goal of the disobedient.[7]

6 If the state authorities come to share (to a sufficient degree) the views of the civil disobedients they should not, other things being equal, prosecute them, for people should not be punished for doing the right thing. If a judge or a prosecutor comes to side with the protesters against the authorities he may find it necessary to resign or civilly disobey or both.

7 Two possible ojections should be mentioned and dismissed. It may be said that the law cannot set the right limits to political action for it cannot set limits to specifically political action. If a road is closed it must be closed to all. If it is open it will be open to all. It cannot be closed to some and open to others, closed to the general public and open to demonstrators. The answer to this objection is just to deny its premiss. It is often possible and practical to permit action for political reasons where similar action for other reasons is proscribed. Admittedly sometimes this is impractical, but there is no reason to think that, given the many alternative forms political action can take, the law cannot set reasonable boundaries to political action.

Some may think that the argument in the essay disregards the desirability of encouraging pluralism in the society. Pluralism would lead to dissent and to civil disobedience and if it is desirable its inevitable consequences should be tolerated. The fallacy in this argument is to suppose that pluralism must lead to dissent and

I said that the practical implications of the absence of a right to civil disobedience in a liberal state affect one person's judgment of another's action and the agent's way of defending his action to others. Does it not affect the agent's own practical deliberations? Having a right to perform an action is no reason to do it. One has to be convinced that the action is right. Otherwise one's action will be an abuse of one's rights. But it is sometimes thought that having a right to act is, in general, a precondition for its being right to do so. No doubt this is sometimes the case. For example, since one has no right to interfere in a stranger's private affairs it is never (or almost never) right to do so, even though having a right to interfere in one's wife's private affairs does not mean that it is generally right to do so. But whether or not having a right to act is a precondition of the rightness of the act depends on the underlying reasoning supporting the claim of a right and its limitation. The reason for the limits on the right to political participation is to set a boundary to one's toleration of unjustified political action. It therefore does not affect the agent's own reasoning so long as he is confident that his action is justified.

Yet more indirectly the absence of a right to civil disobedience in liberal states does affect even the agent's own reasoning. First, he may be less than certain that his action is justified and, therefore, caution may advise desisting from an action to which one may not be entitled. Secondly, civil disobedience is a very divisive action. It is all the more so because of the absence of a right to it (in liberal states). In taking a civilly disobedient action one steps outside the legitimate bounds of toleration and this in itself adds to its disadvantages and should make one very reluctant to engage in it.

The argument above explains the sense in which civil disobedience is an exceptional political action. It is exceptional, in liberal states, in being one beyond the bounds of toleration, beyond the general right to political action. It is not necessarily, as is sometimes said, justified only as an action of last resort. In support of a just cause it may be less harmful than certain kinds of lawful action (e.g. a national strike, or a long strike in a key

disobedience. It will do so if the law does not allow for pluralistic forms of life to flourish. If the law encourages and respects pluralism it need not lead to dissent from law. It can find adequate expression within it.

168

industry or service). It may be wrong not to resort to civil disobedience and to turn to such lawful action first, or give up any action in support of a just cause. The claim that civil disobedience is justified only when all else has failed or is certain to fail, like the claims that it should be open and non-violent, etc., reflects a failure to conceive its true nature. It is an attempt to routinize it and make it a regular form of political action to which all have a right. Its exceptional character lies precisely in the reverse of this claim, in the fact that it is (in liberal states) one type of political action to which one has no right.

11

JUSTIFYING NONVIOLENT DISOBEDIENCE

Kent Greenawalt

This chapter concentrates on [. . .] the status of particular factors that have often been thought to be critical to whether disobedience of law is justified. I consider, in turn, the relevance of (1) claims that behavior is legally justified, (2) the exhaustion of political remedies, (3) the nature of objections to laws, policies, or practices, and the purposes behind violation, (4) the relation between the laws broken and the laws or policies protested against, (5) the interests affected by violations, and (6) the openness of behavior and acceptance of punishment. In this chapter I deal only with nonviolent disobedience, postponing the problem of violence until the next chapter. Here I treat situations in which the reasons for disobedience do not involve any fundamental challenge to the way the political order is constituted.

Placing the factors discussed here in the context of reasons to obey and disobey is complicated because of the variety of those reasons. Morally acceptable reasons for disobedience include overriding obligations to others, conscientious objection to performing required acts, belief that disobedience will promote justice or welfare, and, occasionally, strong personal motivations. Arrayed against these sorts of reasons are nonconsequential duties and consequential reasons in favor of obeying laws and whatever independent moral reasons support doing the acts the law requires. The factors I consider may occasionally affect the strength of a reason to disobey, but more typically their force concerns the reasons to obey. Their presence or absence may

From: Kent Greenawalt, *Conflicts of Law and Morality* (Oxford University Press, 1987), pp. 226–43.

eliminate or mitigate a nonconsequential duty to obey or affect its application. The factors may also have consequential importance.

CLAIMS OF LEGAL RIGHT

People may disobey particular legal norms in the belief that their behavior is justified under a high legal norm. Such situations can arise when an administrative or inferior legislative body exceeds authority granted by a superior legislature, but I shall focus on the familiar American context in which a law is thought to be invalid because it is unconstitutional.[1] The presence of a claim of legal right brings us to the definitional threshold of disobedience to law. If one's claim is upheld, one has not, in retrospect, disobeyed valid law; and if one believes one's claim will be upheld, one has not intentionally disobeyed valid law.[2] More important than the borders of what amounts to disobedience is the question of what effect a claim of legal right has on the moral reasons to comply with legal norms.

Among innumerable variations in circumstances I will consider three basic situations. In each, I assume that the actor's estimation of the likely success of his or her legal claim corresponds with the estimate an objective lawyer would make. I further assume that quick legislative review is unavailable, that a violation of the law is needed to get a judicial determination of validity,[3] and that the actor is willing to submit to the court's disposition.

In the first situation, Clay is reasonably sure his constitutional claim will be upheld. Any reasonable view of an individual's duties in a political order providing judicial review must include the appropriateness of testing the validity of laws that appear invalid.[4] No otherwise applicable deontological principle

1 Often a constitutional claim will be joined with a claim of moral right; here I am concerned only with the moral force of the claim that one's act is justifiable within the legal system itself.
2 People who raise test cases often have radically different motivations from those who engage in civil disobedience. See L. Buzzard and P. Campbell, *Holy Disobedience* (1984), 179, quoting an unpublished dissertation by Thomas Rekdal.
3 Generally, the validity of a criminal prohibition can be tested only by disobedience. Sometimes injunctions or declaratory judgments will afford a means to challenge legal norms without noncompliance.
4 The point is even more obvious if a statute is clearly and blatantly unconstitutional.

would require obedience when disobedience is the only avenue for testing validity. From a utilitarian perspective, a challenge to a probably invalid law serves the objective of eliminating improper legal norms; the existence of the legal claim will also affect perceptions of a violation, making it appear as something other than a challenge to the legal order. The question about obedience becomes somewhat more difficult if already pending cases adequately raise all legal issues, or if these can be raised without anyone's disobeying. Since one's own violation serves no testing objective, disobedience cannot be justified on that score. But, at least if the likelihood of invalidation is very high and disobedience will not be seriously unsettling, one should simply not be thought bound to comply with such 'laws.' [5]

In the second situation, Clay thinks that a significant doubt exists about the law's constitutionality but understands that a legal challenge is more likely than not to fail. Deontological standards and utilitarian considerations should be understood to permit disobedience, since serious but probably losing challenges are a healthy part of the legal order. Such challenges sometimes succeed, and even when they do not they may contribute to the development of constitutional law. When the likelihood of success is not great, however, the justification for disobedience may not extend beyond the cases necessary to raise the legal issues of invalidity.

In the third situation, Clay has a firm personal view about constitutionality that he knows will not succeed in court; he believes, say, that conscription violates the Thirteenth Amendment ban on involuntary servitude. If the courts will predictably dismiss his position as frivolous, his disobedience will not promote legal development; and given people's familiarity with wild ideas being dressed in the clothing of constitutional right, public perceptions of his violation of a draft law will be little influenced by his announcement of a constitutional justification. [6]

How nonconsequential duties are affected by Clay's view is

5 This conclusion would be strengthened if the probably invalid law inhibited an important personal liberty. Were the legal system to demand initial compliance with invalid laws, as the American system does demand compliance with improper injunctions, the conclusion would be altered.
6 The reactions of people who know him well might be significantly affected by his constitutional conviction.

more difficult. Clay might argue that his consent, duty of fair play, or natural duty extends only to laws he regards as valid. But that position would be too simple. A duty to obey the law should be understood in relation to a whole system of governance, including processes of interpretation, and one's own views about what *should* be declared legally invalid should not count for very much. Very few people even have reflective views about the content of constitutional standards; for them the constitutional claim will be little more than an elaboration of a moral or political conviction, one that does not gain greater force by being put in the language of legal validity.[7] Within a stable legal order and with respect to issues that courts adjudicate,[8] the special claim that one is really acting within the law changes the nature of obedience only when a real prospect exists that the norm that is disobeyed will be held invalid.

In the sections that follow, I will assume that no claim of legal invalidity is involved, that the actor is committing what he understands to be a violation of the positive law of his society.

PURSUIT OF LAWFUL ALTERNATIVES

A commonly stated condition of justifiable disobedience is that lawful alternatives for changing a law or policy have been pursued. The illustration [omitted here] involving the faculty resolution about the content of the constitutional law course shows the basic soundness of this position. Presenting one's views in a full and orderly fashion to those who have made or are to make a decision can be an important aspect of duties based on consent or fairness. Even if one is permitted finally to disobey, one at least owes it to one's fellows to try to avoid that impasse by persuading them to change their minds. From a utilitarian perspective, considerations of mutual respect and avoidance of unnecessary disruption counsel a similar course. Of course, in a large political unit, few individuals will have an opportunity to

7 I am not suggesting that the actor should disregard his moral conviction, only that his idiosyncratic view about the scope of the Constitution should carry little weight by itself.
8 If the actor's claim is that a law is unconstitutional and no relatively detached organ of government stands ready to interpret the Constitution with respect to that claim - say, because of the political question doctrine - the individual's interpretation may carry more moral significance, particularly if it enjoys some support by others.

air their views fully; but individuals can wait until the positions they accept have been presented by someone about as well as they can be.

The principle that people should exhaust lawful political remedies before turning to disobedience requires some qualification. It, of course, does not apply when one has no objection to a law or policy, but simply believes he has an overriding obligation, say to a family member. Nor does it apply when the law requires an act that one cannot in conscience perform and one must perform the act before pursuit of lawful alternatives is possible. What the principle reaches are situations in which obedience is aimed at overturning a law, policy, or practice. Even then, pursuit of lawful alternatives may not be required if they are patently futile. When *some* efforts have been made to get ordinary political redress, people may sharply disagree over the adequacy of the efforts and whether they can yet be declared unsuccessful.[9] Though the basic principle itself is widely accepted, and properly so, the way it applies to particular circumstances will often be highly controversial.

THE NATURE OF OBJECTIONS TO LAWS, POLICIES, OR PRACTICES, AND THE PURPOSES BEHIND VIOLATIONS

People disobey the law with some frequency, believing that pursuit of their own personal objectives justifies rather trivial violations or that a competing obligation overrides the duty to obey. But the most serious and notable instances in which people who break the law think they are morally justified are ones in which they object to a law, policy, or practice. If the law compels an act that a person cannot conscientiously perform, say to join the military, an outsider cannot evaluate his justification for refusing to do the act short of assessing all the moral reasons that led him to think the act is absolutely forbidden. Not much of general application can be said about these clashes of conscience and law. Nor can much be said if the actor's position is that the harm done to other persons by a rule of law is so great that its

---

9 The disagreement, of course, will not be merely or mainly factual. People will have different views on how great the efforts must be and how long they must continue without success before disobedience is warranted.

circumvention is demanded by conscience – the position taken by those who aided fugitive slaves and, more recently, by many in the 'Sanctuary' movement who have helped persons they consider victims of injustice to evade immigration restrictions.[10]

Some writers have thought that more definitive guidelines are possible when obedience is mainly aimed at changing a law or policy. Such disobedience is almost always a collective act.[11] Possible guidelines concern the reasons people disobey, the conditions in which they do so, and the tactics they employ. I concentrate in this section on the first of these factors, restricting myself to nonviolent responses to the law.

I ask particularly whether it is crucial to justification of nonviolent disobedience that it is directed at influencing the majority's sense of justice and is responsive to injustices of a substantial magnitude. Such limits have been offered either as part of the definition of civil disobedience or as conditions of justifiable civil disobedience. Although the possibility of otherwise justifiable disobedience may be left open,[12] the implicit assumption is that what does not qualify as justifiable civil disobedience will be harder to justify and may require qualitatively different justification.

Various authors have expressed the ideas that justified civil disobedience must appeal to the sense of justice of the majority[13] or must involve claims of genuine injustice,[14] or both; but since these notions receive systematic explication in John Rawls's well-known account, I will concentrate on that. According to Rawls, a person who engages in civil disobedience 'invokes the commonly shared conception of justice that underlies the political order,'[15] declaring that principles of justice are not being respected[16] and aiming to make the majority reconsider the justice of its actions. Ordinarily, justified civil disobedience will be limited 'to instances

10 See Buzzard and Campbell, op. cit. note 2 at 17, 148; 'Trial Opening in Arizona in Alien Sanctuary Case,' *New York Times*, Oct. 21, 1985, Section A.
11 See M. Walzer, *Obligations: Essays on Disobedience, War and Citizenship* (1970); Flynn, 'Collective Responsibility and Obedience to Law,' 18 Ga. L. Rev. (1984), 845, 859.
12 See, e.g., J. Rawls, *A Theory of Justice*, (1971), 363–68.
13 See, e.g., P. Singer, *Practical Ethics*, (1979) 192, who speaks of civil disobedience as trying to get a genuine expression of majority rule.
14 See, e.g., Buzzard and Campbell, op. cit. note 2 at 100. H. Bedau (ed.), *Civil Disobedience: Theory and Practice* (1969), 23.
15 Rawls, op. cit. at 365.
16 ibid., at 364.

of substantial and clear injustice, and preferably to those which obstruct the path to removing other injustices.' [17] Involving resistance to injustice within the limits of fidelity of law, civil disobedience will help inhibit and correct departures from justice and can contribute to stability in a well-ordered society.[18]

In excluding circumstances in which those who disobey seek mainly to bring the majority around by causing more inconvenience than the majority will tolerate, and also excluding appeals that are not directed at the majority or are not based on the majority's shared conception of justice, Rawls's concept of civil disobedience is a good bit narrower than many other formulations.[19] What I examine is whether disobedience that is either excluded by Rawls's definition or does not fit within his principles of justification is indeed much more difficult to justify than what he treats as justifiable civil disobedience.

Illustration 10-1:
Vegetarians who believe that the killing of nonhuman animals for food violates the animals' moral rights[20] consider whether to lie down in the midst of a stockyard as a protest against that practice. They think that publicizing their position by risking physical harm and suffering arrest may lead some people who already have qualms about the practice to become vegetarians or quit jobs in the meat industry. They hope that others will begin to think more seriously about the problem and that over the long term a majority of society will come to accept their view and will outlaw killing animals for meat; but they recognize the latter development will take generations.

From the vegetarians' point of view, a grave moral wrong is being committed against defenseless beings who deserve protection. They seek to draw attention to this moral wrong in much the same way that other illegal demonstrations attempt to highlight wrongs. Even if human beings can have duties of justice to animals, the vegetarians do not appeal to the majority's shared conception of justice, which recognizes no rights of the

17 ibid., at 372.
18 ibid., at 382.
19 Compare Hugo Bedau's definition, in Bedau, op. cit., note 14 at 218: 'Anyone commits an act of civil disobedience if and only if he acts illegally, publicly, nonviolently, and conscientiously with the intent to frustrate (one of) the laws, policies, or decisions of his government.'
20 Some may quarrel with the terminology of rights and justice for entities that are not potential participants in the moral community. The crucial question is whether we can have moral duties toward such entities. Rawls assumes that we can (see Rawls, op. cit. note 12 at 17, 512), although he apparently believes that the vocabulary of justice is inappropriate for those duties.

sort they claim. No doubt, the vegetarians' hope to influence the views of their fellow citizens is based on a point of connection between their views and ordinary moral sympathies, which include respect for life and a limited concern for nonhuman animals. But when Rawls talks of 'invoking a commonly shared conception,' he requires a much stronger identity between the moral convictions of the majority and those disobeying than any the vegetarians can claim. Moreover, the vegetarians in this particular demonstration are mainly aiming at a passive minority that is already sympathetic to their position, so only in a very long-term sense are the demonstrators really addressing the majority at all. Yet if they are at all successful, the immediate result will be both *some reduction* in a practice they consider barbarous and an initial positive step toward wider reform.

If the aim of civil disobedience must be to keep the nearly just society true to its own present convictions, then the vegetarians cannot engage in justifiable civil disobedience. But what the illustration shows is that the reasons for open and peaceful disobedience are not limited to that purpose. The vegetarians do lack a justification derived from the existing political order that Rawlsian demonstrators will have,[21] but the two aims to transform a society's moral consciousness over time[22] and to reach a minority who themselves can quickly reduce the incidence of serious wrongs might also warrant peaceful disobedience. If the demonstrators submit to physical risk and to legal processes and possible punishment, their tactics are not likely to be so widely replicated as to threaten the society's stability. The claims of obedience are often weighty, and they are especially strong when the law represents the considered opinion of the majority; but these claims do not absolutely preclude every instance of disobedience that is intended to sensitize people to grave moral wrongs that are not yet widely recognized.[23]

21 In *Practical Ethics* (op. cit., note 13, at 182–95), Peter Singer discusses violations of law by Britain's Animal Liberation Front. He apparently supposes that the particular aims of the demonstrators, such as to stop the exploitation of factory farming, are consonant with the majority's moral sense.
22 See B. Zwiebach, *Civility and Disobedience* (1975), 154, who points out 'the historical rule of disobedience in the and articulation of new and valuable rights.'
23 See P. Singer, op. cit., note 13 at 192–5. Rawls himself, it should be noted, does not assert any absolute preclusion, and he does not develop how much harder it may be to justify nonviolent disobedience that does not qualify as justified civil disobedience.

Illustration 10-2:
A neighborhood is undergoing what has come to be known as
'gentrification.' Many buildings in which poor people live are being
torn down to provide luxury housing, and in other buildings rents are
being raised so fast that most present residents must leave. Poor
residents and their sympathizers consider trespassory occupations of
buildings doomed to destruction. They hope to persuade city officials
that the laws and policies that permit such rapid change are unjust in
conception; that, in any event, the strongly held feelings of injustice
by those affected should not be overridden; and that attempts to
override those feelings will cause inconvenience and embarrassment to
the officials.

The potential demonstrators, unlike the vegetarians, have at
least a plausible if debatable argument that failure to protect
poor residents offends present conceptions of justice between rich
and poor as they affect security of dwellings. The triple message
the demonstrators wish to convey is common to most illegal
political demonstrations. The first message is that, in its initial
disposition, the majority or the government acted unjustly given
the facts available to it. On this score, the demonstration is meant
to illuminate the seriousness of the issue and encourage sober
reconsideration. The second message introduces the intensity of
the minority's feelings as a new element in calculations of justice.
It says, 'Even if you are still persuaded you were right in the first
place, you should now change course when you realize the
strength of our contrary feelings.' Perhaps this notion is most
familiar in the claim that a country should not fight a foreign
war over an intense minority opposition. What Rawls says about
appealing to the majority's sense of justice mainly refers to the
basic merits of the issue, but the message that is grounded on the
relevance of a minority's intense opposition is also an appeal to
the majority's sense of justice and we should include it in what is
a proper part of civil disobedience.[24]

24 According to Rawls, 'The intensity of desire or strength of conviction is
irrelevant when questions of justice arise' (Rawls, op. cit. note 12 at 361). One is
hard put to understand how one could determine the justice of a policy that will
lead to dislocation without knowing how strongly people dislike being dis-
located; and their sense of resentment at being treated unjustly would also seem
relevant. Compare Rawls, 'The Justification of Civil Disobedience', in H. Bedau,
(ed.), op. cit. note 14 at 240, 253, in which he indicates that the majority's sense of
justice may be evidenced by an unwillingness to suppress the minority, but even
there he seems to suppose that the sense of injustice does not depend on the
minority's intensity.

The third message, that inconvenience and embarrassment will attend continuation of the present policy, is the most troubling and is not an appeal to a sense of justice at all. 'Coercion' may be too strong a word, but the demonstrators in this respect seek to manipulate costs and benefits in a way that will persuade those in charge that the present course is too expensive. Rawls is certainly right that pressure of this sort involves subversion of ordinary processes of decision-making in a way that appeals to justice do not. Because pressure is less reconcilable with adherence to ordinary processes, it does require stronger reasons to be justified. Both Gandhi and Martin Luther King, Jr, notable and reflective practitioners of civil disobedience, emphasized that the aim must be to transform opponents.[25] For them, civil disobedience was not a sophisticated method of force but one of persuasion. But in their actions, both recognized that inconvenience for oppressors might be a necessary means to focus their attention on the issue of justice.[26] In reality, among instances of civil disobedience *pure* appeals to justice are rare; some element of pressure is usually present. The line between trying to persuade the majority that it is 'unjust' to keep a committed minority in jail and trying to persuade the majority that jailing the minority will be inconvenient and unproductive is very thin indeed. Often those who disobey consciously seek to wear down as well as sensitize opponents; even when they do not, their tactics of disobedience are likely to exert pressure in fact.

Maintaining that success through such pressure is never a legitimate aim of civil disobedience may not be illogical; however, a more sensible position is that those who are willing to suffer to correct an injustice may sometimes convert that willingness into an aim to achieve a concession that the majority would not accord out of its own sense of justice.

Illustration 10-3:
Opponents of civilian nuclear power consider a trespassory demonstration at a site of a nuclear power plant to be built by a privately owned electric company. They hope both to persuade the company to

25 M. K. Gandhi, *Non-Violent Resistance*, (1961); M. L. King, Jr, *Strength to Love* (1963), 54.
26 See King's 'Letter from a Birmingham Jail' (1963), reprinted in Bedau, op. cit. note 14 at 72 [this volume, pp. 68–89].

abandon its plans and to alter public laws and policies that permit and favor such projects. Gerald believes that the public acceptance of such projects represents a clear injustice toward nearby residents and toward future generations. Wilma's view is somewhat different. She thinks that what has happened is an honest and understandable but terribly unfortunate misappraisal of the dangers of nuclear plants. She does not really blame anyone and thinks that the building of the plants would be warranted if the facts were as they are widely supposed. She has enormous respect for the minority of scientists who have estimated the dangers as very great and accepts their judgment.

One point of this illustration is to show how civil disobedience can be directed at decision-makers other than public officials.[27] Often, as here and in many of the illegal protests on private university campuses during the late 1960s in the United States, demonstrators take aim at both private institutional and public targets. As long as it does not seriously threaten the legal order, disobedience to correct private injustice cannot be ruled out on principle, although, like the vegetarian demonstration, such disobedience lacks the particular political justification that may exist when public policy is the target and is claimed to violate prevailing principles of justice.

The main objective of this illustration is to use the difference between George's and Wilma's views to test Rawls's assertion that one must appeal to the majority's sense *of justice*, a claim that follows from his more general position [. . .] that justice takes priority over utility. No doubt, Wilma is artificially drawn; those willing to put their bodies on the line usually find severe injustice someplace. But it is also true that many who consider illegal action draw no clear distinction between injustice and great harm. For Rawls, civil disobedience concerns only injustice, and a demonstration by Wilma and people of like view would be something other than civil disobedience. Rawls's approach would apparently require people considering disobedience to discount their fears about harms that do not derive from injustice. Yet if, as Wilma believes, what has happened is *only* a very bad policy decision[28] *and* disobedience is likely to

27 See, generally, M. Walzer, op. cit. note 11, at 25-43, who discusses illegal strikes mainly directed at changes in company policies.
28 One might argue that any stumbling decision by the government with very bad consequences is unjust to citizens but that extension of the concept of justice would turn any pressing utilitarian basis for public action into an issue of justice. For another interpretation of Rawls that sharply restricts instances of possibly

produce a careful reappraisal and possible reversal, the disobedience might well be warranted.[29] The intensity of opposition demonstrated by self-sacrificing disobedience can serve to promote reexamination of crucial factual data as well as claims of justice.

Illustration 10–4:
Parents in a neighborhood where two children have been killed at a busy intersection that has no stop sign consider whether or not to publicize the need for such signs by blocking traffic for an hour. They have unsuccessfully sought for many months to get the town to install signs.

One may question whether the sloppiness and inertia that prevent stop signs from being placed where they are needed amounts to injustice, but they are common failings of all governments and perhaps all human endeavor. Certainly the failure to install signs is not a major injustice. Yet a contained illegal demonstration of the sort contemplated seems warranted to protect the lives of other children. A sensible approach to disobedience must calibrate the degree of injustice or likely harm to the magnitude of the disobedience. Much less is needed to justify minor localized disobedience than major illegal demonstrations.

The discussion in this section has addressed a number of factors: (1) appeal to the majority, (2) appeal to a sense of justice, (3) appeal to a present sense of wrong, and (4) appeal based on a substantial wrong. Each of these appeals may be important to measuring the magnitude of claims to obey and disobey, but none marks a critical dividing line between justifiable civil disobedience and other disobedience.

RELATIONSHIP BETWEEN THE REASON FOR PROTEST AND THE LAW BROKEN

Disobedience is easier to justify when a close connection exists between the injustice or wrong protested and the law being disobeyed. The force of the example of disobedience will be more

justifiable civil disobedience, see J. Feinberg, 'Rawls and Intuitionism,' in N. Daniels, *Reading Rawls* (1975), 108, 120–1.
29 What is said here also applies to conscientious avoidance of legal requirements. If one believes that following the law will be very harmful for people, one may be warranted in not following the law, although no issue of justice is involved.

contained and the interests that are compromised by disobedience will be less likely to warrant protection. But one cannot move from these matters of degree to the position of Justice Abe Fortas that 'civil obedience . . . is never justified in our nation where the law being violated is not itself the focus or target of the protest.' [30]

A preliminary difficulty with this sharp distinction is the elusiveness of its application. Would a 'sit-in' by parents at a house that a developer has refused to sell to them because they have small children be an improper violation of the general trespass law, to which the parents do not object, or a proper violation of the laws that allow developers to refuse sales on this ground? What of refusal to submit to the draft because one is opposed to an unjust war? Would that be a proper violation, because most draftees are sent to the unjust war, or an improper violation, because the draft itself is acceptable?

These perplexities of application mainly highlight the basic indefensibility of a sharp distinction of this kind. The moral legitimacy of the interests that will be undermined by obedience does not turn simply on the justice or injustice of the law that is violated. Even unjust laws may generate expectations whose disappointment is unfortunate, and some of those who benefit from a just law, say against trespass, may by immoral behavior largely forfeit their moral claim to the protection of that law. A demonstrator against apartheid trespassing on the property of a South African embassy might take such a view about the moral rights of the South African government.

If justifiable protests were limited in the way Fortas suggested, some laws and policies – for example, a highly unjust definition of treason or an egregious use of military force abroad – might be entirely immune from law-violating protest, as would be any injustice that results from a failure to enact laws to prevent great wrongs. A means of protest is more appropriate when it is reasonably related to the matter under protest;[31] a trespassory demonstration at the Pentagon is a better means of protesting an unjust war than setting a fire in a national forest. But the strict

30 A Fortas, *Concerning Dissent and Civil Disobedience* (1968), 63.
31 See J. F. Childress, *Civil Disobedience and Political Obligation* (1971), 33; B. Zwiebach, op. cit. note 22 at 181-4; and W. L. Taylor, 'Civil Disobedience: Observations on the Strategies of Protest,' in H. Bedau, op. cit. note 14 at 98, 104-5.

principle that the very law that is violated must be what is protested makes no sense.[32]

INTERESTS AFFECTED BY A VIOLATION

The power of claims to obey depends in part on the interests affected by a violation of law. In this connection, I discuss both the immediate impact on the interests of others and possible longer-term effects.

Violations of law can have radically different impacts on the interests of other citizens. Some involve no direct and perceivable interference with their interests. A law designed to protect those interests may not do so in the particular circumstances in which it is violated.[33] Other laws are not even designed to protect other people from harm to their interests. Some, such as those against drug use, are meant to protect the persons against whom they are directed; others, such as those requiring payment of taxes, concern shared burdens.[34]

Violations of law that affect people's interests do so in various ways. Some illegal acts cause inconvenience to others. A loud-speaker that exceeds permissible limits of noise disturbs people; a subway strike in a big city can disrupt travel for millions of commuters. In yet other situations, something that people own is taken, destroyed, or interfered with. The line between inconvenience and deprivation of rights[35] is not a clear one, and it depends largely on which interests the legal system recognizes as rights.[36] Some forms of illegality, such as illegal sit-ins, may

32 The thoughts in this section are developed at greater length in Greenawalt, 'A Contextual Approach to Disobedience,' 70 Colum. L. Rev. 48, 67–9 (1970); also in J. R. Pennock and J. Chapman (eds), *Nomos XII, Political and Legal Obligation* (1970), 332.
33 I have in mind here examples such as the low speed limit that is really unnecessary at the time of day it is violated.
34 Of course, the citizenry, as beneficiaries of public expenditures, has an interest of a sort in each person paying his or her taxes, and each taxpayer may have an 'interest' in fair sharing of the burden. I am referring here to more concrete interference with interests.
35 Obvious instances of deprivations of rights are interferences with property rights, but the sense of owning something might extend to other kinds of rights, such as contract rights. I do not pause over the subtlety of whether or not people generally attach a special psychological significance to property rights.
36 A sense of ownership does not always track legal ownership; a member of a family or a corporate employee, for example, may have such a sense about something he or she does not legally own.

involve aspects of both inconvenience and impairment of property or other rights. The most severe harm is physical injury to persons. On some occasions, harm to persons may be a greater or lesser risk of acts that would not be characterized as violent, such as an illegal strike in winter by fuel-oil drivers, but I will disregard this complication.

One reason the nature of interference with the interests of others can affect justifications for obedience is that the independent moral reasons against behavior are stronger when more serious injuries are inflicted. Another reason is that some deontological standards favoring obedience have more force when schemes of social cooperation are designed to protect vital individual interests. There are consequential reasons as well. Human beings come to expect that certain of their interests will be protected by society. When this protection fails, the reaction is not only one of loss but also of frustration and insecurity, and the insecurity, at least, also extends to others who fear similar losses. For commuters and others, delays often translate into economic losses; but people suffer losses from inconvenience more readily than equally costly losses of property.[37] The deprivation of social expectations is felt more immediately and sharply when what is taken is something that one actually 'owns'. Beyond being unpleasant feelings, frustration and insecurity lead to withdrawal and retaliation, which are destructive. No doubt, as radical demonstrators during the 1960s often claimed,[38] on some occasions the person shaken by loss may re-examine complacent assumptions and recognize the injustice of the law or policy those who directly damaged him were protesting. But rejection of those who cause loss is much more typical, especially if the injury is a deprivation of rights.

Regarding many instances of obedience that cause harm to others, an important difference exists between expected harmful consequences and hoped-for beneficial ones. The former are virtually certain, the latter problematic. The greater the uncertainty that any good will be achieved, the greater that good would have to be to outweigh certain or highly probable harm.

I turn now to two longer-term effects that Rawls discusses. One

37 This distinction may not apply when the only property that is injured is property held by the government or a large private institution.
38 Keeping other students away from class was considered a device for radicalizing them.

of his conditions of justifiable civil obedience is that a group's violations of law will not lead to the kind of serious damage to the political order that may occur if too many groups, with various claims of injustice, disobey within a short time.[39] Within a nearly just society, such an overload should be avoided, although Rawls fails to suggest how hard it will be for any single group to decide whether its own choice to disobey will significantly worsen existing conditions.

The second longer-term effect Rawls addresses is provocation of the majority's harsh retaliation. If the danger is great, Rawls says a group may not be 'wise' or 'prudent' to disobey,[40] even though it has met the conditions for justifiable disobedience. Rawls's distinction between what is justifiable and what is prudent is another illustration of his priority of justice over utilitarian considerations. More specifically, he believes here that if victims of injustice are willing to risk further damage to their own interests triggered by their own otherwise justifiable response, the likelihood of further damage to them does not affect the justice of their own actions.

Unfortunately, this idea rests on an unrealistic picture of many large demonstrations against injustice. Typically, the protesters are a small slice of the victimized group plus sympathizers who are not victimized. The incidence of repression often falls on the entire minority that is the subject of the original injustice, including large numbers who have not violated the law and may have disapproved those tactics.[41] The caution of prudence is a heavy moral responsibility the demonstrators must bear with respect to the interests of all those they purport to represent.[42]

OPENNESS OF BEHAVIOR AND SUBMISSION TO PUNISHMENT

If obedience is to be justifiable within a generally just system, must those who disobey act openly and submit to punishment? I have already said enough to indicate that this cannot be an

---

39 Rawls, op. cit. note 12 at 373-5.
40 ibid., at 376.
41 Rawls does recognize that possible injury to innocent third parties must be considered, but he does not seem aware of how typical the risk of such injury is.
42 See, generally, Peter Singer's account of escalating force in Northern Ireland. *Democracy and Disobedience* (1973), 139-45.

absolute rule about morally justified disobedience. Some applications of some laws are not reached by any obligation to obey, and many violations in these situations will not be open. Moreover, when an obligation to obey is outweighed by a more pressing moral duty to prevent severe injustice or harm to individuals, one's effectiveness may depend on secrecy. To take an extreme example, a person who *openly* tries to help a fugitive slave escape is likely to make escape impossible, and someone who surrenders to authorities after aiding a successful escape will compromise the chance of giving future assistance to others. Relieving people from the bonds of slavery justifies secretive violation of law, at least if it is nonviolent. Finding a non-controversial example for more just societies is not as easy, but in the United States some concerned people now think that application of our immigration laws in certain instances is so unfair and inhumane that covert evasion is warranted.

The claims about openness and acceptance of punishment are mainly relevant to illegal protests.[43] The actual publicness of one's act may have some intrinsic significance, but its main importance is its linkage with submission to the operation of law. When people act openly, enforcement officials can arrest them and can also prosecute with clear evidence of their behavior. But two illustrations show that openness of the act itself is not critical. If people who sneak into a draft office and pour blood on the files come forward immediately and admit what they have done, the covertness of the illegal behavior at the moment it happened does not affect the quality of their whole course of action. And if easily identified illegal strikers use their economic power to ensure that no punishment is imposed, the unwillingness to submit to the law is not much affected by the openness of their actions.

A willingness to submit to punishment, which may combine two distinguishable elements, is often a critical ingredient of justified disobedience. One element is that the actor behaves so that authorities may impose punishment if they wish. The

43 These matters are explored in a somewhat different way in Greenawalt, op. cit. note 32 at 69–71 [this volume, p. 183]. The discussion here proceeds on the assumption that the punishment to which one submits is one seriously intended by society. For the interesting suggestion that such was not the case when Socrates was sentenced to death, see Olsen, 'Socrates on Legal Obligation: Legitimation Theory and Civil Disobedience,' 18 Ga. L. Rev. (1984), 828, 844–7.

second element, not necessarily present with the first, is that the actor acknowledge the appropriateness of punishment if it is determined that the law has been violated. Raising possible legal defenses is not, of course, inconsistent with either element.

Acceptance of punishment often mitigates the force of a violation of a deontological duty. I have suggested that in some situations such acceptance may wholly satisfy the demands of a duty of fair play. Even when acceptance of punishment falls short of this, it can lessen unfairness by eliminating any unjust advantage the actor might derive. The ultimate commitment of one's fate to legal process means that under an obligation of consent or a duty to support just institutions, one's breach is also substantially lessened.

The actual effects of an illegal action are likely to be significantly different if the violators submit to punishment. In the first place, the frustration, resentment, and insecurity people feel when their interests are jeopardized are reduced if they realize that those who threaten them are willing to pay an even more costly price. Acceptance of punishment signifies the respect, even the love,[44] the protestor has for his opponents. Submission to punishment also demonstrates the depth of the actor's conviction, showing that his claim of substantial injustice is not just hypocritical rhetoric, rationalization of self-interest, or simple overstatement. Protestors wanting to convince others of the magnitude of their grievance are likely to be more persuasive if they submit to punishment.

Submission to punishment also serves as a helpful test of the actor's strength of conviction and contains the force of his example. When someone asks himself the hard question whether or not he is willing to be punished, he will be careful to consider his course of action and its value; thus, submission to punishment imposes some check on irresponsible judgment. It also sets an important limit on the message communicated to other persons considering disobedience, suggesting that they can think themselves justified in disobeying only if they believe a law or policy is so unjust that they are willing to suffer serious penalties to alter it.

The reasons so far suggested for willing submission are largely satisfied by a course of action that allows the authorities to

44 See King, op. cit., note 26 at 78.

187

impose punishment. An acknowledgment of its moral appropriateness goes even further, demonstrating a commitment to the fundamentals of the existing social order. Although the actor does not accept the judgment of society as expressed in the law about the proper course of behavior, he or she does ultimately accept that judgment in the form of punishment for behavior society considers wrongful. In so doing, the actor may express a certain humility about his moral judgment, but even if he does not, he reaffirms his sense of being a member of the community by admitting the appropriateness of enforcement efforts.[45] Such acknowledgments will reduce anger directed at protesters and minimize the chances of massive repression.

45 See ibid.

12

DEFINING CIVIL DISOBEDIENCE

Brian Smart

The meaning of quite diverse social and political acts has been the subject of a broadly converging interpretation in several disciplines over the last twenty years. In philosophy H. P. Grice[1] has studied conversation and ringing bells on buses. In economics and politics Thomas Schelling[2] has studied bargaining and brinkmanship. In sociology Erving Goffman[3] has studied walking in public places and smiling. Underlying these actions and mutual interactions is the triad of intentions first explicated by Grice: let U stand for the Utterer (in the appropriate broad sense covering the above examples), A the Audience, and x the Utterance, then:

(1) U intends to produce an effect on A (that A should believe p or do $ø$) by the utterance of x;
(2) U intends that A should recognize the first intention;
(3) U intends that the effect on A should be produced because of A's recognition of the first intention.

That is the primitive model for the underlying structure of these diverse actions, though of course much refinement has taken place since the publication of Grice's first paper. The first aim of this paper will have been achieved if I can provide arguments which establish that civil disobedience belongs to this range of actions. In the second half I attempt to add the

From: Brian Smart, 'Defining Civil Disobedience,' *Inquiry*, 21 (1978), pp. 249–69.
1 H. P. Grice, 'Meaning,' *Philosophical Review*, 66 (1957), pp. 377–88.
2 Thomas Schelling, *The Strategy of Conflict* (New York: Galaxy Books, 1963).
3 Erving Goffman, *Relations in Public* (Harmondsworth: Allen Lane, The Penguin Press, 1971).

definitional flesh of civil disobedience to these rather dry theoretical bones.

I. NON-NATURAL MEANING

Rawls writes:

> I shall begin by defining civil disobedience as a public, nonviolent, conscientious yet political act contrary to law usually done with the aim of bringing about a change in the law or policies of the government. By acting in this way one addresses the sense of justice of the majority of the community and declares that in one's considered opinion the principles of social cooperation among free and equal men are not being respected.[4]

In this part I shall concentrate on the notion of 'address'.

In 'Meaning' Grice drew a broad distinction between natural and non-natural meaning including within the latter class not only linguistic utterances and inscriptions but such non-linguistic actions and gestures as ringing a bell on the bus, hoisting a flag, and deliberately frowning. The contrast between the two kinds of meaning is this: with natural meaning, e.g. 'Those spots meant measles', we *cannot* infer that *somebody* meant something by those spots, but *can* infer that *somebody* (the conductor) meant that the bus was full from 'Those three rings meant that the bus was full' in the case of non-natural meaning; also we can paraphrase 'Those spots meant measles' as 'The fact that he had those spots meant that he had measles', but we cannot paraphrase 'Those three rings on the bell meant that the bus was full' as 'The fact that the bell had been rung three times meant that the bus was full'.

Now ringing the bell is not a linguistic act since it does not consist of lexical items or proper names strung together by a grammar. But since it does have non-natural meaning let us call it an NLNN action. My proposal is that in spite of Rawls's emphasis upon the linguistic notion of 'address', standard cases of civil disobedience are to be construed as NLNN actions. Though non-linguistic they may of course be protests, vehicles of information and persuasion, and arguably threats. Just as

---

4 John Rawls, *A Theory of Justice* (Oxford: The Clarendon Press, 1972), p. 363: henceforth referred to as *TJ*.

explicit inscriptions inside the bus allow us to decode the rings on the bell, so accompanying leaflets or speeches allow the decoding of acts of civil disobedience. The necessarily non-standard exeptions are provided by cases where the civilly disobedient act involves the performance of a speech act in direct violation of law, e.g. making a speech from the Public Gallery of the House of Commons, writing slogans across buildings or sky-writing.

I shall look first at Grice's reasoning for the triad of intentions in acts of communication and mention some possible improvements arising from subsequent discussion. I shall then review a series of conscientiously illegal acts lacking the complete triad and indicate how they must fall short of civil disobedience.

He argues for (1) by the following example. By putting on a tail coat a man might unintentionally induce in someone the belief that he is going out to dance, but he has not communicated with the onlooker: he has not meant anything non-naturally. So we need (1) for communication: U must at least intend to induce a belief or bring about an action or response. But

(1) is not sufficient for non-natural meaning. For A might leave B's handkerchief at the scene of a murder and induce in a detective the belief that B is the murderer. But A does not communicate with the detective for A does not intend him to recognize his primary intention: indeed the detective's recognition of (2) would frustrate A's purpose. Nothing less than (1) and

(2) is required yet they are jointly insufficient for an act of communication.

Grice contrasts two cases to show why (3) is needed:

(a) I show Mr X a photograph of Mr Y displaying undue familiarity to Mrs X;
(b) I draw a picture of Mr Y behaving in this manner and show it to Mr X.

Both (1) and (2) feature in (a) and (b) and yet, for Grice, only (b) is a vehicle of non-natural meaning, since A's recognition of (1) there figures as a reason for Mr X's acquiring the belief U wishes to induce. In (a) by contrast Mr X recognizes (1), but the recognition is irrelevant to his forming the belief – he has natural evidence to go on. Grice mentions another case which he treats like (a) where Herod presents Salome with the head of St John the Baptist: Salome recognizes (1), but her recognition is irrelevant to her learning that St John is dead, and so, according to Grice, Herod has not non-naturally meant anything by his act. For Grice in his paper 'Meaning' (1), (2), and (3) are jointly necessary and sufficient for non-natural meaning.

Let me mention just two points of criticism that have been raised over the Gricean analysis, points that bear upon the applicability of the model to civil disobedience.

Stephen Schiffer[5] has questioned the need for (3). He finds plausible the suggestion that Herod non-naturally meant that St John the Baptist was dead when he showed Salome the head. By showing his bandaged leg a man might non-naturally mean (according to the question asked) either that he cannot play squash or that his leg is bandaged. I should like our concept of communication or non-natural meaning to be indeterminate on this issue, since people have different intuitions about these cases. Yet that very indeterminacy supports the main thesis of this paper, since our concept of civil disobedience becomes blurred at the very same point. We shall later be looking at some cases where people will have different intuitions about conscientious illegalities lacking (3).

Many writers, including Grice in a later paper,[6] have raised the question of whether an infinite regress of intentions is generated by the Gricean triad: whether that regress is vicious and, if so, how a non-arbitrary cut-off point can be decided upon. It will be enough for our purposes if we rule that U does not rely for the success of his evoking A's response upon some misunderstanding of U's intentions.[7] This rule together with (1) and (2) and (indeterminately) (3) supplies the necessary and jointly sufficient conditions for non-natural meaning and bypasses the need to establish whether an infinite series of intentions is inherent within acts of communication,[8] and makes our analysis of civil disobedience easier to handle.

5 Stephen Schiffer, *Meaning* (Oxford: The Clarendon Press, 1972), pp. 56-7.
6 H. P. Grice, 'Utterer's Meaning and Intentions,' *Philosophical Review*, 78 (1969), pp. 147-77; also P. F. Strawson, 'Intention and Convention in Speech Acts,' *Philosophical Review*, 73 (1964), pp. 439-60; and Schiffer op. cit.
7 I roughly follow Jonathan Bennett, *Linguistic Behaviour* (Cambridge University Press, 1976), pp. 126-7.
8 In their introduction to *Truth and Meaning* (Oxford: The Clarendon Press, 1976), the editors, Gareth Evans and John McDowell, are so anxious to avoid

I now turn to a series of remarks about civil disobedience to see how useful a yardstick our Gricean model is.

An example of a definition which does not require intentions (1)–(3) is Robert T. Hall's:

> An act of civil disobedience is an act in violation of a law (or a specific group of laws) which is undertaken for moral reasons.[9]

But since this allows the civil disobedient to be ignorant of the fact that he is violating at least one law let us take a better version of a definition not requiring (1)–(3). Michael Bayles writes:

> For purposes of this discussion civil disobedience may be defined as selective and public performance of actions (commissions or omissions) truly believed to be illegal for reasons which the agent takes to be morally compelling.[10]

It is worth noting that Bayles intends 'public' to be taken in the sense that the person does not try to hide his violation of the law from the authorities. Now it is clear that by defining civil disobedience as deliberate and conscientious violation of the law Bayles does not even require intention (1). I suggest that the absence of (1) is sufficient to destroy both Hall's and Bayles's definitions. My point is that (1) introduces both an *audience* and a *response* that *U* intends to elicit from the audience and that the proffered definitions introduce neither. In a democracy, for example, the audience is the government or the public or both. The response may be acquiring the belief that a law or governmental policy or public attitude is wrong and that appropriate action should be taken. My contention is that conscientious illegalities constitute a much wider class that includes civil disobedience and more. An example of what this more includes is someone who continues to practise his religion privately even though he knows that it has been banned: he chooses *to ignore* the law but does not intend to induce in anyone the belief that the

ascribing superhuman capacities to language-users and money-users that they prefer to eliminate altogether the positive ascription of belief and intention in the understanding of non-natural meaning and put their faith in the unreflective use of language and money. But this is going too far.
9 Robert T. Hall, *The Morality of Civil Disobedience* (New York: Harper & Row, 1971), p. 15.
10 Michael Bayles, 'The Justification of Civil Disobedience,' *Review of Metaphysics*, 24 (1970), p. 4.

ban should be lifted. He has no audience and hence no response in mind: *ergo* he is no civil disobedient.

In his advocacy of 'civil disobedience' Bertrand Russell clearly includes (1) but, on the interpretation I shall adopt, does not include (2) or (3):

> We advocate and practise non-violent civil disobedience as a method of causing people to know the perils to which the world is exposed and in persuading them to join us in opposing the insanity which affects, at present, many of the most powerful governments in the world.[11]

Within the Gricean framework the expression 'causing people to know (or believe)' has of course a simpler structural interpretation than 'informing'. Since I wish to see whether (2) is an essential component in acts of civil disobedience I shall construe 'persuade' as bearing the same simpler interpretation. My warrant is the *Shorter Oxford English Dictionary*, which distinguishes between the simpler 'to seek to induce (a person) to (or from) a belief, a course of action etc.', and the non-natural meaning 'to commend to adoption, advise, advocate, recommend (an act, course etc.)'.

The difficulty with Russell's formulation as so understood is that civil disobedience could be practised without anyone except the civil disobedient either knowing or being intended to know that it had been practised. Proof of the perils to which Russell refers could be illegally obtained and placed where it can be brought to public attention in such a way that the public would acquire the intended knowledge or belief and oppose their government's insanity in the way intended. So on this account civil disobedience could have (1) and lack (2), as in the case of the man who left B's handkerchief at the scene of the murder for the detective to see. And the trouble with an act of this structure is that while a response is intended to be elicited, it cannot be from an *audience* that the response is forthcoming. The relation between the handkerchief-planter and the detective is not that of 'utterer' and audience but that of manipulator and intended spectator.

Since in many contexts there are no structural differences

11 *The Autobiography of Bertrand Russell*, III (London: Allen & Unwin, 1969), p. 139.

between audiences and spectators except for the implication that audiences are primarily hearers or listeners and spectators are viewers, I now propose to substitute the word 'addressee' for 'audience', so long as addressees are not thought of as the recipients of linguistic utterances and inscriptions alone. My contention is that ordinary speech acts and other kinds of communication with non-natural meaning, including acts of civil disobedience, involve the Utterer/Addressee relationship. Both (1) and (2) are clearly necessary conditions of such a relationship.

Hugo Bedau offers a definition which can be construed as requiring both (1) and (2):

> Anyone commits an act of civil disobedience if and only if he acts illegally, publicly, nonviolently and conscientiously with the intent to frustrate (one of) the laws, policies or decisions of his government.[12]

Here, unlike the Bayles definition, it is reasonable to assume that the public nature of the act involves (2). The following case has been taken to be an example of civil disobedience and indeed has persuaded at least one lawyer that civil disobedience is in principle justifiable.[13] The law of the Pawnee prescribed the annual sacrifice of a maiden who would be captured from a neighbouring tribe, tied to a stake, and shot through with arrows by the Pawnee braves riding round her on horseback. One summer solstice at dawn Peshwataro, a young brave of great renown, galloped to the stake before an arrow could be fired, untied the girl and returned her safely to her tribe. He then rode back and submitted himself to his own tribe, but no action was taken against him: it was felt that it was high time the practice should end and that this courageous act had made that clear.

Let us suppose that Peshwataro intended (1) that the law prescribing the sacrifice should be revoked and (2) that his tribe should recognize his intention (1). A necessary condition of civil disobedience is that there should be an addressee: is Peshwataro's tribe the addressee or just a spectator of his act? According to the original Gricean model it was essential for non-natural meaning

12 Hugo Bedau, 'On Civil Disobedience,' *Journal of Philosophy*, 58 (1961), p. 661.
13 See Robert T. Hall, 'Legal Toleration of Civil Disobedience,' *Ethics*, 81 (1971), p. 128.

that Peshwataro should have intention (3), i.e. that he should intend that the tribe's recognition of (1) should be one of their reasons for realizing what a hideous practice the sacrifice was and for revoking the law that prescribed it. But I doubt whether (3) can be plausibly ascribed to Peshwataro. The mechanism inducing the tribe's response involves natural meaning: the moral nature of the practice is revealed or shown to the tribe by the fact that a brave with his qualities should be moved to save the girl: *that fact meant that the practice had to be abandoned* – a case of natural meaning.

Still Peshwataro did have intention (2) and did not rely upon cross-purposes to secure the tribe's response, and so the case is structurally identical with Herod showing the head to Salome or to the man who shows his bandaged leg. We might have doubts about whether any of these are vehicles of non-natural meaning. To that extent we might have doubts about whether Peshwataro's act involved any addressee and so about whether it was an act of civil disobedience essentially having a non-natural meaning component since in this respect at least it is isomorphic with other acts of communication. Here intuitions may differ and I shall follow the liberal Schiffer line in insisting on only (1) and (2) on condition that no cross-purposes are involved. I shall now argue that protest is the infrastructure of civil disobedience.

Clyde Frazier writes:

> If the defining feature of traditional civil disobedience was that it could be characterized as a form of speech, the more radical position I wish to explore defends the right of a citizen not only to appeal to the state but to resist it as well.[14]

As I read him Frazier wishes to expand the traditional notion of civil disobedience to embrace not only resistance but resistance which does not incorporate speech at all. Though the only vehicle of non-natural meaning to which he alludes is that of speech or of linguistic communication in general, I shall assume that he would wish to reject my thesis that civil disobedience must have a non-natural meaning component in the sense that it must have intentions (1) and (2) and be free of any cross-purposes

14 Clyde Frazier, 'Between Obedience and Revolution,' *Philosophy and Public Affairs*, 1 (1972), pp. 324–5.

mechanism: such a requirement might take a linguistic or a non-linguistic form and might or might not involve natural meaning. Frazier's objection might be twofold:

(A) While I have claimed that civil disobedience must have an addressee and so be an act of communication I have not really provided any argument for that claim.

(B) Even if, as must be conceded, communicative civil disobedience is one kind of civil disobedience, why must it be the only kind? There might be many other kinds of civil disobedience falling between revolution and obedience to the law.

My answer to (A) rests on the further claim that civil disobedience is essentially a form of protest and that it is this communicative feature of the act that binds together the civil disobedient and the government or the public in the relationship of Utterer/Addressee. Naturally this appeal to 'protest' as the explanatory concept would be merely *ad hoc* if the *only* feature essential to civil disobedience generated by it were the Utterer/Addressee relationship. At least two other essential features are also generated by the fact that acts of civil disobedience are essentially forms of protest.

Civil disobedience is necessarily a protest *against* something, there must be *an object of protest*. In the case of Peshwataro it was the law prescribing the annual sacrifice. There is clearly no object of protest for the man we considered earlier who committed the conscientious illegality of continuing to practise a banned religion: he obviously considered the ban to be wrong, but as he did not protest there could be nothing protested against. Or consider those who harboured or otherwise protected slaves from their owners in defiance of the Fugitive Slave Act but did so in secret. The Act might well have been an object of their contempt, but their conscientious violation of the law did not constitute a protest – how could the government be addressed if the main condition of success was secrecy? It does seem to be essential to any act of civil disobedience that it should have an object of protest.

The second essential feature I have in mind is *the principle or principles invoked, appealed to or cited by* the civil disobedient. Both acts of civil disobedience and other conscientious acts are *governed* by principles (moral and otherwise). This means that certain principles form part of the explanation of how the acts came to be performed. Furthermore, both acts of civil disobedience and other conscientious acts may be *justified* by the principles that govern them. That is, the governing principles may be good principles, or the best applicable or the least evil applicable in the circumstances. But in the case of civil disobedience it is essential that not only does a principle govern the action and therefore in principle is able to justify it, but also that the principle may be appealed to, invoked, or cited. For this to be possible the act must convey non-natural meaning, and civil disobedience as protest meets this requirement. Peshwataro can be construed an appealing non-linguistically to some principle that sacrifices of a certain kind should not be tolerated.

Thus my reply to (A). Discussion of (B) requires a brief excursion into natural-kind theory and the nature of cluster concepts.

An illuminating parallel can be drawn between civil disobedience and gold. Consider the following remarks of Saul Kripke:

> Given that gold *does* have the atomic number 79, could something be gold without having the atomic number 79? Let us suppose the scientists have investigated the nature of gold and have found that it is part of the very nature of this substance, so to speak, that it have the atomic number 79. Suppose we now find some other yellow metal, or some other yellow thing, with all the properties by which we originally identified gold, and many of the additional ones that we have discovered later. An example of one with many of the initial properties is iron pyrites, 'fool's gold' . . . we wouldn't say that this substance is gold.[15]

Clearly Kripke does not intend to suggest that gold and iron pyrites share *all* of their superficial characteristics but only some of them.[16] Chemical experimentation no doubt leads to differences observable by the naked eye, just as it does with the different colour of litmus paper according to whether it is an acid or alkali that is being tested. But it does mean that without a theory of metallurgy or chemistry one might be forced to treat

15 Saul Kripke, 'Naming and Necessity,' in Donald Davidson and Gilbert Harman (eds.), *Semantics of Natural Language* (Dordrecht: D. Reidel, 1972), pp. 319–20.
16 For some of this clarification of Kripke cf. Colin McGinn, 'A Note on the Essence of Natural Kinds', *Analysis*, 35 (1974–75), pp. 177–83.

gold and iron pyrites as one kind of metal. And even if some superficial differences could be detected, lack of a theory might simply lead to one of the metals being regarded as a deviant type of the other.

We can contrast the *natural kind concept* of 'gold' with the *cluster concept* 'jade'. Hilary Putnam uses 'jade' to illustrate the fact that cluster concepts are not based upon the possession of a unique infrastructure:

> Although the Chinese do not recognize the difference, the term 'jade' applies to two minerals: jadeite and nephrite. Chemically, there is a marked difference. Jadeite is a combination of sodium and aluminium. Nephrite is made of calcium, magnesium, and iron. These two quite different microstructures produce the same unique textural qualities![17]

For certain visual purposes jade can be treated as one kind of thing, just like real and plastic lemons. But chemically jade is not one kind of thing, while only real lemons belong to biology.

Can we carry over these distinctions from the natural sciences to the social sciences? I think we can. For certain untheoretical purposes the cluster concept 'conscientious illegality' is useful. When engaged in political activity between revolution and obedience to the law all kinds of illegal tactics may have to be contemplated: the sub-class of those which are conscientious are not likely to share a specifically social scientific infrastructure, even though they do share some superficial features that are relevant to the social sciences, viz. illegality and conscientiousness. But philosophico-linguistic theory certainly provides us with an infrastructure for a sub-class of conscientious illegalities. It is of course a structure which ordinary language-speakers *know how* to wield and recognize even though they *cannot give an account* of it, any more than they can give an account of the rules of English grammar: that needs theoretical expertise. Nor is this infrastructure idle. We have seen that it gives rise to various features – an addressee, an object of protest, a principle appealed to – which other conscientious illegalities necessarily lack.

17 Hilary Putnam, 'The Meaning of "Meaning", ' in *Mind Language and Reality: Philosophical Papers*, 2 (Cambridge University Press, Cambridge 1975), p. 241.

II. EXAMINING THE RAWLSIAN DEFINITION

A detailed survey of Rawls's definition will allow me to construct a more refined one together with its infrastructure of non-natural meaning. His definition has the following seven features. Acts of civil disobedience must be,

(1) in violation of a law, and intended to be so;
(2) nonviolent;
(3) public and with fair notice given;
(4) accompanied by willingness to accept the legal consequences;
(5) usually performed to bring about a change in the law or in policies of the government;
(6) addressed to the majority's sense of justice;
(7) addressed to a sense of justice that is mainly incorporated in the law and social institutions.

In fact not one of these conditions (in the way Rawls understands them) seems to be definitionally necessary.

1. Violation of a law, and the intention to violate the law

Two issues are raised here. The first arises over Rawls's narrow reading of law and the second over the nature of test cases.

Rawls intends the condition of law-violation to provide a contrast with the notion of *conscientious refusal*.

Conscientious refusal is noncompliance with a more or less direct legal injunction or administrative order. (*TJ*, p. 368)

Two examples are the refusal to serve in the armed forces and the refusal to pay one's taxes. Rawls's point is that an administrative injunction or order, unlike a law, is addressed to the refuser personally and, normally at least, the refusal does not escape the notice of the authorities. There is, however, no recognition of this distinction in the theory and practice of civil disobedience from Thoreau[18] to Chomsky.[19] Why does Rawls wish to exclude

18 See Thoreau's essay 'Civil Disobedience', in Hugo A. Bedau (ed.), *Civil Disobedience* (Pegasus: New York 1969), pp. 27–48 [this volume, pp. 28–48].
19 Cf. Noam Chomsky, 'Intolerable Evils Justify Civil Disobedience,' in Bedau, op. cit., p. 201: 'What justifies an act of civil disobedience is an intolerable evil. After the lesson of Dachau and Auschwitz, no person of conscience can believe that authority must always be obeyed. A line must be drawn somewhere. Beyond that line lies civil disobedience. It may be quite passive, a simple refusal to pay war taxes: refusal to serve in Vietnam is a far more meaningful, far more courageous example.' Cf. also Gandhi, *Non-Violent Resistance* (New York, 1961), p. 142, quoted by Bedau in his Introduction to Bedau, op. cit., p. 22: 'Civil

conscientious refusal from civil disobedience? The reason lies in false theory. For Rawls, conscientious refusal *may* be grounded on an appeal to a shared conception of justice but *need not be*. Civil disobedience by definition must be so grounded for Rawls. When we come to discuss (6) we shall see that civil disobedience need not make any appeal to a shared conception of justice either so any theoretical point in excluding conscientious refusal from civil disobedience will have been lost.

The question of whether civil disobedience should include the presentation of test cases is problematic. According to Rawls:

> A second gloss [on his definition, B. S.] is that the civilly disobedient act is indeed thought to be contrary to law, at least in the sense that those engaged in it are not simply presenting a test case for a constitutional decision; they are prepared to oppose the statute even if it should be upheld. (*TJ*, p. 365)

It is unclear in the above passage who is to think that the act is contrary to law: the civil disobedients or the courts? It appears from the context that Rawls intends the civil disobedients, and so they might even accept the highest court's ruling on the law but persist in breaking it. This is of course a possibility under many constitutions and much civil disobedience will conform to such a pattern. But is it necessary that the civil disobedients should think they are violating the law even when, say, the Supreme Court's decision goes against them? Ronald Dworkin thinks not:

> Sometimes, even after a contrary Supreme Court decision, an individual may still reasonably believe that the law is on his side; such cases are rare, but they are most likely to occur in disputes over constitutional law when civil disobedience is involved.[20]

This passage reflects one of the main themes of Dworkin's book – his attack on legal positivism. He holds that under the U.S. Constitution the interpretation of the law involves moral judgment and not some detached assessment or prediction of what

nonpayment of taxes is indeed the last stage in noncooperation. We must not resort to it till we have tried the other forms of civil disobedience.'
20 Ronald Dworkin, 'Civil Disobedience,' *Taking Rights Seriously*, (London: Duckworth, 1977), p. 211.

some rules or courts enjoin. The possibility he cites is one that any comprehensive definition of civil disobedience must permit.

To resolve these difficulties I propose that Rawls should have meant that the act is regarded as illegal by at least one court and that at the time of acting no higher court has decided otherwise. The act therefore does not have to be illegal but is so regarded by the appropriate organs of the civil authorities; nor does the civil disobedient have to believe that his act is illegal.

'Civil' disobedience is not necessarily courteous or polite: it is either a deliberate violation of the laws and orders of the civil authorities or at least appears to the civil authorities to be so at the time of action.

One kind of civil disobedience is an exception to these remarks. Indirect civil disobedience is where the object protested against is perhaps not a law or an order addressed to the civil disobedient but is something like foreign policy. Here it is important for communication that both the civil disobedient and the authorities know that he is deliberately violating a law or injunction in protest at a policy that has no direct bearing upon the nature of the law or injunction violated: the civil disobedient may hold the particular law violated to be good or just law and the injunction to be justifiable.

2. Non-violence

Non-violence is particularly associated with Gandhian *Satyagraha*. But is it a defining condition of civil disobedience? Rawls claims it is:

> to engage in violent acts likely to injure and hurt is incompatible with civil disobedience as a mode of address. Indeed, any interference with the civil liberties of others tends to obscure the civilly disobedient quality of one's act. Sometimes if the appeal fails in its purpose, forceful resistance may later be entertained. Yet civil disobedience is giving voice to conscientious and deeply held convictions; while it may warn and admonish, it is not itself a threat. (*TJ*, p. 366)

What is violence? Rawls's formulation would appear to exclude damage to property, which is rather surprising in view of his including among the basic civil liberties the right to hold personal property (*TJ*, p. 61). In the light of discussions by Ted Honderich[21] and John Morreall[22] let me propose the following definition of violence:

> Violence is a considerable or destroying use of force against persons or their property, a use of force which violates their human rights.

For Morreall civil disobedience can include violence since violence is a form of force and force can certainly be used in civil disobedience as in the case of sit-ins, lying down in the road, and mass tax refusals. As I read him, Morreall envisages such civil disobedience as a form of threat, using force and the threat of force as a lever to attain the aims of the civil disobedients. I agree that this is a form of civil disobedience but I shall argue that both violence and force can enter civil disobedience without it constituting a threat either in the speech act sense or in the sense of imminent danger.

Honderich too believes that civil disobedience may involve violence and, again, only on condition that it consists of a threat, but not *any* kind of threat. He distinguishes between the *coercion of force* and the *coercion of persuasion*.[23] Coercion of force is illustrated by my giving up my wallet at the point of a gun: while the threat poses two theoretical alternatives only one action is humanly possible: 'I am not left room for effectual reflection and

21 Ted Honderich, *Three Essays on Political Violence* (Basil Blackwell, Oxford 1976), p. 9: 'Political violence, roughly defined, is a considerable or destroying use of force against persons or things, a use of force prohibited by law, directed to a change in policies, personnel or system of government, and hence also directed to changes in the existence of individuals in the society and perhaps other societies.' I want to omit the political element of the definition and change the reference from law to human rights, since the law might not protect one from wrongful uses of force, e.g., execution or corporal punishment which violate human rights, and might paternalistically protect one from force which does not violate human rights, e.g., boxing or ice-hockey.
22 John Morreall, 'The Justifiability of Violent Civil Disobedience', *Canadian Journal of Philosophy*, 6 (1976), pp. 38-9: 'we should add that although all acts of violence involve the treatment of a person in a manner contemptuous of his *prima facie* rights as a human being, not all acts which disrespect persons are of sufficient magnitude or intensity to be labelled acts of violence [this volume, p. 134]. I want to omit reference to 'prima facie' rights since if these are to be understood as rights which can conceivably be overridden then there are no non-prima facie rights.
23 Honderich, op. cit., pp. 109-15.

judgement about what I do.[24] I illustrate the coercion of persuasion by a director threatening to resign if his board votes against a takeover, and where the director is regarded as valuable but not indispensable. The threat presents the board with two practicable alternatives, leaving it room for effectual reflection and judgement: it may incline but it does not necessitate.

Where a threat has been made and will be backed up, then with both kinds of coercion the total number of theoretical alternative courses of action has been diminished by the threat.[25] Honderich's idea is that at least in those cases where the distinction between the two kinds of coercion is tolerably clear then it is only the coercion of persuasion that can feature in civil disobedience: for Honderich the coercion of force appears to be an act of revolution, not civil disobedience. Again, I agree that some kinds of civil disobedience may involve violence via the coercion of persuasion, but I shall suggest that civil disobedience may also involve the coercion of force, and that other kinds of civil disobedience do not have to be threatening at all even when violence and force are involved.

It will help if I preface a sketch of the range of possibilities with the following chart:

either Threatening by		(a) Coercion of Force of Violence
		(b) Coercion of Force of Nonviolence
Civil Disobedience		(c) Coercion of Persuasion (with or without violence)
or Non-threatening but with		(d) Violence
		(e) Nonviolent Force
		(f) Persuasion

Rawls accepts as the only possibilities (e) and (f), Morreall (a), (b), (c), and (f), Honderich (c), (e), and (f). I understand (a) and (b) to exhaust the Coercion of Force, and contend that (a) – (f) are *all*

24 ibid., p. 111.
25 Cf. J. P. Day, 'Threats, Offers, Law, Opinion and Liberty,' *American Philosophical Quarterly*, Vol. 14 (1977), pp. 252–72. For example, I can no longer perform the complex action of both holding on to my wallet *and* living; the board cannot vote against the takeover *and* retain the director.

forms of civil disobedience with violence entering via (a), (c), and (d).

Let us take (a)-(c) first. As we saw, Rawls holds that by definition no act of civil disobedience can constitute a threat. A threat does not have to be an explicit speech act but, in this context at least, has two features: it is non-naturally meant by the threatener and, given its effectiveness, reduces the number of theoretical alternative courses of action open to the threatened. There is therefore a *requirement* that the threat should be a mode of address: Rawls provides no argument for restricting such address to warning and admonishing in the case of civil disobedience. In the case of (c), for example, a protest might be made against the government's policy of allowing into the country cricket teams which have been selected in a racially discriminatory manner: having exhausted legal means of protest without success the protestors might trespass and destroy the cricket pitches with the threat that this kind of action will continue until the policy is changed. The government is not *forced* to change its policy for it certainly has room for effectual reflections; but it will be incommoded if it does not change its policy and so we have a case of the coercion of persuasion. Even if the players were kidnapped, which would undoubtedly require the use of some violence, I see no reason why the use of violence should, in principle at least, obscure the appeal to principles of equal opportunity.

But (a) and (b) raise the issue of force and both Rawls and Honderich are agreed that the coercion of force is incompatible with civil disobedience. But why? I suspect that they are thinking of kinds of goal – seizure of power, overthrow of all authority – that can accompany the use of force. But suppose there were a sustained mass tax refusal and the destruction of missile bases to prevent the implementation of the government's policy to remain a member of NATO? The protesters might make it perfectly clear that they want the elected government to continue in office but that on just this one policy many members of the public would prevent the government from taking any action. The threat might be accompanied by appeals to justice, and as this is not a case of a revolution there seems no reason why it should not be a case of civil disobedience, exemplifying (a) and (b). It must however be conceded that not only the government but many members of the public not directly involved in the dispute will be forcefully inconvenienced. But then so are otherwise uninvolved commuters when civil disobedients sit down on the tracks or in the road to lodge a protest.

Simply by varying one feature of the above case we can construct (d) and (e). Suppose they violate the law on one occasion but do not threaten to do likewise in future. Given some background knowledge of sincerity the illegality cannot be construed as a threat or as involving coercion: that the law is broken simply serves to emphasize the deeply felt nature of the protest. In the case of (d) the protestors might kidnap an official or destroy a building and then submit themselves voluntarily to the due legal processes, making it clear that they will not be followed by others doing likewise until the government capitulates. Passive resistance in violation of the law unaccompanied by threat would exemplify (e): there is force directed against the police but no violence and certainly no coercion either of force or persuasion against the government. (f) is uncontentious and is to be distinguished from (c) by the fact that no threat is made and no pressure is brought to bear. (d)–(f) are merely dramatic guises of protest as pure address and are conceptual possibilities for civil disobedience, though whether they can be sharply distinguished from (a)–(c) in practice is obviously doubtful.

3. Publicity and fair notice

A further point is that civil disobedience is a public act. Not only is it addressed to public principles, it is done in public. It is engaged in openly with fair notice; it is not covert or secretive. (*TJ*, p. 366)

Rawls's arguments for this feature are dealt with under (2) and (6). There are of course many dimensions in which something can be a 'public' act, and there seems to be no reason why an act of civil disobedience should be public in all of them. It must of course be addressed to the public or the government, but this is compatible with secrecy in various respects. For example, the requirement of fair notice might well frustrate the performance of the civil disobedience and prevent it from being made public, so advance publicity cannot be a requirement of all civil disobedience: a public declaration of intention made after the act is all that need be required to decode the meaning of the civil disobedience.

4. Willingness to accept legal consequences

Here the Rawlsian argument is that voluntary submission to the legal consequences of one's act is evidence of sincerity in the protest: the onus is on the civil disobedient to distinguish himself from a 'mere' criminal. However, there are other ways of establishing sincerity: a man might publicly break the law against taking cannabis but elude the police and seek asylum abroad where he attacks his home country's legislation through publications and filmed interviews distributed in the home country. He may have no intention of returning until amnesty is granted: why should unwillingness to suffer imprisonment for the breaking of a (to him) repressive law automatically impugn his honesty?

5. Usually done to bring about a change in the law or policies of the government

It is conceivable that both the laws and governmental policies should be universally acceptable or almost so. The object of protest could mainly be the public's moral sense as it expresses itself outside the scope of law and the main social institutions. Discrimination in social relations or even a divisive sense of humour amongst the general public might be the object of protest, and yet the protesters might share with the general public the belief that this is no matter for a change in either legislation or governmental policy. This might be the form that civil disobedience usually takes with the public as the addressee.

6. Address of the majority's sense of justice

It should also be noted that civil disobedience is a political act not only in the sense that it is addressed to the majority that holds political power, but also because it is an act guided and justified by political principles, that is, by the principles of justice which regulate the constitution and social institutions generally. (*TJ*, p. 365)

Rawls is expressing himself elliptically: it is of course the majority or the government or the public who are generally the addressees. But who are the definitionally permissible addressees of civil disobedience? The answer to this depends upon what kind of principles may be invoked.

(i) *Invocable principles*. Rawls's own view is very restrictive for he would allow appeal only to the majority's principles of justice. Peter Singer offers two criticisms.[26] The first is that even if the only invocable principles were those of justice, why should they have to be the very principles that the majority had adopted? Clearly a minority within the state might have a conception of justice which they believed the majority should adopt but have not. Perhaps, and here the question of addressees is seen to be raised, the conception of justice which the minority wish the majority to adopt is the conception of justice prevalent in international opinion and international courts. Singer's second criticism is that he sees no reason why civil disobedience should be restricted to justice. Rawls explicitly excludes appeal to principles of personal morality or to religious doctrines (*TJ*, p. 365) and Singer points out that this rules out civil disobedience over cruelty to animals and over the legal prevention of the use of hallucinogenic drugs as part of religious ceremonies by various American churches.

How are we to capture both Rawls's cases and Singer's counterexamples? Inevitably our attempt is going to be vague, but the formula 'moral principles relating to matters of public concern' will suffice, though it will suffice *only* as a way of capturing Singer's broader and better notion of invocable principles. It is doubtful if the formula will cover the following grounds for civil disobedience: the damage to the national interest of laws permitting any works of art to leave the country; the ruin of a minority's pleasure by allowing the construction of motorways across moorlands; the irrationality and waste of much government bureaucracy. Here we must note that Rawls's idea was to exclude not only personal moralities and religious doctrines but also any reference to group or self-interest. Let us agree that reference

26 Peter Singer, *Democracy and Disobedience* (Oxford: The Clarendon Press, 1973), pp. 86-92 [this volume, pp. 122-29].

to self-interest must be excluded, but what about groups such as of those who share a distinctive interest like walking or a culture?[27] There seems to be no good reason for excluding reference to their interest from our invocable principles.

We are driven to the very broad formula that 'invocable principles are only those relating to matters of public concern'. But the formula does have some support from the fact that it helps to yield an intuitively acceptable answer to the question of who the possible addressees of civil disobedience are.

(ii) *Definitionally possible addressees*. Given the nature of the invocable principles it is clear that the public of one's own state is to be normally included among the addressees. In the quotation from Russell we saw the possibility that while the protest may be directed at the government the primary non-natural meaning of an act of civil disobedience may be to *inform* the public and to *urge* it to put pressure on the government. Yet there is no reason why the addressees should be restricted to one's own state in an era of mass communications: other governments and peoples may be informed and urged to put pressure on one's own government. Within one's own state a repressive majority may be protested to, but the primary aim may be to inform and urge the minority to put pressure on the government or to resort to further campaigns of civil disobedience and so forth. The addressees do not therefore have to be restricted to either the authors or victims of the violations of invocable principles but to any public which, consistent with those principles, can put pressure on one's government. So we can rule out the case in which a man breaks the law in order to get the public to put pressure on his wife to return to him: it is not the government's or the public's business.

---

27 Cf. Vernon Van Dyke, 'Justice as Fairness: For Groups?,' *The American Political Science Review*, 69 (1975), pp. 607–14. Van Dyke convincingly argues that recognition of group interest should be built into a conception of justice.

7. The sense of justice is mainly incorporated in the law and social institutions

Both Brian Barry[28] and Vinit Haksar[29] have rightly criticized Rawls for so defining civil disobedience that it is questionable whether it is ever needed. Either the society in which it is contemplated is not nearly just, in which case Rawls seems to think other illegal means to one's end are required, or the point of the protest can be achieved by perfectly legal means in a nearly just society. Haksar in particular points out that Rawls's theory seems to have little application to real societies and cannot cope with Gandhi's campaigns in India. Though Gandhi's campaigns were directed at the overthrow of British rule they were not conducted in a revolutionary manner: persuasion and the coercion of persuasion were the main forms it took. So it is just not true that civil disobedience need have no practical role, let alone no conceptual recognition, in a far less than just society.

III. CONCLUDING DEFINITION

It is time now to construct our own definition out of the non-natural meaning core of Part I and the polemical material of Part II. Just one complication prevents us from proceeding directly to it, for there is an apparent tension between allowing coercion by violence and Gandhi-like campaigns into civil disobedience but excluding revolutions from it. The difficulty is that disobedience with Gandhi-like aims - the overthrow of a régime and replacement of the constitution - combined with the coercion of force through violence just is revolution, not civil disobedience. One response to this might be to give up the idea that Gandhi and his followers practised civil disobedience since their aims were revolutionary.[30] But that Gandhi did practise civil disobedience is one of those hard pieces of data which one should ignore or

28 Brian Barry, *The Liberal Theory of Justice* (Oxford: The Clarendon Press, 1973), p. 153.
29 Vinit Haksar, 'Rawls and Gandhi on Civil Disobedience,' *Inquiry*, 19 (1976), pp. 151-92.
30 Cf. Clyde Frazier, op. cit., who thinks it is the aim rather than the manner of disobedience which is decisive for its classification as *either* civil *or* revolutionary. For the standard view that Gandhi did practise civil disobedience see Haksar, op. cit., and Marshall Cohen in a generally Rawlsian paper, 'Liberalism and Disobedience,' *Philosophy and Public Affairs*, 1 (1972), pp. 283-314.

explain away only as a last resort. Another response is to exclude violence as coercion as many writers do, but for bad reasons. I suggest the solution lies in neither of these responses but in the exclusion of the conjunction of revolutionary aims with coercion by violence. In this way we can contrast civil disobedience quite sharply with revolution and yet retain the many varieties of civil disobedience that on reflection seem to be possible.

I conclude with a definition of civil disobedience which may also serve to summarize my paper:

> Civil disobedience must be a vehicle of non-natural meaning: it is a protest and may also be a threat and information addressed to governments and the public; it is *either* a deliberate violation of the law or of an injunction *or* a deliberate challenge of the official interpretation of the law; it involves an appeal to principles of public concern that are held to have been breached; it may involve violence either as the coercion of force or as the coercion of persuasion or as a merely dramatic device but it cannot combine the coercion of force by violence with the overthrow of the government and the constitution.[31]

31 I am very grateful to Clive Borst, Jonathan Dancy, Patrick Day, David McNaughton, John Rogers, and Richard Swinburne for acute and helpful discussion of an earlier draft. I am also indebted to Alastair Hannay for criticisms and clarifications at the final stage of preparation.

SELECT BIBLIOGRAPHY

Bedau, H. A., 'On civil disobedience,' *Journal of Philosophy*, 58 (1961): 653–65.

Bedau, H. A. (ed.), *Civil Disobedience: Theory and Practice*. New York: Pegasus, 1969.

Childress, James F., *Civil Disobedience and Political Obligation: A Study in Christian Social Ethics*. New Haven: Yale University Press, 1972.

Cohen, Carl, *Civil Disobedience: Conscience, Tactics, and the Law*. New York: Columbia University Press, 1971.

Crawford, Curtis (ed.), *Civil Disobedience: A Casebook*. New York: Thomas Y. Crowell, 1973.

Fortas, Abe, *Concerning Dissent and Civil Disobedience*. New York: New American Library, 1968.

Gandhi, Mohandus, K., *Non-Violent Resistance*. New York: Schocken Books, 1961.

Greenawalt, Kent, *Conflicts of Law and Morality*. New York: Oxford University Press, 1987.

Haksar, Vinit, *Civil Disobedience, Threats and Offers: Gandhi and Rawls*. Delhi: Oxford University Press, 1986.

Hall, Robert T., *The Morality of Civil Disobedience*. New York: Harper & Row, 1971.

Harding, Walter, *The Variorum Civil Disobedience*. New York: Twayne Publishers, 1967.

Kent, Edward (ed.), *Revolution and the Rule of Law*. Englewood Cliffs NJ: Prentice-Hall, 1971.

Kraut, Richard, *Socrates and the State*. Princeton NJ: Princeton University Press, 1984.

Madden, Edward H., *Civil Disobedience and Moral Law in Nineteenth Century American Philosophy*. Seattle: University of Washington Press, 1968.

Murphy, Jeffrie G. (ed.), *Civil Disobedience and Violence*. Belmont CA: Wadsworth Publishing Co., 1971.

Schlissel, Lillian (ed.), *Conscience in America: A Documentary History of Conscientious Objection 1757–1967*. New York: E. P. Dutton, 1968.

Sibley, Mulford Q., *The Obligation to Obey: Conscience and the Law*. New York: CRIA, 1970.

Simmons, A. John, *Moral Principles and Political Obligations*. Princeton NJ: Princeton University Press, 1979.

Singer, Peter, *Democracy and Disobedience*. Oxford: The Clarendon Press, 1973.

Tolstoy, Leo, *On Civil Disobedience and Non-Violence*. New York: Bergman Publishers, 1967.

Van den Haag, Ernest, *Political Violence and Civil Disobedience*. New York: Harper & Row, 1972.

Whittaker, Charles E. and William Sloan Coffin, Jr., *Law, Order and Civil Disobedience*. Washington, DC: American Enterprise Institute, 1967.

Woodcock, George, *Civil Disobedience*. Toronto: CBC Publications, 1966.

Woozley, A. D., *Law and Obedience: The Arguments of Plato's Crito*. London: Duckworth, 1979.

Zashin, Elliot M., *Civil Disobedience and Democracy*. New York: The Free Press/Macmillan, 1972.

Zinn, Howard, *Democracy and Disobedience: Nine Fallacies on Law and Order*. New York: Vintage Books, 1968.

Zweibach, Burton, *Civility and Disobedience*. New York: Cambridge University Press, 1975.

INDEX

214